other books by Ray Miller:

Vol. 1 FROM HERE TO OBSCURITY	Model T Fords
Vol. 2 HENRY'S LADY	Model A Fords
Vol. 3 THE V-8 AFFAIR	Early V-8 Fords
Vol. 4 THUNDERBIRD!	Ford's T-Bird
Vol. 5 NIFTY FIFTIES Fords	Post-War V-8 Fords
Vol. 6 MUSTANG Does It!	Ford's Mustang

Vol. 1 CHEVROLET: Coming of Age	1911-1942 Chevrolets
Vol. 2 CHEVROLET: USA #1	1946-1959 Chevrolets
Vol. 3 The Real CORVETTE	Chevrolet's Sports Car

ABOUT THE AUTHORS—

Ray Miller and Bruce McCalley are names well known to the several thousand members of THE MODEL T FORD CLUB OF AMERICA. Among the half dozen founding members, this unusual pair has carved out time to continue chartered duties to the present day. Ray serves as Executive Secretary and Bruce as Editor of the Club's journal *The Vintage Ford.*

Ray Miller, whose interest had remained dormant since an active planetary youth, involved himself all over again in the hobby of restoring Model T Fords about ten years ago. He has since owned and restored several cars of the pre-1915 era. By keen observation, search and interview Ray has educated himself as to the nuances and distinguishing features of early models with a diligence that has brought him recognition as an authority for the brass radiator production years.

Bruce McCalley, whose interest in such matters also ranges back to school days, has combined an unusual capacity for preparing and presenting technical information in a non-technical manner with in-depth knowledge of the later black age models. He holds his focus by driving his restored 1923 Touring Car to town. Bruce has researched and presented penetrating chapters examining the variation in major component parts for all the production years.

The authors, long time residents of Southern California, regard the Model T as a car for all seasons. Strictly as a lark, Bruce (along with another Club founder John McInnis) trail-blazed tandem in their Model T's to New York only a few years ago. Today the authors go by flivver wherever modern iron goes and sometimes even wheel along the Los Angeles Freeway system — where they are committed to keep well up with normal traffic flow.

SIXTH PRINTING
1978

From Here to Obscurity

. . . . . "An Illustrated History of the
Model T Ford" 1909 – 1927

ISBN 0-913056-01-4

Library of Congress Catalog Card No. 75-27314

By Ray Miller and Bruce McCalley
©1971 Ray Miller

All rights reserved. No part of this book may be reproduced or used for any purpose without the written consent of the authors, except in the case of brief quotations embodied in critical articles and reviews.

Printed by SIERRA PRINTERS, INC.

The Model T Ford

From Here to

"An

Obscurity

Illustrated History

of the Model T Ford"

1909 - 1927

by Ray Miller and Bruce McCalley

acknowlegements

Despite the enthusiasm of the Authors, this book could never have been compiled without the support and assistance of so many people that a listing must necessarily be incomplete. Owners of the cars featured are generally mentioned in the text and are, herewith, again thanked for their help. Material submitted by the Henry Ford Museum, Harrah's Automobile Collection; catalogs furnished by Gerald Maginnis, Winston Oliver, Bob Landreth, Gordon Chamberlain and so many more aided greatly.

A great part of this material appeared originally in THE VINTAGE FORD, journal of The Model T Ford Club of America. The gratitude of the Authors is extended to the Board of Directors, MTFCA, for reprint permission.

Above all else, the photographic work and encouragement of Glenn Embree was of indescribable aid.

On October 1, 1908, the infant Ford Motor Company, which had been established a brief five years before, announced its newest and, it was believed, most satisfactory entry into the growing automobile market.

When the last of the model was assembled, in May of 1927, a virtually unbroken line of over fifteen million Model T Fords had been produced. Although the concept persists that they were all alike, this was not the case. The familiar accusation that "you could have any color you want — so long as it was black", while true for the greater part of the production run, was not always so. Early cars, up through 1913 were available in bright colors, as were those produced in 1926 and 1927.

The changes made in the Model T were incomprehensible in number. Yet, with them all, almost all of the critical parts of the car were interchangeable from one model year to any other. Very little was permitted to be changed on Henry Ford's pet that would obsolete parts previously produced, and for this reason most changes were minor and were made almost imperceptibly. Changes, when made, did not occur at any given time; they were incorporated during production as the supply of the older parts became exhausted.

Those to whom "restoration" is a word denoting a serious attempt to return a car to its pristine factory-issue will find these pages a truly significant contribution to their efforts. Those whose curiosity is active will find an aid which is unmatched. Even those who have never had a Model T will find hours of pleasure in watching the successive changes appearing in the Model T Ford.

CONTENTS

"... And here it all began" 11

The "Early '09" Model T Ford 13

The "Production" 1909 Model T Ford 30

The 1910 Model T Ford 48

The 1911 Model T Ford 64

The TWO 1912 Model T Fords 84

The 1913 Model T Ford 102

The 1914 Model T Ford 118

The 1915 Model T Ford 136

The Transitional Years — 1916-1917-1918 162

The Ascending Years — 1919-1920-1921-1922 179

The Golden Era — 1923-1924-1925 200

die Gotterdammerung — 1926-1927 220

Let There Be Light — a review of Model T headlights 245

A Baedeker of Model T Transmission Covers 254

Model T Ford Carburetors 260

The Fords before the "T" — Models N, R and S 273

Serial Numbers 289

The Defeat of Obscurity 293

"AND HERE IT ALL BEGAN"

𝕋his book is dedicated to the almost fifteen million pioneers who first acquired those over-fifteen-million Model T Fords as they rolled in an uninterrupted stream from the assembly lines. It is to those ordinary people who, through their extraordinary oversight of the Model T's limitations and shortcomings, persisted in pushing back the barriers and limits so that at the end of the line there might be enjoyment. From their perserverence on cold mornings, their patience on long, hot climbs, and their willingness to overlook the lack of creature comforts, was derived today's American mobility.

𝕋o them, therefore, the Authors gratefully dedicate this book.

The reader will find disappointment if he anticipates the lens-cut polish of a Rhodes scholar in the pages of text that follow. But such facility with the English language is not required. This is not a tale of Rolls-Royce, but of the earthy Model T. The chronicle is told through the low-key succession of informal notes and captions, tied together with a rough-hewn structure more characteristic, perhaps, of the country tongue once typical among mid-western Fordists in the time of Model T.

The reader should not look always for a subject and a predicate, nor try to freeze his vantage in a fixed tense. He will more fully enjoy the bounty this book offers if he bounces over the syntactic bumps he may encounter down this rustic memory lane.

The authors knew who their readers would be. Their intentions were to "get these readers told." To this end they have succeeded with an unpolished charm.

THE EVERGREEN PRESS

Production figures for the Ford Motor Company during the fiscal year 1908, indicate that the company's production dropped from almost 8500 cars the previous year to just over 6000, an indication that something significantly new had to be built to obtain an increased market share. That significantly new something was Henry Ford's Model T which was introduced in October of 1908 with double-page ads in the trade magazines, and an "Advance Catalog". Portions of both are reproduced here.

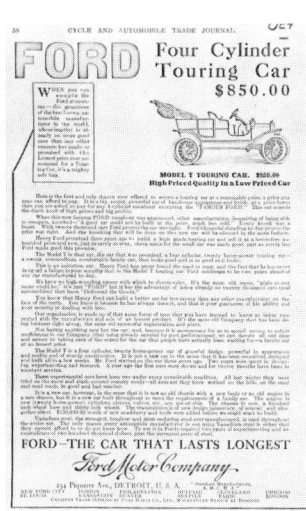

Model T was not the first Ford produced. Indeed, the Ford Motor Company was a major manufacturer of automobiles by the time of the T's birth. The Model T was but a logical extension of Henry Ford's policy of an inexpensive but not 'cheap' car "for the multitudes."

The first Ford produced by the Company was the Model A, a simple, two-cylinder, open car, introduced in 1903. This was followed by the Model B, C, F, K, N, R and S. In the period from its founding in 1903, the Company produced two-cylinder cars (A, C and F), four-cylinder cars (B, N, R and S), and a six, the Model K. The Model B was offered in only a Touring Car. The Model C

Ford Model N

Ford Model R

Ford Model K

was a refined Model A, as was the Model F. The large Model K was a financial disaster; Ford never forgot it and was prejudiced against sixes for years to come. Of spectacular success were the Models N-R-S. Basically alike except for body and trim, these models, built from 1906 to 1908, set the stage for the Model T. In this span of six years, Ford produced and sold about 16,000 cars.

Introduced in October of 1908, the Model T was an instant success. Years ahead of its time and priced at the bottom of the low-price field, it had innovations galore. The Model T introduced left hand control for the first time in any mass-produced car. The advantages of driving from the left side became obvious and it was not long before all U.S. auto manufacturers followed Ford's lead.

Another major departure from standard was the en-bloc casting of the cylinder block. General practice in those days was to cast the cylinders in pairs and bolt the pairs to a crankcase. The Model T engine was one casting and featured a removable cylinder head. Again, the advantages were many; the industry followed.

The Model T was priced at $850. This price did not include such luxury items as headlights, windshield or top. These were offered as options at additional cost. The necessary iron work to support the top came whether or not the top itself was purchased.

Early catalogs illustrated a number of body types. In addition to the Touring, a Runabout, a Coupe, a Town Car and a Landaulet were offered. The Touring and the Runabout were by far the more popular; there is little evidence that the others were ever produced. Colors were offered. Tourings were Carmine (red) at first and Brewster Green in later production. Roadsters were grey. Fenders, at least in the earlier stages of production, were the same color as the body. Later, fenders, running boards and splash aprons were dark blue or black.

The earliest cars used a running board of wood covered with a rubber matting. Later, a steel one with a series of embossed ridges running lengthwise was used. Rear fenders were changed at the time to fit the new board. The new-style board is shown in the "Production 1909" coverage in the next chapter.

Model T Touring Car—4 Cylinder 20 H. P.—Left Side.

Bodies were of wood in most cars but there were quite a few made of aluminum in 1909, apparently experimental.

The use of Vanadium steel in all parts that were subject to strain enabled Ford to make the Model T light in weight, yet stronger than many cars weighing twice as much. The lack of weight, coupled with the great (for the time) power of the engine made this new Ford a great performer. Nothing at anywhere near the price could match it for power.

The Model T frame was also light in construction, allowing it to twist with the poor roads of the day. By using what was termed "three point suspension" of the engine assembly, the rear axle and the front axle, Model T could take any surface in its stride. Its great road clearance, power and ease of handling made it an ideal car for the day — and indeed, for the years to come.

The initial cars were expensive to produce; featured many items which were later found unnecessary. One of these was a latching device at the front of the engine to support the crank when not in use. Another was the use of a riveted-in-place reinforcement inside the frame rails, eliminated early in production.

The first 2500 Model Ts were constantly changing. Innovations were added, parts were changed and general design altered with almost every car. By car number 2500 (April of 1909) the general design was finalized and remained stable, comparatively, for years. The first 2500 Model Ts were generally so unlike the 15,000,000 that followed that they required a separate section of the parts catalog. The engine, while of similar basic design,

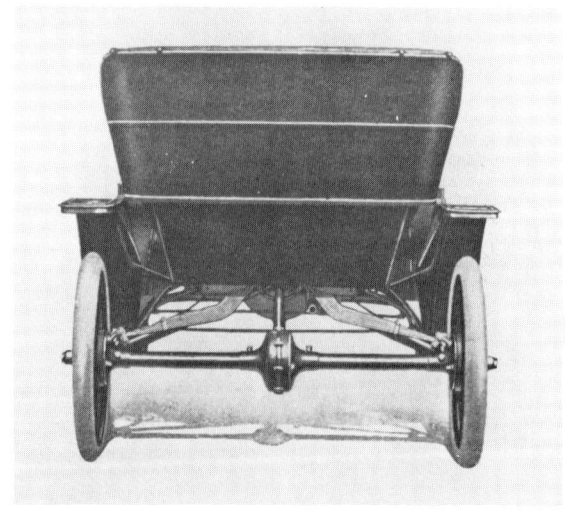

Rear view from an illustration in the 1909 Ford catalog. Most of the pictures were artist's renditions; can not be relied on for accuracy. In this picture, for example, the rear end is incorrect. It appears to be more like that used on the N-R-S Models of 1906 to 1908.

16

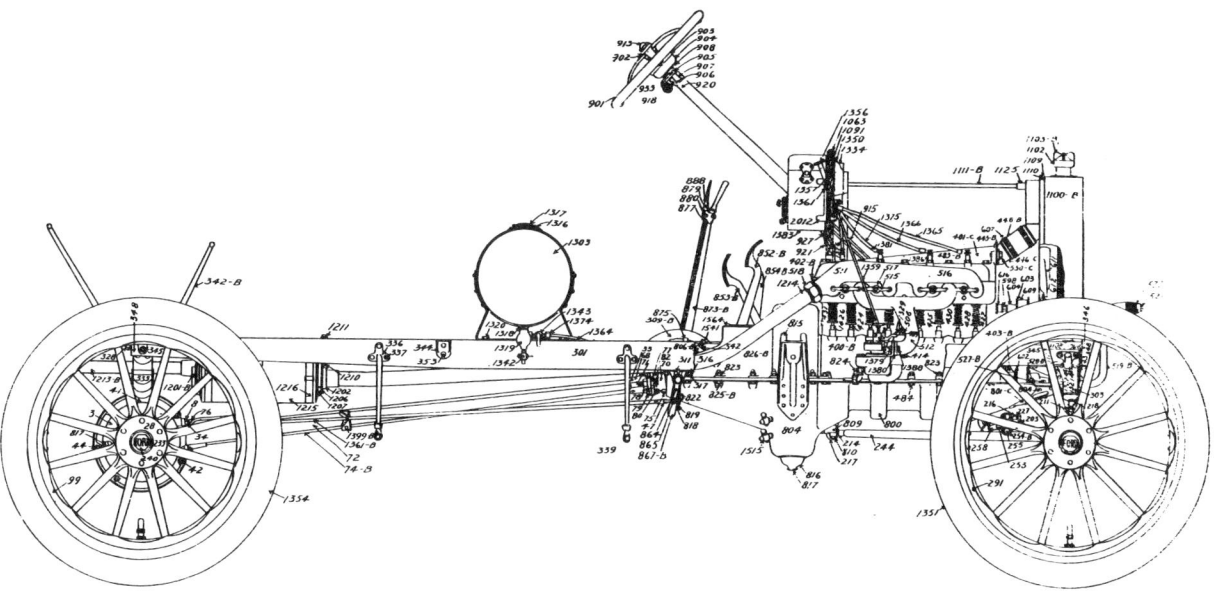

Showing side elevation, Chasis with location of Parts by number

Another obvious error in the catalog is this illustration of the front compartment. Note the two levers — and the three pedals. All two-lever cars had only two pedals. All three pedal cars had just one brake lever.

featured an integral water pump which was driven from the timing gear. The fan was mounted on an extension of the water pump shaft.

Lubrication of all engine parts was assured by the basic design of the engine. The flywheel, running in oil, splashed it everywhere as owners found out as shafts wore or gaskets were misplaced. No longer were the external oilers with their separate reservoirs needing constant attention necessary.

The need for external batteries was eliminated by incorporating a magneto in the basic design of the engine. Magnets, mounted on the flywheel, induced a current flow in a series of coils mounted on a ring just ahead of the flywheel. Simple, trouble-free and very effective. The magnets also aided in the circulation of oil.

The engine pan, which extended to include the transmission, was of one-piece design. It had no provision for adjusting rod or main bearings without disassembly of the engine.

The transmission cover was, at first, also of pressed steel. After less than a few hundred cars the cover was changed to one of cast aluminum. The inspection hole in both types was square and its cover was secured by a lever arrangement operated by a single large bolt head in the center. Later, this cover was secured by four screws and the general design remained unchanged until the 1911 models.

After car number 2500, the water pump was eliminated. The cylinder block was redesigned to include a water jacket at the front. The head was modified for more capacity and to fit the new block. The change made it necessary to increase

 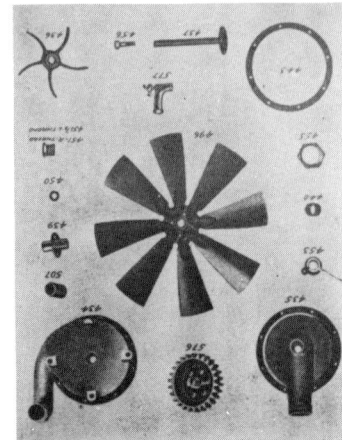

the length of the crankshaft so that the pulley for the fan belt could be added.

All engines had the manifolds on the right side; the reverse of the previous Models N-R-S. The valve lifters and stems were exposed and required occasional oiling by the owners for lubrication. The lifters and the valves themselves ran in removable insert bushings.

The radiator, too, went through several changes. Early ones featured a one-piece brass shell; some as an integral part with the core; others as a separate shell. Some featured a "Ford" in a winged script; others had no identification at all. The filler neck was a low casting and was soldered in place. In later production the shell was an assembly of brass pieces and integral with the core. Although it featured the "winged script" 'Ford,' it set the pattern of all brass radiators on Model Ts until they were discontinued in 1916.

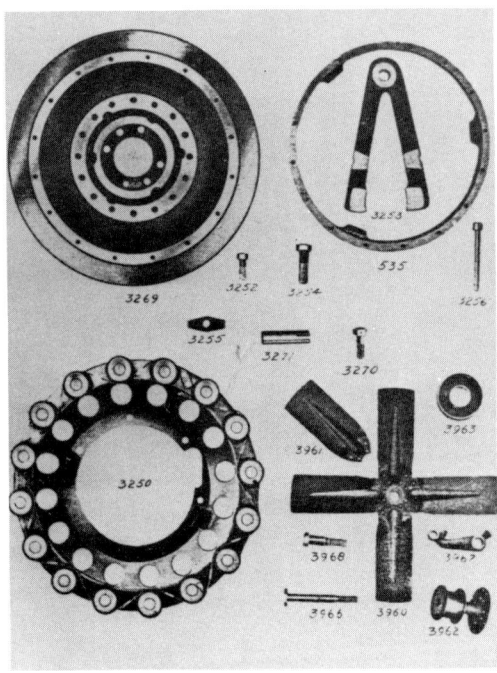

Top — Water pump parts used on the first 2500 engines. The fan, with eight blades, was quite small and was driven by an extension of the water pump shaft.

Center — The magneto featured elaborate magnets and relatively small coils which were mounted on a pressed steel ring. Part number 535 is a brass spacer which supported the outer ends of the magnets on the flywheel.

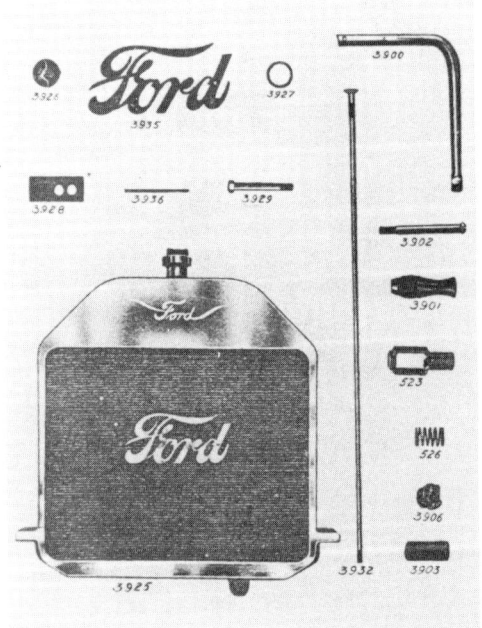

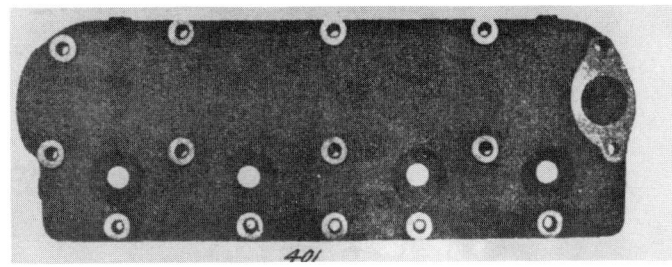

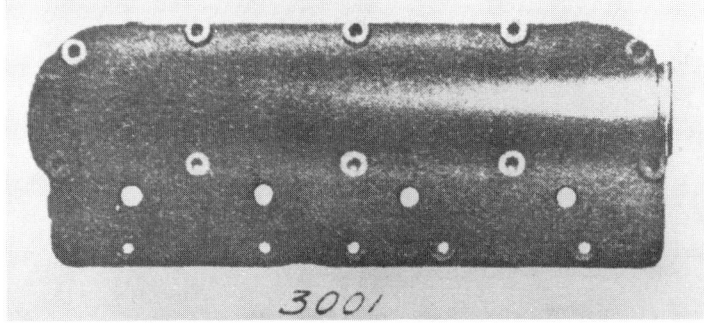

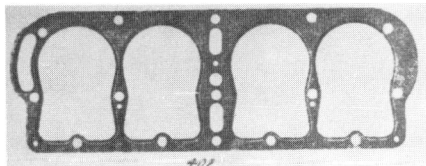

These illustrations, from the June 1909 Parts List, show three of the four (apparently) cylinder heads used in early production. The earliest heads (401) were drilled for 3/8-inch cap screws. After a short period, these holes were enlarged to accept 7/16-inch cap screws (401A and 401B). The later heads had, in addition, greater water jacket area. From available evidence, all three of these early heads came with or without the "Ford Motor Co." identification.

The fourth head became standard at car number 2500, when the water pump was discontinued. The design was altered to provide greater water capacity. Oddly, the Ford identification appeared on some but not all. When it did appear, it was in the familiar Ford script between numbers two and three cylinders.

Top view of engine number 77, owned by the Los Angeles County Museum. The manifolds and carburetor are incorrect for this engine.

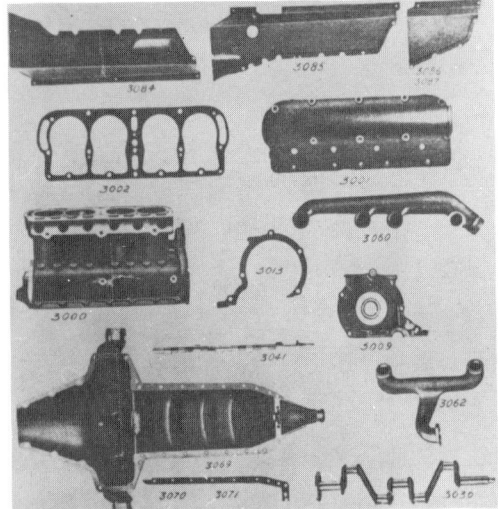

Engine parts (after 2500). Note the one-piece engine pan. It was necessary to completely disassemble the engine to adjust the rod bearings. An inspection plate was not added until during 1911.

Note the addition of a hole in the front of the head gasket for additional water circulation, as compared with the earlier style shown on Page 19.

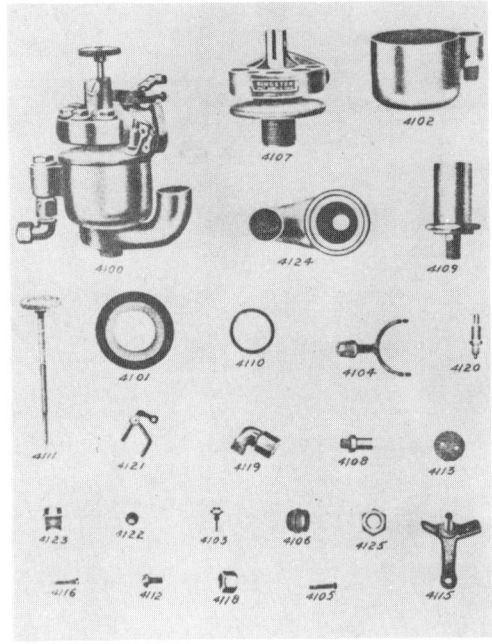

The commonly used carburetor was the Kingston five-ball, illustrated here. A Holley, Part Number 4150, was also used.

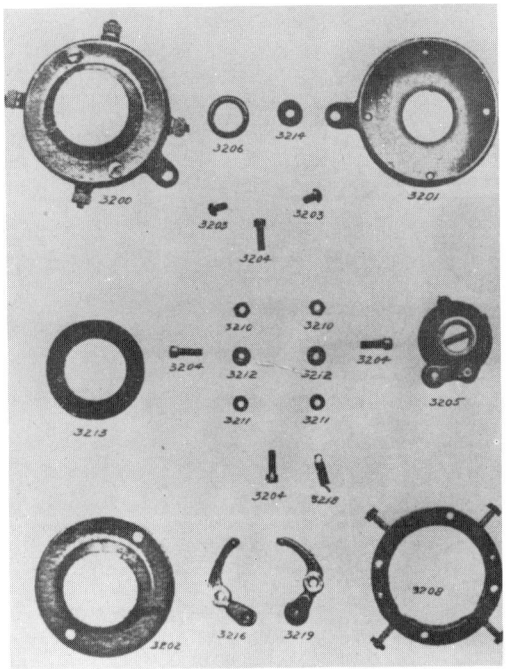

The commutator (timer) was of the so-called two piece design and was smaller than that used on the later Model T Fords.

The early 1909 engine. Note the lack of a water inlet on the left side; the unusual oil filler tube. The serial number is located on the right side between the two center exhaust ports.

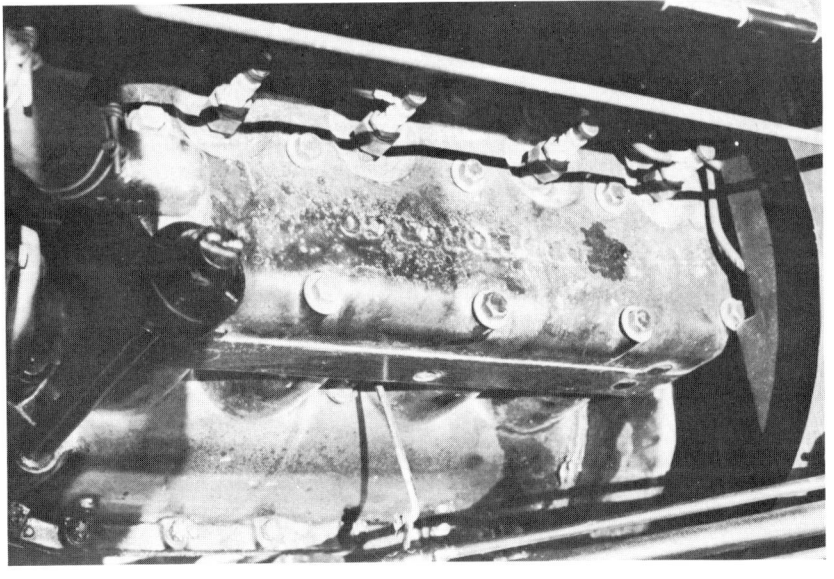

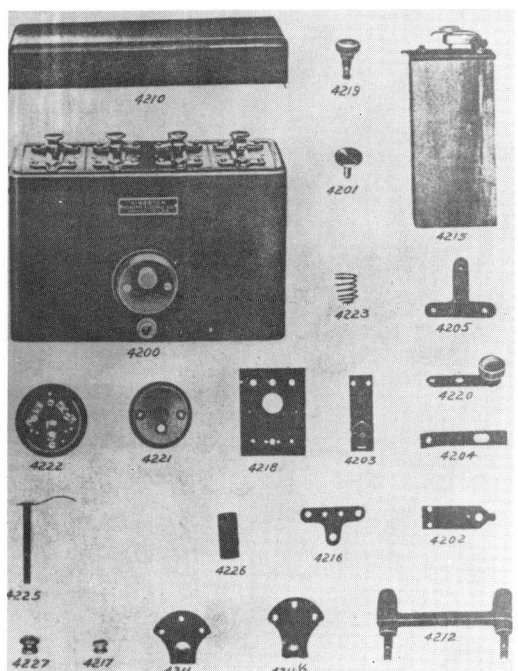

The Kingston coil box is illustrated in the Parts List. Heinze units were also used. The earliest cars used the same box as the Models N-R-S; the electrical connections came out of the bottom of the box. Later models used this type in which the connections came out the rear, through the firewall.

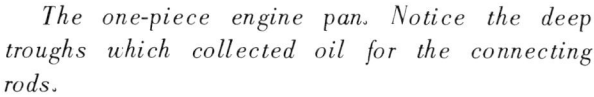

Serial number, in this case, 77, is located above the center of the intake manifold.

The one-piece engine pan. Notice the deep troughs which collected oil for the connecting rods.

21

Views of engine number 77 showing the unique water pump and six-bladed fan. Note the exposed valve stems and the unusual oil filler location. With the introduction of the new engine at number 2500, the oil filler was moved to the timing gear cover, where it remained thereafter.

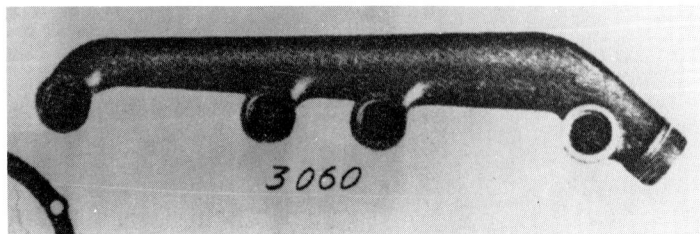

The exhaust manifold differed from the bulk of production in that the exhaust pipe fit into it and was packed with asbestos and secured with a large nut. The pipe was flared and the manifold outlet beveled to fit in 1911. It was still secured with the large brass nut but the asbestos packing was eliminated.

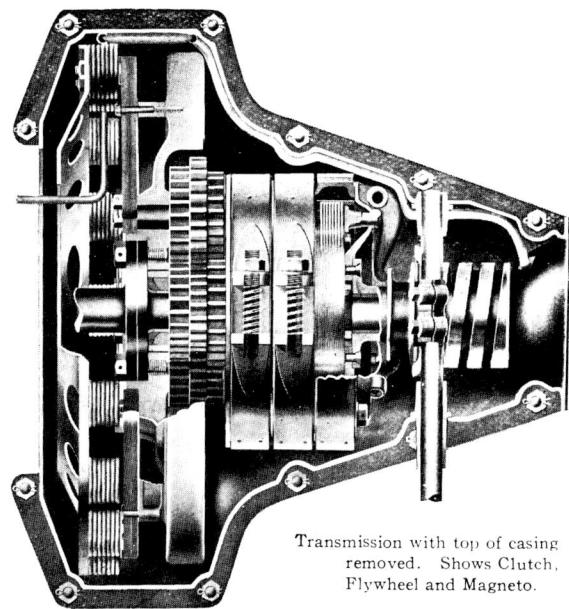

Transmission with top of casing removed. Shows Clutch, Flywheel and Magneto.

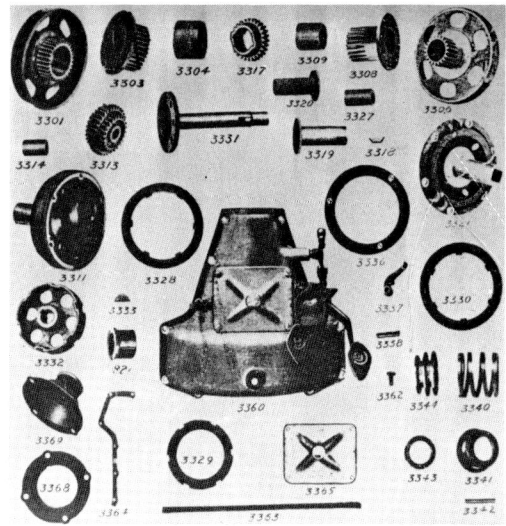

Transmission parts. This shows the later style transmission cover. The first ones used an inspection plate which was secured by a single lever, rather than the four screws.

Below — The early pressed steel transmission cover.

The transmission, of the planetary type as in all previous Fords, was now enclosed in the engine assembly where it was safe from dirt and assured plenty of lubrication. This design proved to be quite trouble-free and easy to operate.

The transmission was controlled (on the first 1000 cars, approximately) by two pedals and two levers. The left of the two pedals controlled low and high gears. Push it to the floor and you were in low; release it and you were in high. Somewhere in between these two extremes was neutral. The right-hand pedal applied the transmission brake which acted on the drive shaft and was used for stopping the car in normal operation. The two

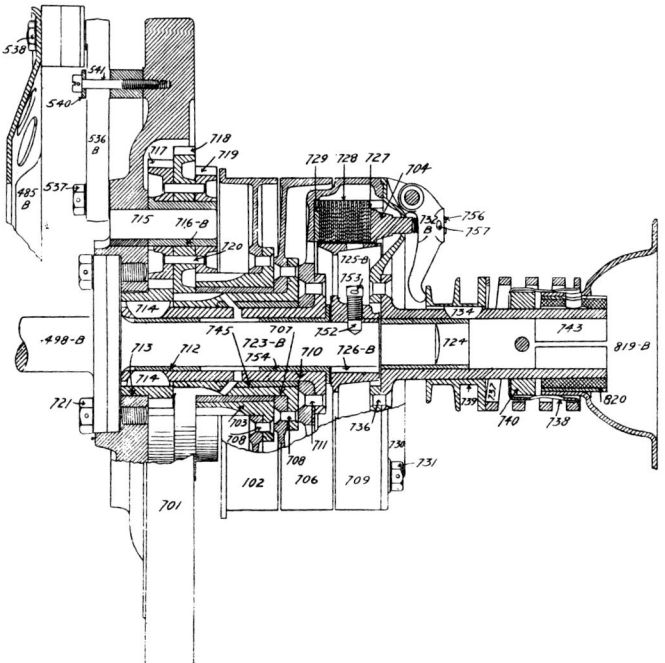

levers, located at the driver's left, controlled the parking brakes at the rear wheels, and the reverse gear. The outer of the pair was the brake. Unlike the later models, it acted only on the rear brakes; did not disengage the high speed clutch. The inner lever, when pulled back, applied the reverse band. As it was pulled from the extreme forward position, it also released the high-speed clutch, putting the transmission forward gears in neutral by means of a cam and roller arrangement similar to the later system used on the brake lever.

This system did not prove too satisfactory and at somewhere between car number 850 and 1000 a third pedal was added between the first two. This pedal was used to apply reverse. At the same time the brake lever was modified so as to release the high-speed clutch as it was pulled back slightly.

Details of the two-lever, two-pedal transmission control system. This engine is owned by the Los Angeles County Museum.

Note the single bolt in the center of the inspection hole cover. This turned a lever which engaged the edges of the hole. The four 'dimples' at each corner serve to locate the cover and prevent its shifting in position.

Note, too, the use of rollers in the clutch linkage; discontinued with the introduction of the three-pedal system after car number 850 (approx.).

This is engine number 77.

Further pulling kept the car in neutral and applied the rear brakes. The idea was to put the brake lever in the neutral position and then apply the reverse pedal but almost every driver learned to find neutral with the low-high pedal with the left foot and to apply reverse with his right. Simple, easy to learn, and easy to use. It was impossible to "clash" the gears. In an emergency, applying any one pedal, or any combination of pedals would slow or stop the car.

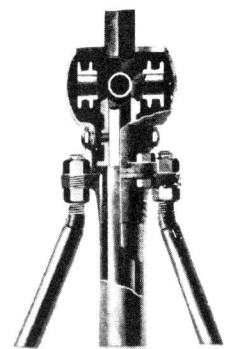

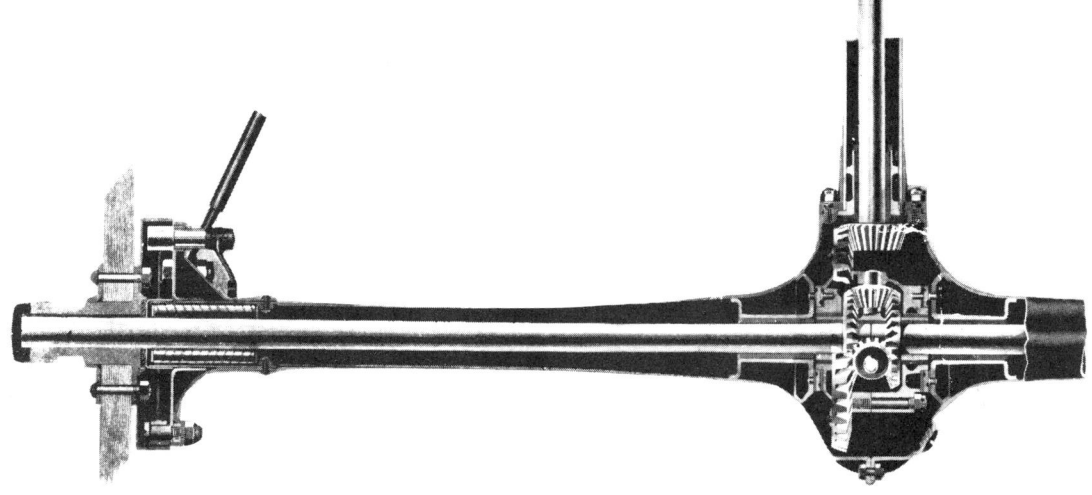

Conversion kits were offered to the owners of the early cars so that they could have the three-pedal system, at a price of just $15 and the old parts. Due to the limited production of the two pedal system, and to these kits, there are few original two-pedal Model Ts surviving today.

Like the engine-transmission assembly, the entire drive line was enclosed in oil proof, dust proof housings. The early 1909 cars featured a pressed steel rear axle/differential housing which had no rivets in evidence on the differential housing. The drive shaft pinion bearing was a babbitt sleeve. The pinion gear was keyed and peened to the drive shaft; the assembly was

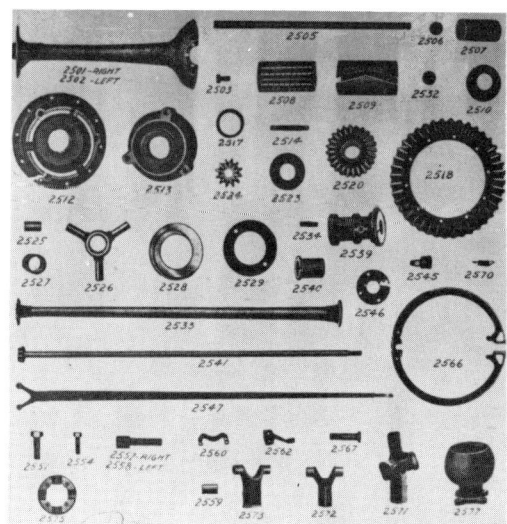

The earliest cars used a babbitt pinion bearing in the rear axle. This was changed to a roller early in production.

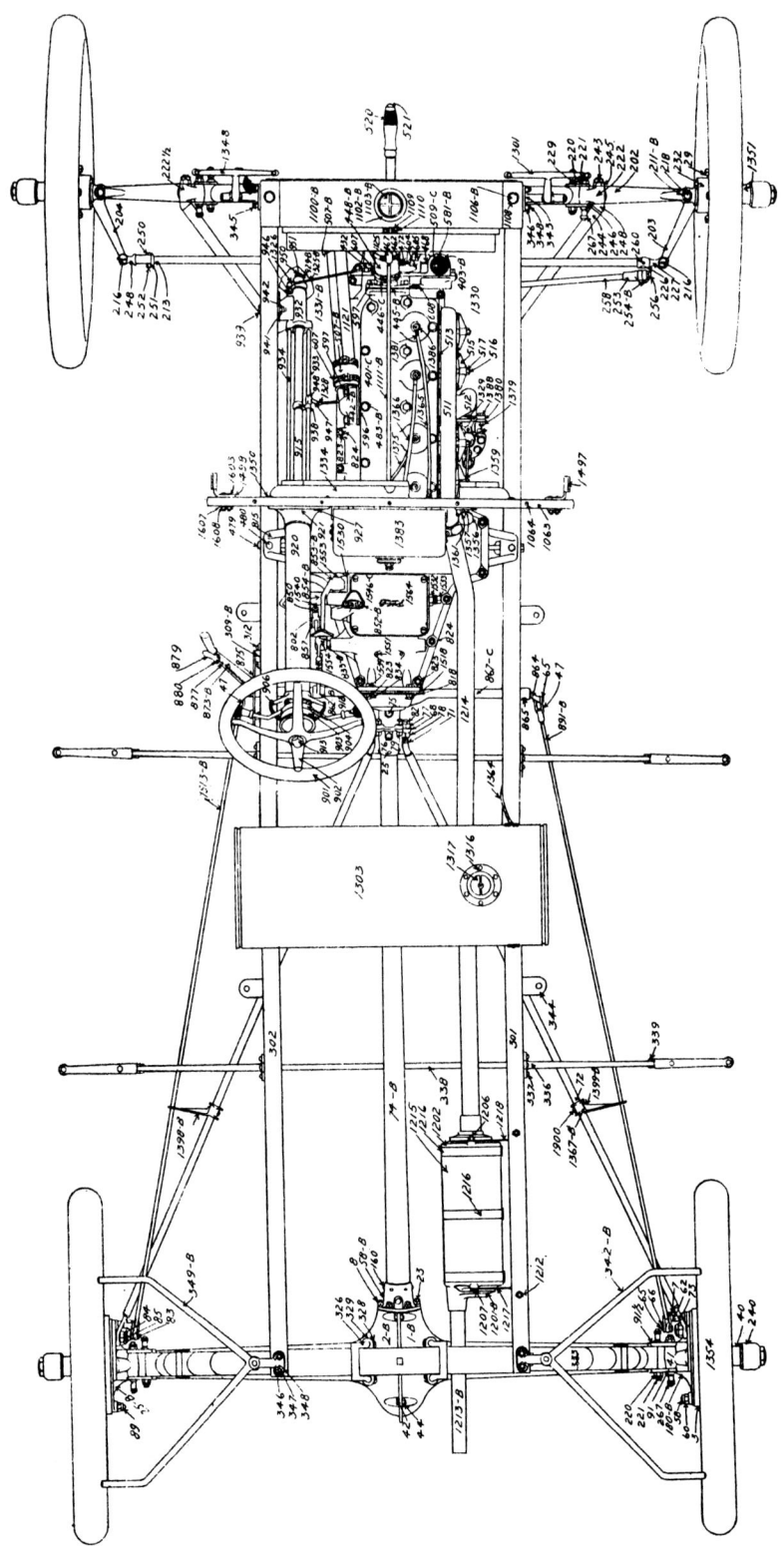

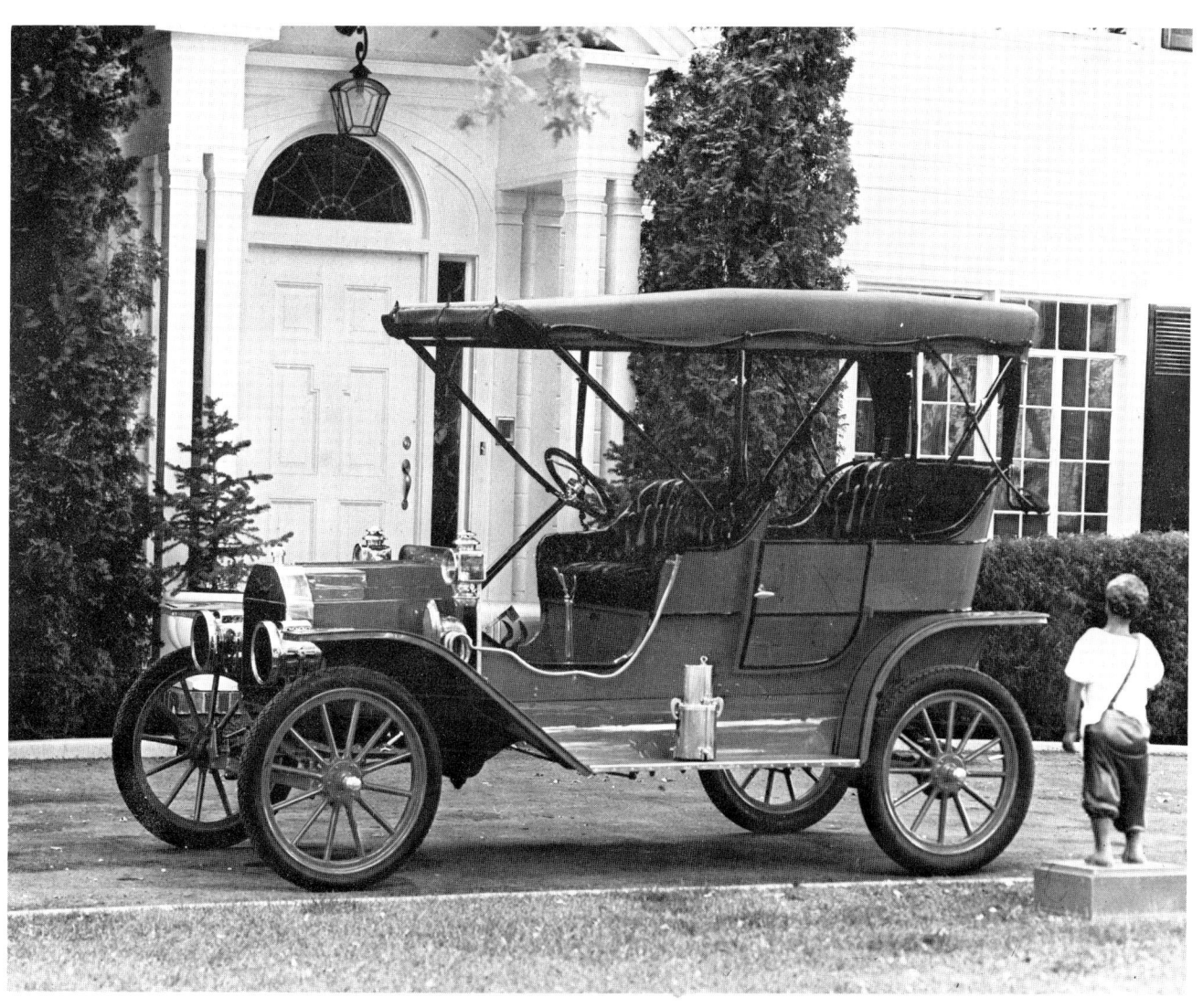

Early, two-lever, 1909 Model T Ford Touring. Courtesy Harrah's Automobile Collection.

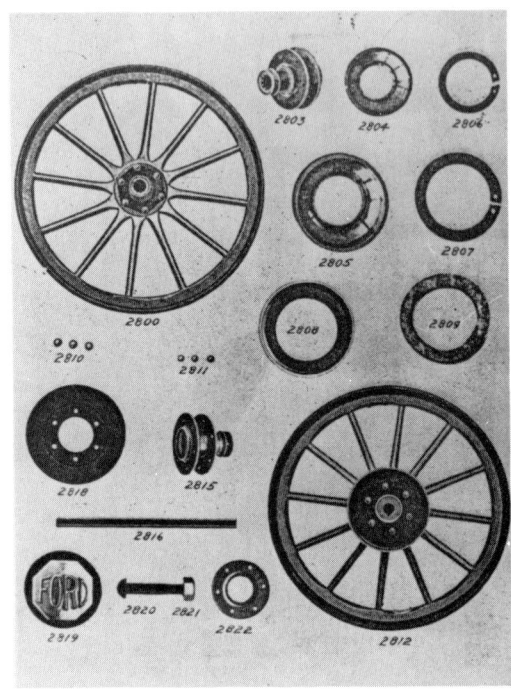

Wheels featured thin spokes; were painted to match the body color. Tires were 30 by 3 in front, 30 by 3½ in the rear. Notice the "Ford" in block lettering on the hub caps.

serviced as a unit. The ring gear was riveted to the differential carrier, rather than being bolted as in later production. The inner axle bearings were babbitt bushings, similar to that used on the pinion bearing. Outer axle bearings were roller. The axles were straight and non-tapered at the ends. Each end was milled for a key, and drilled for a retaining pin. The key kept the hub from turning and the pin kept it in place. The pin was held in place by the hub cap. The design had been used in the Models N, R and S.

This simple design proved unsatisfactory. The housings were too flexible; the pinion bearing would not stand up; the rivets in the ring gear and differential carrier made servicing a major chore; and the axle-hub design wore rapidly. Early in 1909 production the entire assembly was modified to include a roller pinion bearing; a bolt-on ring gear; a strengthening plate around the pinion area; and reinforcing plates in the inner bearing section. Six rivets on each side of the center section; plus the reinforcing plate around the pinion bearing were the identifying features of the later design. The axles remained without change until mid-1911, at which time they were changed to the tapered end type. The rear axle continued to be modified and it was not until late 1914 or early 1915 that the design became stable.

Wheels were carried over from the Model S. They featured very thin spokes; were painted to match the body color of the car. Tires were 30 by 3 in the front; 30 by 3½ in the rear.

Thus began the production of the major factor in the growth of the automobile industry. Model T made Henry Ford a billionaire. For years to come there were to be more Fords on the highways than *all other makes combined!*

The "Production" 1909 Model T Ford

Ford-Motor-Cars

FORD-MOTOR-COMPANY
DETROIT · MICH · U·S·A
Standard Manufacturers — American Motor Car Manufacturers' Association

Without a doubt, the smell of success attended the Model T Ford from the day of its introduction on October first, 1908. In six months, by April 30, 1909, the Ford Motor Company had built and shipped over 2500 cars! As its fantastic acceptance became evident, Ford authorized the first essential re-designs of the car, and after 2500, the Model T became substantially a different car. This, then is the nature of the "production" 1909 Model T Ford.

April, 1909: Model T Ford No. 2500
December 31, 1909: Model T Ford No. 14,161

The above statistics tell the story! Almost 12,000 of these "improved" Model T Fords were produced in 1909. Not all of these cars were the same though, for Ford made changes in his car during production.

Foremost of these changes was the simplified and more positive three-pedal transmission control, introduced at about car Number 850. Another was the re-design of the engine block to eliminate the unreliable (and costly) integral water pump, after car Number 2500. Other changes, of mechanical or trim nature, were less significant.

With the "production" 1909 Ford came the introduction of additional body styles beyond the Touring — the Runabout, the enclosed Coupe, the Town car, and the perhaps-never-produced Model T Landaulet.

Fundamentally though, and for years to come, the five passenger Touring Car provided the bulk of the production. While early Touring Cars were carmine (red), and Roadsters, grey, an additional color, introduced in June, permitted a Brewster Green to be added to the colors on the road. Striping was confined to the center of the black highlight area (see following illustrations) and was done in a narrow red line.

Just as is true today, accessories were offered, and in the "production" 1909 Ford, the list was long. For example: Headlights (!), windshield — even the top was an accessory! No instruments, such as a speedometer, were provided.

Come with us now, for a photographic essay defining the "production" 1909 Model T Ford.

The restored 1909 touring car used to illustrate this article is owned by Hy Pingree and Ray Miller. This is engine (and body) number 4888. The body of this particular car is made of aluminum, one of the few that still exist, but the style is typical of all "production" 1909 Model T Fords.

FORD MOTOR CARS

Summary

MOTOR: 4 cylinder, 4 cycle, vertical, 20 h. p. 3¾ in. bore, 4 in. stroke, Cylinders cast in one block with water jackets and upper half of crank case integral, water jacketed cylinder head detachable, fine grain gray iron castings.

VALVES: Extra large, all on left side and offset.

SHAFTS: Crank and cam non-welded drop forged heat treated Ford Vanadium steel, bearing surfaces ground, cams integral and ground.

CRANK CASE: Upper half integral with cylinder casting. Lower half pressed steel and extended to form lower housing for magneto and transmission.

COOLING: Gear driven centrifugal pump.

IGNITION: Ford magneto generator, low tension, direct connected to engine drive.

CARBURETOR: New design, float feed automatic with dash adjustment.

TRANSMISSION: New design Ford spur planetary, bathed in oil,—all gears from heat-treated Vanadium steel, silent and easy in action.

LUBRICATION: Combination splash and gravity system—simple and sure. Insures against insufficient or excessive lubrication.

CLUTCH: Multiple steel discs, operating in oil.

CONTROL: All forward speeds by foot pedal. Reverse by hand lever. Spark and throttle under steering wheel.

FINAL DRIVE: By cardon shaft with single universal joint to bevel drive gears in live rear axle. Ford three point system (patented in all countries) with all moving parts enclosed in dust proof casing, running in oil. Vanadium steel throughout.

FRONT AXLE: One piece drop forging in I-beam section, specially treated, Vanadium steel.

STEERING: By Ford reduction gear system; irreversible.

BRAKES: 2 sets. (a) Service band brake on transmission; (b) Internal expanding brakes in rear hub drums.

WHEELS: Artillery wood type. Hubs extra long.

TIRES: Pneumatic; rear 30 x 3½ inches, front 30 x 3 inches.

NUMBER OF PASSENGERS: Normal load touring car, 5 adults.

SPRINGS: Front and rear, semi-elliptic.

FENDERS: Enclosed full length of car.

WHEEL BASE: 100 in.; tread 56 in.; 60 in. for Southern roads where ordered.

GASOLINE CAPACITY: 10 gallons. Cylindrical gasoline tank mounted directly on frame.

STANDARD EQUIPMENT: Side oil lamps, tail lamp, tube horn and gas lamp brackets. Touring Car and Roadster ironed for top.

WEIGHT: 1200 lbs.

PRICE: Touring Car, $850.00; Roadster, $825.00; Coupe, $950.00; Landaulet, $950.00; Town Car, $1000.00. F. O. B. Detroit.

HIGH PRICED QUALITY IN A LOW PRICED CAR

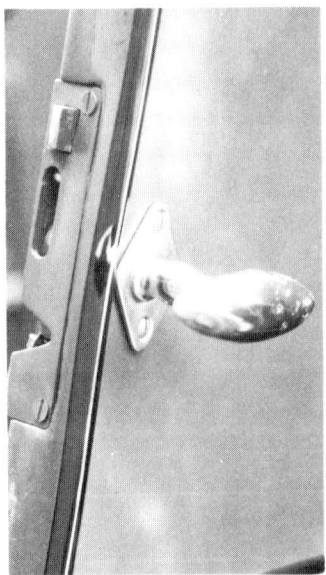

Rear doors were "safety-latched" by means of a double acting latch. When latched, both a conventional sliding latch and a rotating hook were engaged. (Left photo) A half-turn (next photo) would retract the rotating hook, still permitting the sliding latch to hold the door shut. Action of the hook was initiated by an ingenious taper (second photo from right) assuring complete close of the door before activating. Right hand photo illustrates inside-door view of this clever latch.

Bodies were of wood, carefully constructed with panels bent to shape over inner wooden struts. Joints and edges were generally dressed with half-round mouldings, and great care was taken, after the then-current fashion, to finish these bodies in highly polished lacquer, applied, rubbed out, and re-applied endlessly. These wooden bodies, often appearing to be metal to a casual observer of a fine restoration, were installed on a chassis that was all metal.

A very few experimental bodies were built of aluminum skin panels installed over similar wooden struts. Several of these unusual cars have survived and in their survival have justified Ford's curiosity in building this advanced-thinking "metal" Model T Ford. Generally their appearance is similar to the wooden body car, but the use of the half-round in some places seems to have been for effect rather than need.

Upholstery was "full leather" and the diamond tufts were carefully folded, not sewn, in place. Door panels occasionally included integral pockets, but generally were plain. Leather door stops were installed to protect the rear door hinges.

On the first 5000 cars, the top, when ordered from the factory, was lined with a woolen blanket-like material colored, invariably, red or maroon. These interlined tops were among the first casualties in the move to cut prices.

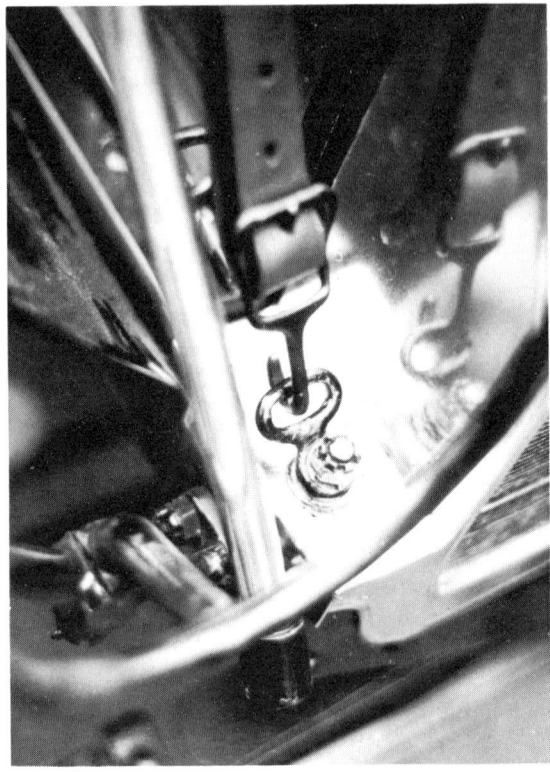

Top is held in place by a most ingenious hook arrangement. Pressure (pull) of top against the strap causes hook to be placed in such a position that it cannot be released from the eye. Top straps must be loosened to permit hook to be rotated far enough for its tongue to clear the eye. Note the clamp which secures lower end of windshield support rod to chassis.

Crank handle, of hard rubber, is secured by a machine bolt, and nut.

Crank is disengaged from crankshaft by pressure of wirewound spring. Note the seven-leaf, tapered-ends, front spring. Taper leaf springs were also used at the rear.

The radiator is now made of several pieces, carefully soldered together. Gone is the smooth-sided shell. The dimensions of this new radiator are such that it could be used on any of the "brass era" Model T Fords. Featuring a winged-script "Ford," its cap was cast and machined, fitting into a low filler neck which was soldered in place.

Headlamps then available for the "production" 1909 Model T were the E&J No. 466, illustrated above, and below. Curious is the fact that although they were manufactured in pairs (right and left doors), the author has found several pairs, like those shown, in which the holes in the smoke bonnet were elliptical in the right and circular in the left lamps! We have yet to find a truly identical pair!

Apparently, E&J's die was worn when they stamped the nameplates for some of their lamps, in that the "4" was incomplete in the "466", with the result that many reproductions have been made with the identification made incorrectly. Note that the correct number is 466!

The running boards are now of metal and are embossed with rows of uninterrupted ridges. The running boards are interchangeable from the right to the left side of the car. Note the sharp curve of the splash apron at the rear edge (also see photo at the lower left).

Although headlights were not furnished as standard equipment, there were brackets supplied onto which the lamps could be installed.

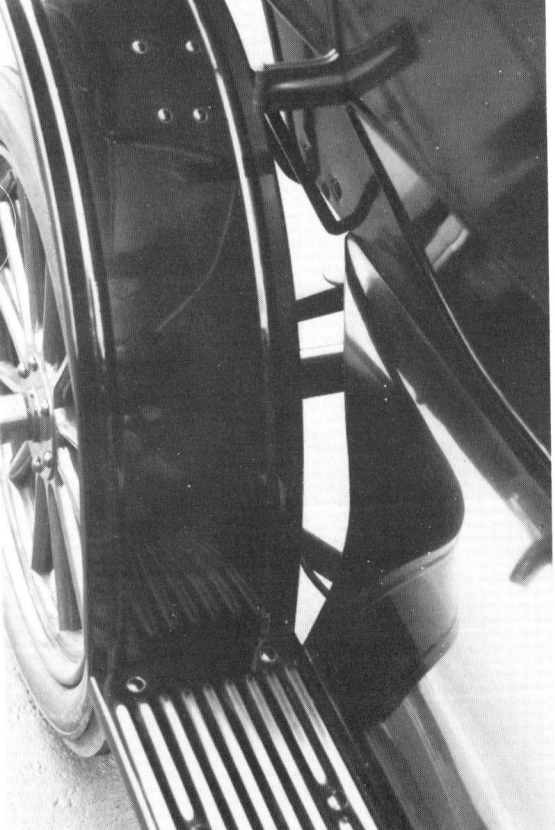

Fenders are secured by means of brackets which are riveted to the fender and clamped to the "butterfly" brackets extending from the chassis. Two bolts, front and rear of the running boards, passing through wooden spacer blocks further support the fenders.

Wheels were painted body color and, when striped, the striping on the individual spokes was "closed" to produce a dart-shaped design.

Front wheels are 24" diameter (30 by 3 tires); rear wheels are smaller (23", 30 by 3½ tires). Front wheel hubs employ ball bearings in the inner and outer races. Brass hubcap nearly meets shoulder of the outer bearing support.

One-piece spindles are secured to tie-rod ends by non-lubricated end bolts. Steering wheel position (rotation) can be adjusted by means of the forged connecting link end. Spring-loaded ball caps, seen on some cars, are an accessory developed to overcome ball wear, and are not standard or original.

Axle is of what may be Ford's most little-understood development, vanadium steel. This tough, malleable alloy permitted lighter-weight structural members, virtually unbreakable in service. A complete knot has been "tied" in a Model T front axle without breaking it! The one-piece spindles nestle snugly in the curve of the axle.

Hubcaps, of brass, contain the "Ford" in block letters. Wheel bolts are of a much higher crowned head than modern bolts. Note the closed-dart striping design.

Open valves are lubricated only by such externally applied lube as the owner may remember to use. Engine serial number is now on a boss located at the lower front right side.

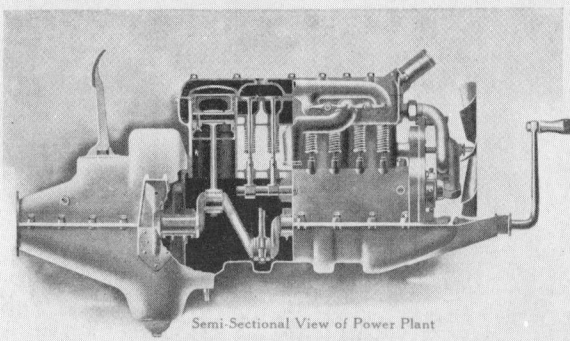

Cylinder head bears the script "Ford," but does not include the "Made in USA."

Illustrating two styles of the Kingston five-ball carburetor. The larger one, on the right, is earlier and is typical of Ford usage, and contains a smaller throat than the one with the smaller bowl (left).

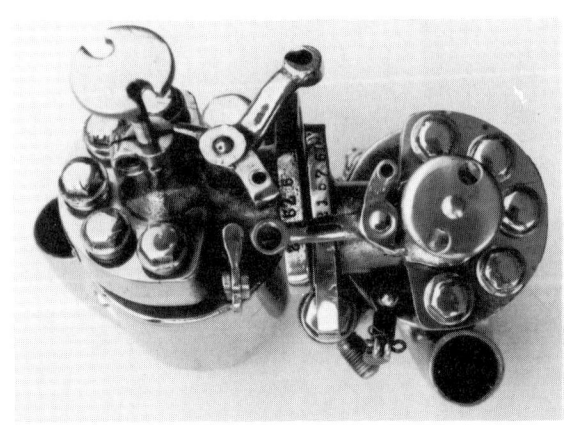

Cam on the hand brake lever is cast, and when rotated by the action of the hand brake, causes the clutch to become disengaged, enabling the subsequent application of either 'low', 'reverse', or the service handbrake.

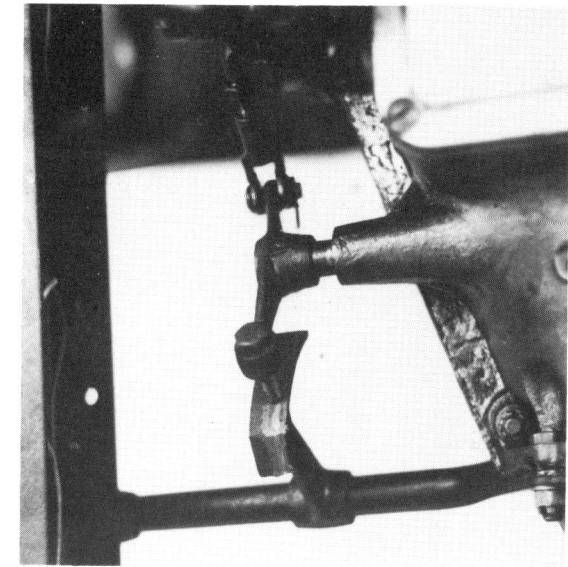

The transmission is now controlled by three pedals, and the cover is of cast aluminum, featuring an internal ramp directing lubrication to the rear transmission (fourth main) bearing.

Tail pipe is designed to slip INTO the exhaust manifold; is not flared nor is the manifold flared to receive it. Inlet manifold is of cast aluminum and is of "gooseneck" style. Carburetor is Kingston five-ball.

Low-speed band can be adjusted without removal of the inspection cover. Note the square adjustment screw.

Magnets are horseshoe-shaped and are secured to the flywheel by screws passing through brass spacers. At this time the screw heads are brass safety-wired to prevent them from backing off. Not clearly illustrated in this view is the date which is stamped into the face of the stub-shaft flange, which is the date on which the transmission, engine and car were assembled. The car used to illustrate this article (No. 4888) was assembled on June 14, 1909.

Early in the production, the inspection hole cover was cast. Later it was stamped of sheet metal. Illustrated (left) is the casting; on the right is the stamping. While externally about the same, the underside clearly shows the strengthening ribs in the casting which do not appear in the stamping.

The field coil ring is of pressed steel and round, cylindrical coils of wire are mounted thereon. Pole pieces virtually cover the face of the coil and must be removed to permit removal of the coils. Coils are linen-wrapped for insulation, and baked in what appears to be enamel. Field coil is adjusted for normal .030'' gap by shimming from the block.

The lower crankcase was the so-called 'one piece pan.' This pan is essentially the same as the style described earlier but the front hanger (bearing) is a bit shorter. A pattern of six rivets secures the motor mounting bracket to the pan.

Front end of the drive shaft housing is of two parts; the ball and the housing itself. Six bolts pass through the flanges; four securing the two halves, the other two being the forward ends of the rear radius rods.

During 1909, a rear roller bearing was inserted in the drive shaft (pinion bearing) and this bearing was carried in a cast spool, as illustrated. A reinforcing plate was added to the differential housing for additional strength.

The thin, pressed steel axle housings, commonly called the "six-rivet rear end" were standard. Rivets secured an internal strengthening disk to the housings. Left and right halves were bolted together with the right half fitting snugly into the flared lip of the left half. A round-headed, screwdriver-slotted filler plug was provided for adding lubricant in the right half housing.

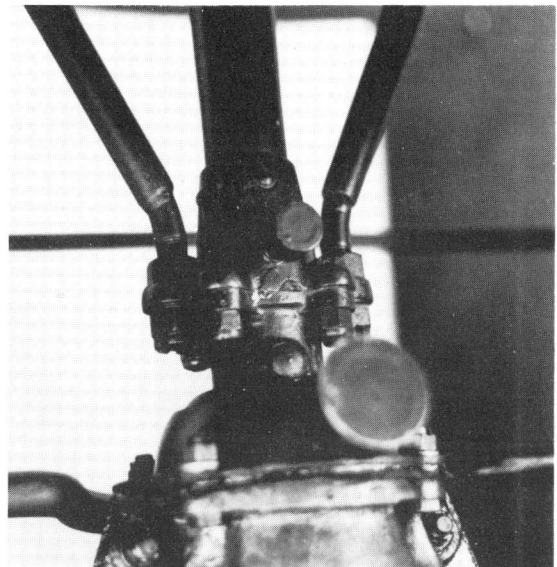

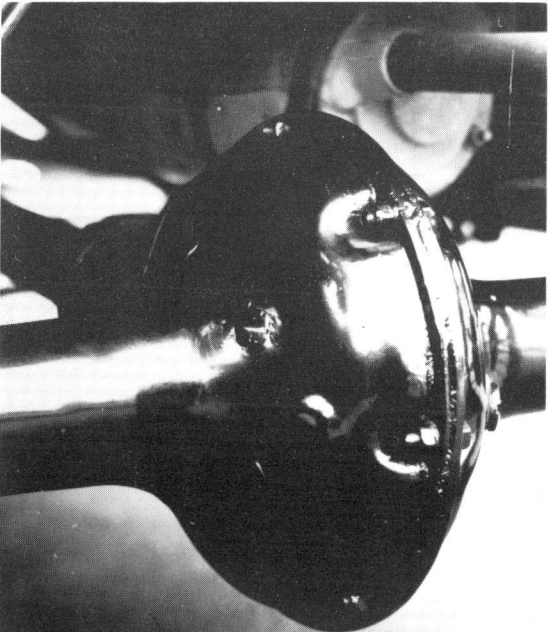

The muffler had cast ends and was asbestos-wrapped, the wrapping being held in place with three metal bands.

Steering wheel was fourteen inches outside diameter; spider is cast bronze (brass), as is the acorn nut. The gear box below the spider is also of brass. The spark and gas knobs are of hard rubber.

Side lamps, standard equipment with the car, were similar to Jno. Brown number 60, square and somewhat less costly than the more elaborate flared sidelamps previously used. An acetylene gas generator was used to provide the illuminating gas for the headlights, and was furnished with the lamps.

Triple-twist Rubes horn is secured to the dashboard. The picture illustrates one early method of mounting the horn bulb; later it was mounted to the body directly. It has been suggested that this unusual mounting is necessary due to the aluminum body construction of this particular car.

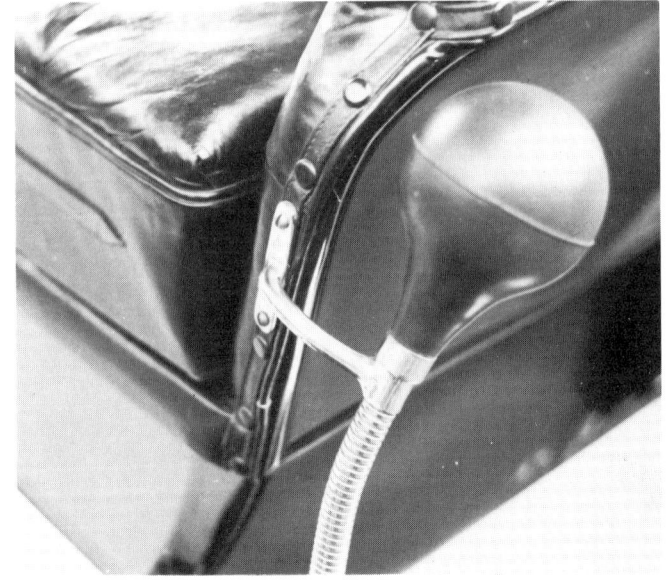

The windshield was not furnished with this "production" 1909 Model T car. When and if the owner wanted one, there were several that he could obtain. Generally, the AUTOMATIC (a brand name, not a description) was used. This made necessary an additional wooden piece that was attached to the lower dashboard and became known (and later produced as standard) as the "two-piece" dashboard.

Illustrating the ingenious latching mechanism of the Automatic windshield. The spring is used to provide a pull on the upper half, in its folded position, in order to keep it from rattling against or damaging the lower half.

Floorboards were of three pieces and were embellished with all-brass pedal trim plates as shown. A fourth, narrow floorboard section is permanently secured to the body as a forward stiffener at the lower edge of the heel kickplate.

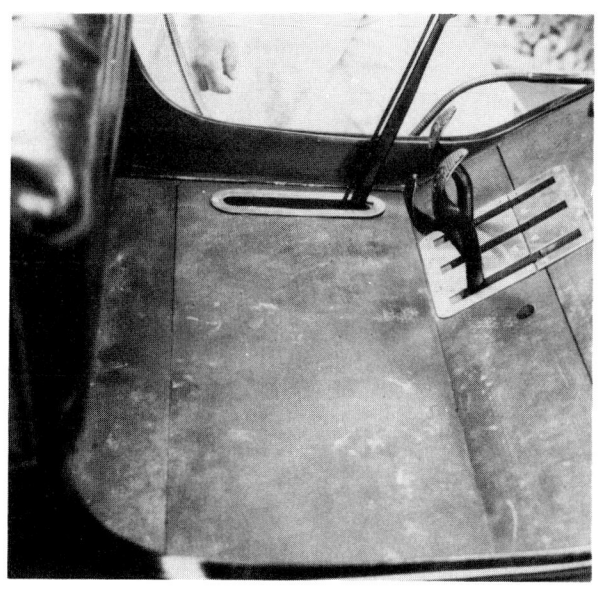

45

A white rubber floor mat of non-slip design was furnished with the car, with cut-outs for the pedal and brake operating area.

The three-pedal, single lever control. The coil box of the car is correctly, a Kingston No. 4200, which is now built so that the coil leads pass through the dashboard instead of under it as in the early series. The "ignition key" is a plug which is inserted into the round, bakelite switch housing.

"Pictures are worth a thousand words." We have tried to tell the story of the 1909 Model T Ford with pictures, as you have seen. Yet, there are some things that cannot be shown, and these things need the words. Less than a thousand, perhaps.

It seems that almost from its conception, the Model T was found lacking. Indeed, Ford must have been engineering the "production" model by the time the first T was produced. There is so much difference between the first 2500 cars and those that followed that one might wonder why the post-2500 cars weren't called the Model "U". A look at the parts manual for 1909 shows pages dedicated to "those cars built before 2500," which were different from the 2500-plus. The past two chapters have covered many of the changes but we will go through some of them here as a sort of synopsis.

No mechanical assembly in the early '09 escaped the eyes of the engineers. From the radiator to the differential, a new design was evolved. Many parts of the early series carried through 1909 and even through 1910, but look what happened after 2500.

The radiator was modified at the time the water pump was dropped, and remained dimensionally standard through the 1916 models.

The engine was redesigned, adding more water jacket area at the front, and eliminating the gear housing that ran the water pump in the earlier engines. The oil filler tube on the left front side was eliminated. The engine number was located on a boss at the lower right front of the engine, just to the rear of the timing gear case. Internal changes included new pistons and connecting rods (early engines had a bushing in the rod which rotated on the piston pin; after 2500, the rod was clamped to the pin as in the later engines), a different crankshaft (longer to take the fan pulley), a new crankcase and transmission cover, cylinder head, crank, commutator (timer) and numerous small items associated with the above. The valves and valve push-rods moved in removable guides in all of the earlier T engines, a feature which continued until Ford really got into high-gear during the teens.

A number of changes were made in the transmission, including new triple gears, clutch disk drum and main shaft, rear ball cap bearing; not to mention the change to the three-pedal system which occurred at about car number 850.

The differential — drive shaft assembly was modified during the model year, as well as at the 2500 point. The first cars had the ring gear riveted to the gear case. This was changed to a bolt-on design at 2500. The troublesome, non-tapered, rear axles remained, however, through the 1910 and into the 1911 model year. Later, Ford advised owners to change to the tapered axles (1911) and offered an exchange deal to those who did so. The rear axle housings were modified during mid year (the third change here) when Ford installed a roller pinion bearing at the rear of the drive shaft. At this time, too, a reinforcing plate was added to the front of the axle housings to better support this new bearing assembly. The inner ends of the axles still ran in the babbitt bearings, however.

Changes throughout the car were so numerous that an entire book might be devoted to them. Let it just be noted that this was truly a *new* Model T. The "production" (after 2500) Model T Ford started a chain of fifteen million that were to follow.

Contrary to popular belief, all were not "peas in a pod." Changes were made all the time to improve the product, cut the cost, or both. As we progress through the model years we will see that it is impossible to say that *any* T is absolutely correct, because to be *correct*, one must compare with a *correct* car, and where can we find such an item — *Ford never made one!*

The 1910 Model T Ford

48

Ford Cars for 1910
1910 for Ford Cars

Control

Model T Touring Car, $950.
Complete equipment
included.

The 1910 Model T Touring featured in this chapter is number 24330, manufactured in May of 1910. Except as noted, it is believed to be authentic, and appears to be largely original.

Model T
Roadster, $900.
Complete equipment
included.

Having produced over fourteen thousand cars by the end of calendar year 1909, The Ford Motor Company was remarkably well along in their plans for a twenty thousand unit year! However, this achievement was not yet to be; the records indicate that calendar year 1910 saw the delivery of *only* 19,739 cars!

January 1, 1910; Number 14162
December 31, 1910; Number 34900

Model T Coupe
$1050.00

Model T
Town Car
$1200.

50

The 1910 Model T Ford was a further refined version of the "production 1909" car which we reviewed in the last chapter. Major changes were limited in nature, and aside from the inclusion of the windshield, headlamps and top, one was hard-pressed to find significant changes. True, running-board design was changed, and bodies were subtly modified to offer easier manufacture, but the essential lines and design of the 1910 car were identical with the earlier late 1909 Obviously, it had not yet occurred to the automobile manufacturers, with their then-unlimited market, to design planned obsolescence into their cars, and Henry Ford set out to make what he believed would have been an unchanged design until his market was saturated.

From the 1910 Sales Catalog, portions of which are reproduced here, we learn that the basic Touring Car, the Roadster, the Coupe and the Town Car were carried over from 1909. Eliminated was the Landaulet, but added was the latest model, the Tourabout. This very practical car appears to have incorporated a second front seat assembly in the rear, mounted on a low deck and removable to enable conversion to a roadster. The "sports car" of its day, the Tourabout, due to the lack of rear doors, was not a "family car", and very few appear to have been sold as compared with the Touring car.

FORD MOTOR CARS

THERE is but one car built in the immense Ford factory, and all the energy, ability, and knowledge of the entire organization is directed to the perfection of this one car, the Model T four-cylinder, twenty horsepower, low priced car of high priced quality. The result is a car that Mr. Ford can well be and is proud of, one that, at the end of twelve months, showed no sign of a waning popularity, a car good enough to warrant its continuance as the 1910 product of the Ford Motor Company.

This car has been tried out in service, it has proven its ability to successfully compete with higher priced cars in tests of serviceability, in trials of endurance and in the every day requirements of the average automobile user.

Fifteen thousand Model T Ford cars delivered prior to December 1, 1909, proved that the Model T car is right, proved it regardless of the low price of which the world generally was skeptical, because they did not appreciate the possibility of making quick sales of a large output offset small sales occasionally made.

Model T Tourabout, $950.
Complete equipment
included.

Model T Tourabout or Roadster, with
rear seat removed and flat deck
and rail ($9.00) substituted.

Typical on the 1910 Fords are the lips on the front fenders.

SUMMARY OF SPECIFICATIONS

BRAKES—Two sets: (a) Service band brake on transmission controlled by pedal; (b) internal expanding brakes in rear hub drums controlled by hand.

CARBURETOR—New design, float feed automatic with dash adjustment.

CLUTCH—Multiple steel discs, operating in oil.

CONTROL—All speeds forward and reverse by foot pedals. Spark and throttle under steering wheel.

COOLING—Thermo syphon and fan.

CRANK CASE—Upper half integral with cylinder casting. Lower half pressed steel and extended to form lower housing for magneto and transmission.

EQUIPMENT—The Touring Car, Tourabout and Roadster include, at the prices shown, an extension top, an automatic brass windshield, a speedometer, two 6-inch gas lamps and generator, three oil lamps, a tubular horn and a kit of tools. The Coupe and Town Car include three oil lamps, horn and tools.

FENDERS—Enclosed full length of car.

FRONT AXLE—One piece drop forging in I-beam section, specially heat treated Vanadium steel.

FINAL DRIVE—By cardon shaft with single universal joint to bevel drive gears in live rear axle. Ford three-point system (patented in all countries) with all moving parts enclosed in dust proof casing, running in oil. Vanadium steel throughout.

GASOLINE CAPACITY—10 gallons. Cylindrical gasoline tank mounted directly on frame.

IGNITION—Ford magneto generator, low tension, direct connected to engine drive.

INTERCHANGEABLE BODIES—

LUBRICATION—Combination splash and gravity system—simple and sure. Insures against insufficient or excessive lubrication.

MOTOR—4 cylinder, 4 cycle, 20 horsepower, 3¾ inch bore, 4 inch stroke. Cylinders cast in one block with water jackets and upper half of crank case integral, water jacketed cylinder head detachable, fine grain gray iron castings.

NUMBER OF PASSENGERS—Normal load, touring car, five adults.

PRICES—Touring Car $950; Roadster $900; Tourabout $950, with full equipment; Coupe $1050; Town Car $1200 F.O.B. Detroit.

SHAFTS—Crank and cam non-welded drop forged heat treated Ford Vanadium steel bearing surfaces ground, cams integral and ground.

SPRINGS—Front, and rear, semi-elliptic transverse.

STEERING—By Ford reduction gear system.

TIRES—Pneumatic; rear 30 x 3½ inches, front 30 x 3 inches.

TRANSMISSION—New design Ford spur planetary, bathed in oil—all gears from heat treated Vanadium steel, silent and easy in action.

VALVES—Extra large, all on right side and offset.

WEIGHT—Touring Car 1200 pounds. Others in proportion.

WHEEL BASE—100 inches; tread 56 inches; 60 inches for Southern roads where ordered.

Side curtains were, and continued to be, a matter of standard supply, furnished with all open cars. Note the flap installed to permit the driver to extend his arm for signaling a turn. This flap is not authentic, but is considered a good safety item, along with safety glass windshield, stop lights and accessory (outside) brakes. Other openings in the side curtains are authentic as to size and placement.

Top sockets were "dog-legged" and in giving the top a wider aspect, also served to emphasize the antique appearance of the car. Note the forged "buggy rail" which ran across the top of the back seat and provided lower-edge fasten point for the top which was now factory-issue, along with the windshield and gas headlamps and generator. Note that front sockets pivot at the seat; tend to block entrance into the front seat of the car.

Bodies were of wood as in the bulk of the 1909 production. Unlike 1909, though, we have no evidence of any aluminum bodies.

Included for the first time as standard equipment, with the 1910 car, was a Stewart speedometer, Model 26, which reads up to 60mph! This speedometer was driven by a ring gear mounted on the right front wheel, through a reducer, with a chain-link cable in a brass shield.

The two-piece "Mae West" or "Figure Eight" type shackles. Although the top five leaves of the front spring had tapered and rounded ends, the sixth leaf appears to have been flat and square-ended. The seventh leaf, of course, joined the shackle.

A small notch was cast into the rear of the axle to allow clearance for the steering arm. This was eliminated later on perhaps to prevent the wheels from turning too far.

Wheels were painted body color which would have been Brewster Green. Striping, when it appeared, was similar in placement to the 1909 car although darts on the spokes of the wheels were left open at their ends to speed up the striping process. Controversy still ranges regarding the authenticity of colors other than Brewster Green, such as black, red or gray, but research to date seems to indicate that all 1910 mid-year cars were originally Brewster Green with black highlighting and striping, if any, in red.

Tires are 30 by 3 in the front; 30 by 3½ in the rear. Wheels are 24" diameter in the front; 23" in the rear.

Illustrating the "butterfly" rear fender irons used only in 1909 and 1910. These passed through holes in the fender vertical aprons to pick up the two eye bolts in the fender mounting plates. The curve in the 1910 splash shield rear edge was less severe than that on the 1909 car.

Typical is the rear roller pinion bearing housing and the clearly-seen reinforcing gusset set into the rear axle housing.

The six-rivet rear axle housing. Note the screw type of filler hole plug. Truss rod is an accessory, not standard equipment.

The "seven-rivet" mounting of the one-piece pan mounts; concealed by the ingenious oil level float housing (see view of dashboard for upper end of this accessory) is the rear ball cap of the front radius rod, which is secured with a cap screw rather than studs and nuts.

The hood is made of aluminum; has no louvres. Note the configuration of the 1909-10 hood former which has an unexplained notch in the edge above the steering column.

The leading and trailing edges of the hood are strengthened with a gusset which also acts to retain a leather strip which serves to cushion the hood on the former and on the radiator.

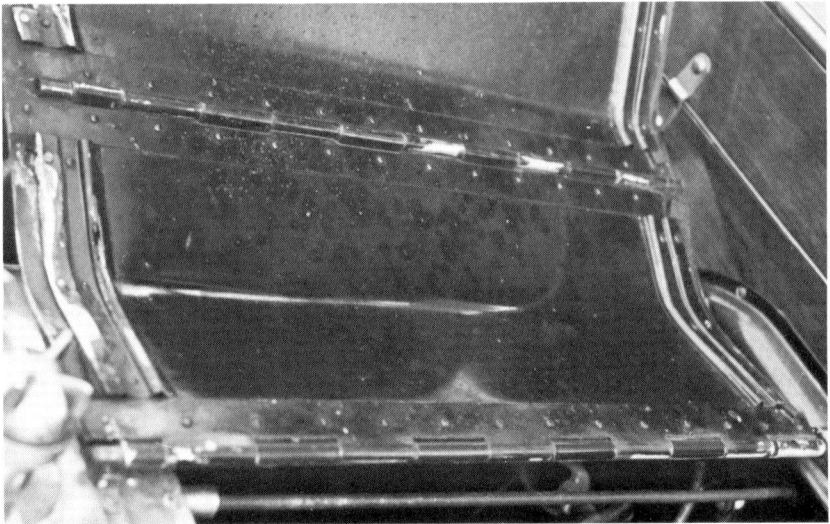

Hood clamps at this time had one ear only; were made of iron, not brass. Dashboard molding is a flat half-round and does not extend beyond the front and rear surfaces of the dashboard. Of brass, the molding was secured by oval-headed brass wood screws.

Steering column lower housing has no provision for lubrication. Owners were cautioned to oil frequently and felt washers were provided as seals.

Engine (and car) number (24334) appeared on a boss at the forward, lower end of the engine block immediately behind the timing gear. Also clearly seen in this picture is the forward valve stem, the lifter for which operated in a brass guide inserted into the block.

Overall view of the right side of the engine. Carburetor is incorrect and should be a Kingston 5-ball. Also incorrect is the explosion whistle mounted on number three cylinder. Note the open-valve block which requires external valve stem lubrication.

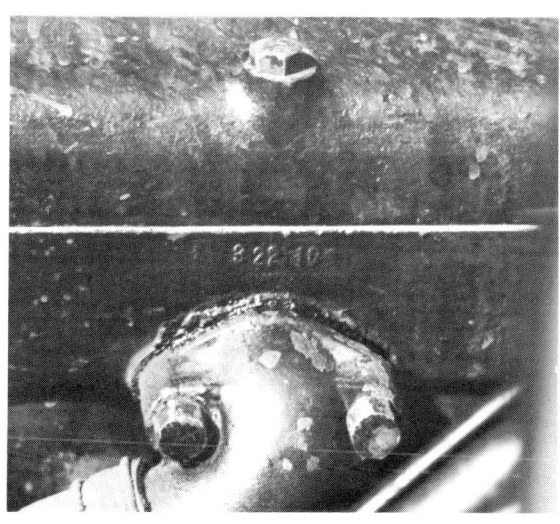

Block casting date is clearly seen in this picture. Located on the left side of the block, immediately above the water inlet, this reads "3 22 10", but the date above indicates that the block was held for aging about two months after casting as was then the custom.

Square-hole transmission cover. Note that the inspection hole cover is a flat steel plate that has been pressed to provide the embossed ridge and script name.

One of the most interesting and little-known identifications appears on the face of the transmission stub shaft which mates with the crankshaft flange. On this surface appears a date which is the day on which this car was assembled. In this case, engine number 24334 was cast on March 10, 1910, but was not assembled until May 4, 1910 (1910-5-4).

The unique 1910 running board with the straight rows of interrupted ridges. These boards are symmetrical in the sense that they could be used on either side. This style of running boards have become extremely scarce.

A brass carbide generator was furnished with the headlights. In the lower tank, a supply of calcium carbide was placed. Water was dripped slowly from the top tank on the carbide and the acetylene gas thus formed was routed to the headlamps via red rubber tubing to furnish a flickering, but effective, illumination. Side and tail lamps were kerosene burning.

Horn is Rubes, triple twist. Seen in this view is an unusual accessory clock made by Stewart and Clark, and furnished in a brass case identical to the speedometer housing. Clock was not factory issue.

Nameplate mounted in the lower front-center and illustrating the brand name "Automatic". These windshields were serialized and each bears its own number which has no relation to the car number.

58

1910 headlamps are Jno. Brown Model 15 and are made in pairs. Lamps are mounted with both doors opening from the center to facilitate lighting burners.

Sidelights are Jno. Brown Model 60, all brass, and have slightly rectangular glass rather than square. Note the two-piece dashboard with the extension supplied to raise the windshield. The extension is not brass-bound. Sidelamp brackets are steel, not brass, and are painted black.

Original leather seat-backs illustrate the careful folding done in upholstering seats. Diamond tufts were not sewn; were only tacked into position after folding. Leather was used throughout and was installed over thick pads of horsehair. Remarkable condition of seats in this car tend to justify the the original choice of material.

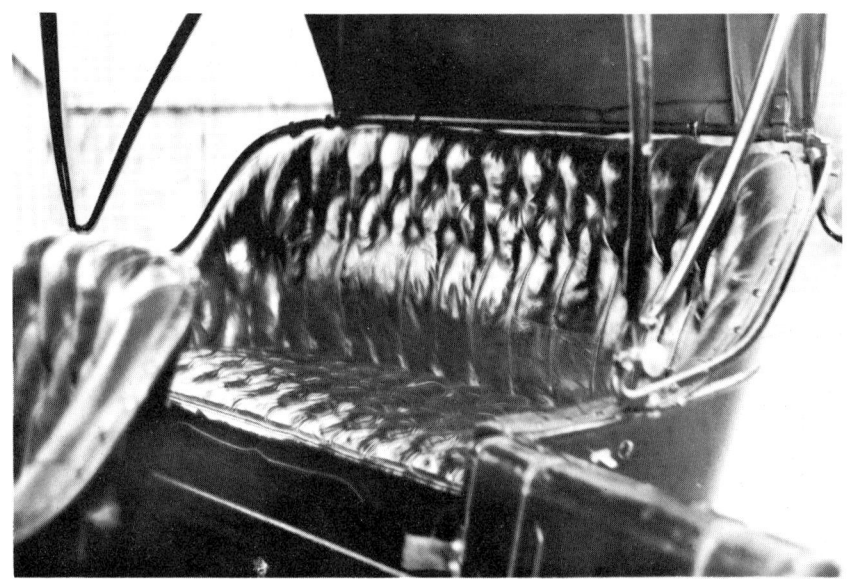

Door panels and check straps were also of leather. Check straps were screwed directly to door; footman's loops were not used. An access panel under the rear seat was hinged at the lower edge and a brass knob was turned to undo the flat steel latch bar and release the panel. Floor covering in the rear was carpet; rubber matting in the front.

We have seen examples of 1910 Touring cars in which a cocoa mat was used in the rear, and which fit up in the "toe area" behind the front seat.

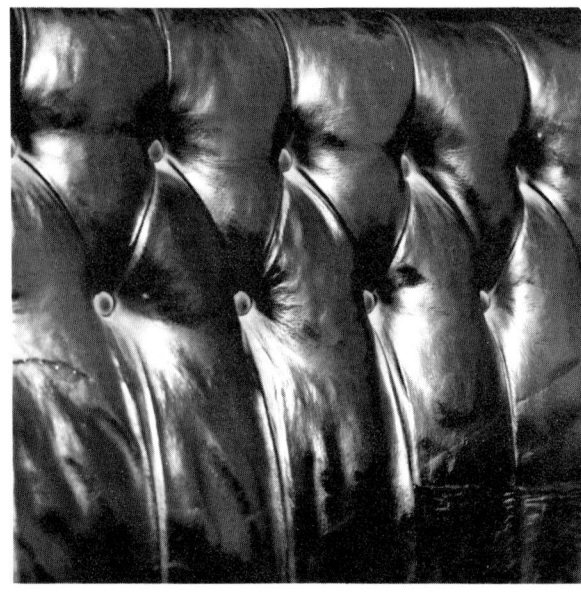

Steering wheel spider, and wheel itself are slightly larger than the same items in the 1909 model. Although still known as a 14'' wheel, this one actually measures 14¼'' outside diameter.

Coil box on this car is Heintz. Box and coils are somewhat different than later units, with location of the contacts and physical size differing and making interchange impossible.

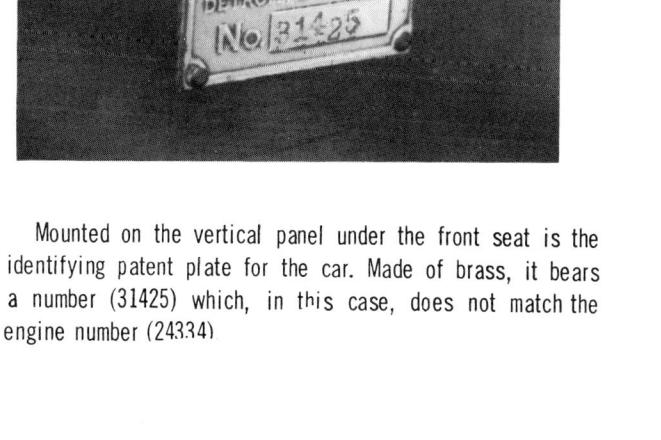

Mounted on the vertical panel under the front seat is the identifying patent plate for the car. Made of brass, it bears a number (31425) which, in this case, does not match the engine number (24334).

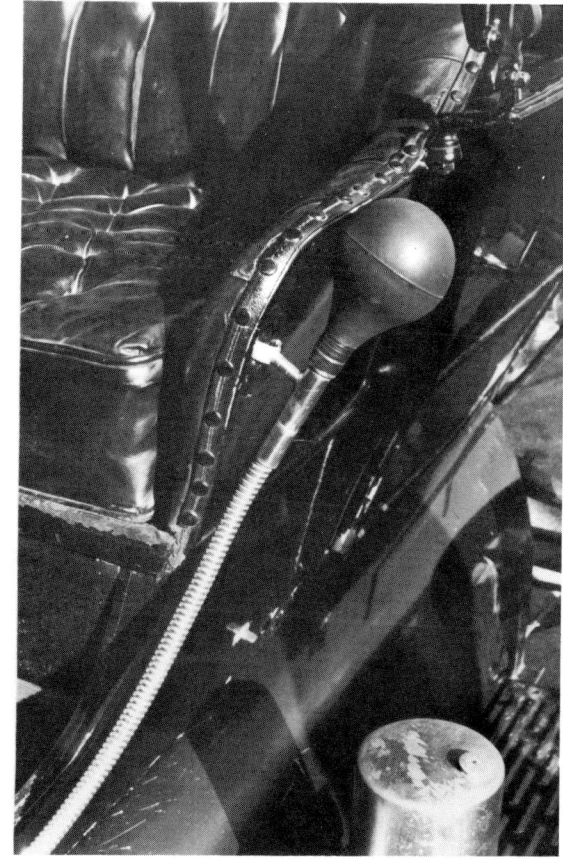

Illustrating the more conventional horn bulb mounting on this car. Contrast with that on the late 1909.

The radiator tank bears the "Winged Script" imprint. Core of radiator is adorned with flat-stock brass "Ford" in the familiar script.

The fasteners used at the lower edge of the top along the "buggy rail" are known as "buggy loops" and are made of circles of leather enclosed by a metal ring. The leather is slotted to provide an opening into which a spool-shaped head on a pin secured to the buggy rail is inserted.

The Automatic windshield was soon replaced with one having far simpler (and cheaper) latching mechanism. Note the large spring used to provide pull on the upper half to prevent rattling in either the up or down position.

These fasteners are known as "Murphy fasteners" and these early versions have cast latches with a large letter "M" impressed in them. They are used throughout the upper portions of the top essentially to (1) lock the rear curtain in place, or (2) secure the side curtains.

The 1911 Model T Ford

Ford Motor Cars 1911

Transitional cars aside, the production version of the 1911 Model T Ford was another step in the constant improvement of the automobile. Perhaps foremost in the changes was the use of the metal body, made of sheet metal formed and installed over wooden stringers. Other significant changes are illustrated in the following article, but some which must be mentioned are the incorporation of the new crankcase cover with access to the lower end bearings of the engine, the transmission cover with the larger access hole for easier band adjustment, the enclosed valve chamber, and the tapered-end rear axles. Illustrations of these major changes, plus identifications of other areas of distinction follow.

PRODUCTION FIGURES
Jan. 1, 1911, number 34901
Dec. 31, 1911, number 88,900

From just under 20,000 units to almost 55,000 in one calendar year! These figures start to tell a story of customer acceptance of this still-new, light-weight family car. In only its third year of production, the car is being produced at an average rate of over 200 per day, and that rate is still increasing!

Despite this then unheard of production rate, Ford was already introducing major mechanical changes, and this car, the 1911, became more nearly representative of the later models than either of its predecessors.

Ford Model T
Torpedo Runabout
Fully Equipped $725
Unequipped $645

The Torpedo Runabout illustrated here on first glance seems to be similar to the Open Runabout, and it in turn resembles the Roadster.

The Torpedo Runabout, in addition to having factory-installed doors to add a sporty appearance, had a lowered seat and steering column which tended to give it a somewhat more racy appearance than the Roadsters. It, and the Open Runabout also had a longer hood (24" versus the conventional 22") and a body that was made to join at the dashboard which was now moved back by two inches. On the rear deck of these two models was a fuel tank, generally oval with an increased capacity (16½ gallons verses ten gallons for the Touring cars).

Ford Model T
Open Runabout
Fully Equipped $680
Unequipped $600

Note that missing from the 1911 catalog is, in addition to the Landaulet which was dropped in the 1910 catalog, the Tourabout. Nevertheless, two original examples of the 1911 Tourabout are known to the author and one of the two is herewith illustrated. This beautiful restoration, engine number 38471 (Feb. 1911), belongs to member Irv Geeslin, of Bakersfield, Calif. Note that the Tourabout was formed by repeating the front seat assembly on the rear deck with the result that an open four-passenger car was obtained of extremely sporty lines.

Ford Motor Cars

"Buy a Ford because it is a Better Car, not because it is Cheaper."
—Henry Ford

Ford Model T
Roadster
Fully Equipped $680
Unequipped $600

GENERAL SPECIFICATIONS

BRAKES—Two sets: (a) Service band brake operates on the transmission and is controlled by a foot pedal; (b) Emergency brake is controlled by hand lever at side of car acting on the drums of rear wheels.
CLUTCH—Multiple steel discs, operating in oil.
CONTROL—Three foot pedals. By pressing the first pedal "C" the slow speed is applied; by releasing, it is in the high speed. The center pedal "R" is for reversing the car. The third pedal "B" is the brake. The FORD Model T can be entirely manipulated either by use of the pedals or by the controlling lever at the side of the car. The carburetor lever and throttle just under the steering wheel will regulate the speed of the car from a walk to 40 miles an hour, without shifting a lever or applying the foot pedals.
COOLING—Thermo-syphon and fan.
CRANK CASE—Upper half integral with cylinder casting. Lower half of pressed steel and extended to form lower housing for magneto and transmission.
EQUIPMENT—The Touring Car, Torpedo Runabout, Open Runabout and Roadster include at the fully equipped prices, a top, automatic brass windshield, speedometer, two gas lamps and generator, three oil lamps, tubular horn and a kit of tools. The Town Car and Coupé equipment include three oil lamps, tubular horn and tools only.
FINAL DRIVE—By cardon shaft with single universal joint to bevel drive gears in live rear axle. FORD three-point system (patented in all countries) with all moving parts enclosed in dust proof casings, running in oil. Vanadium steel throughout.
FRONT AXLE—One piece drop forging in I-beam section, specially heat treated Vanadium steel.
IGNITION—Alternating current magneto, but with no moving parts. Entirely enclosed as an integral part of the engine and running in oil. The FORD magneto always insures a powerful spark. No batteries or dry cells are required.
LUBRICATION—Combination splash and gravity system—simple and effective.
MOTOR—Described in detail on opposite page.
SHAFTS—Crank and cam, non-welded, drop-forged, heat-treated FORD Vanadium steel, with all surfaces ground to absolute accuracy.
SPRINGS—Front and rear, semi-elliptical transverse, all Vanadium.
STEERING—By Ford reduction gear system.
TIRES—Pneumatic; front 30x3 inches, rear 30x3½ inches. Standard makes. Best quality. Larger tires than ordinarily used for weight of the car, which means longest service and greatest comfort.
TRANSMISSION—New design FORD spur planetary, bathed in oil. All gears are of Vanadium steel, silent and smooth running in action.
VALVES—Extra large, all on the right side and offset.
WHEEL BASE—100 inches; tread 56 inches; 60 inch tread for Southern trade when ordered.

All prices are f. o. b. Detroit

Ford Model T
Touring Car
Fully Equipped $780
Unequipped $700

Ford Model T
Coupé $1050
With equipment of 3 Oil Lamps, Horn and Tools only

Ford Model T
Town Car $1200
With equipment of 3 Oil Lamps, Horn and Tools only

Curious is the fact that, as previously, the Town Car was still offered *without* headlamps! Priced at $1200., it was the most expensive of the models, over $400. more than the Touring car at $780. or the lowest-priced model, the Roadster at $680.

67

The proud owner of the 1911 Model T Ford employed for the major illustrations in this article is Chad Champlin, of Los Angeles, Calif. Chad is the third owner of this unusually original car. This particular automobile, engine number 83913, and body number 85522, appears to be largely original although the unusual rear window glass does not appear to be. The top itself could well be original, but most of the 1911 Fords examined appear to have a window style similar to the 1909-10. This car, manufactured in November of 1911, employs essentially all 1911 model year improvements. Cars made earlier that year may differ slightly.

Interesting early pictures of this same car were supplied by the owner and show the original owner, Capt. W. F. Markham and friends on a coyote hunting trip in the Mojave Desert early in the car's life. Note the luggage carrier and the camping equipment. Capt. Markham sold this car in 1934 to another Los Angeles resident who in turn parted with the car in 1964. Careful evaluation of the condition of this particular automobile appears to support the authentic condition.

TRANSITIONAL STYLES

A word about "transitional styles" is in order here. Most unusual of such cars were those manufactured in the change-over period of January-February of 1911 when Ford actually produced cars combining both "metal" and "wooden" bodies. Several of these cars are known to exist which have wooden seat assemblies mounted on metal lower body sections. In addition, it has been established that the engine pan was changed from a one-piece style, including the widening of the diameter across the flywheel and addition of the access holes, but the SQUARE HOLE COVER DESIGN WAS NOT IMMEDIATELY CHANGED! Some few early 1911 cars had, therefore, a very unusual "wider" square hole cover.

Dominating the changed appearance of the 1911-style top is the forward socket which is now hinged to the second socket at a point about two-thirds of the way up, enabling front seat occupants to enter and leave with less interference. On folding the top, this pivot was removed and replaced at the lower pivot of the second socket to enable a smooth folding of the top. Note in the illustration of the Touring Car with top lowered that, since the rear of the body has been lowered, the top now lies flat in the folded position, and contrast this with the earlier body styles.

In front view, the changed appearance of the top is more obvious. Gone are the "dog-legged" top sockets, to be replaced with straight sockets and the consequently narrower top. Note also the two piece dashboard and the less costly "Rands Manufacturing Company" folding windshield.

The radiator is now embellished with the more familiar FORD script. The filler neck, still a machined casting, is higher and is soldered in place. At the lower sides, holes were provided for the passage of the acetylene lines to the headlamps. Ford script on the radiator itself appears to be original and apparently was provided on most cars as standard equipment.

At this time a major change in the front axle appears. Note that the front spindles are now of the more conventional "two-piece" style. In making this change from the earlier "one-piece" spindle, a change in the design of the axle itself was necessitated. In order to clear the new spindle, the axle is now recessed.

Speedometer was standard equipment, and its lower end was attached to a bracket inserted in the arm of the spindle. Special need for this support bracket resulted in design of the right-side arm with the mounting hole. Other details of the speedometer drive are generally similar to earlier styles.

Tie rod ends are now fitted with lubrication cups. Capped oil-filler holes were provided for this purpose. Shackles are still of the "Mae West" style; springs are seven leaf tapered as previously.

71

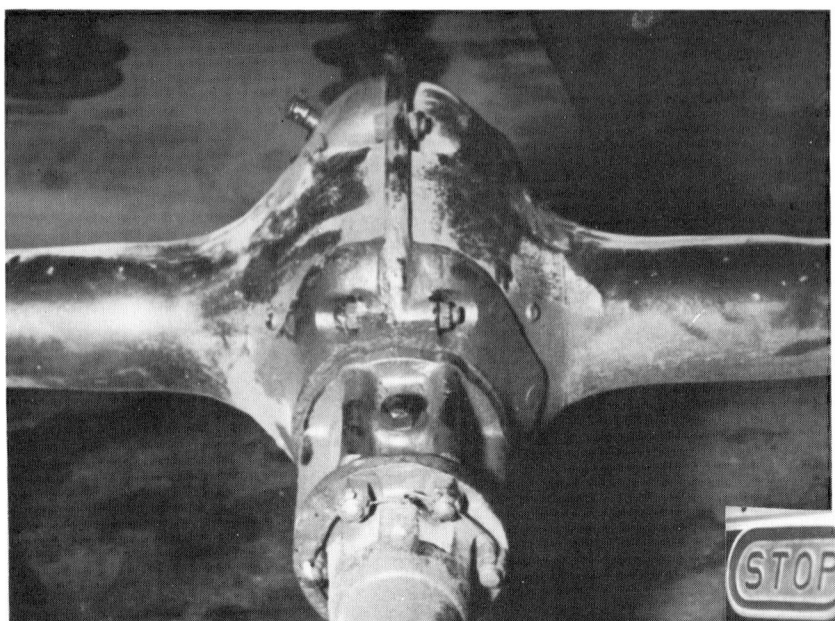

Early 1911 cars had a six-rivet rear end similar to that on the 1910 cars. This style carried through the late spring and possibly in connection with the introduction of the tapered axles (although not necessarily), a newer, more rugged twelve-rivet rear end was introduced.

The twelve-rivet rear end housings were similar in outline to the earlier style but now, with the introduction of the additional reinforcement, were of two-piece construction with the outer section secured to the cast inner section by means of the rivets. Car number 55988 employs the six-rivet rear end; the one on car number 83913 is of the twelve-rivet style. The change was made apparently between May and November of 1911.

The forward end of both driveshafts is of the six bolt hole pattern as last illustrated.

Body styles, although similar through 1911, changed somewhat. Early in the year, the metal body still included an access panel under the rear seat similar to the 1909-10 style (see illustration). Hinges and exposed portion of the latch were of brass.

Later in the year, this access panel was omitted as per the illustration of that section of car number 83913, made in November of 1911.

Wheels are generally similar to the last styles, perhaps a bit thicker in the spokes, but there even seems to be a bit of variation in these areas. Wheels are 24" front (30 by 3 tires and 23" in the rear (30 by 3½ tires).

Although the "straight axle" appears on many cars well into 1911, the later part of the year saw the changeover to the familiar "taper axle." Illustrated is the straight axle assembly of a car assembled in May of 1911. Note the hole in the end of the axle which was used to allow insertion of a pin through the hub, acting as a key. The pin was secured in place by the hub cap and was considered a major weakness as these would often drift through if the caps were lost or defective.

When the change to a tapered axle was made, during 1911, the wheel was fitted snugly to the axle by the taper and a generally more effective assembly resulted. Action of the axle nut forced the tapers firmly together with the result that a mechanical wheel-puller has to be used to remove the wheels.

Earlier hub flanges were smaller in diameter than the conventional six-inch flange. They appear to have been approximately 5½ inches in diameter. Reason for the increase is not clear.

Possibly one of the most significant changes during 1911 was the provision of the tapered-hole transmission cover. This construction enabled the owner to adjust the bands and clutch with greater ease. He still had to remove the cover to change the bands, though. Internally at about this time, there was also a change in the construction of the field coil to a pressed steel ring in place of the earlier casting, and a simplification of the shape of the magnets to the more familiar U-shaped style.

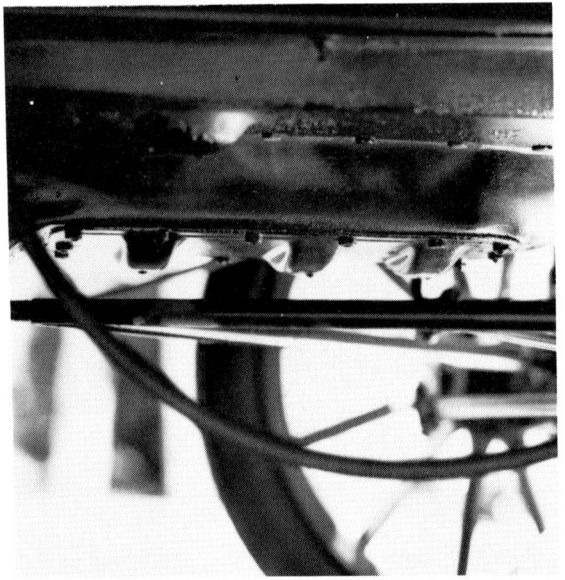

The crankcase was modified to provide an inspection plate enabling adjustment of the rod bearings without removal of the engine from the car. Access to the fourth rod and the front and rear main bearings remained limited for some time to come.

The radius-rod ball fits into its cap and is secured by cap screws, the heads of which are safety wired to prevent backing out. Also visible is the round, screwdriver-slotted drain plug at the lower crankcase drain.

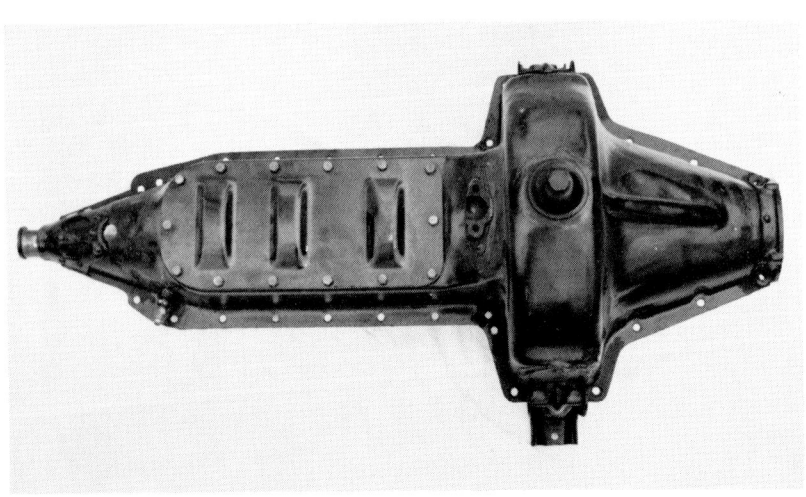
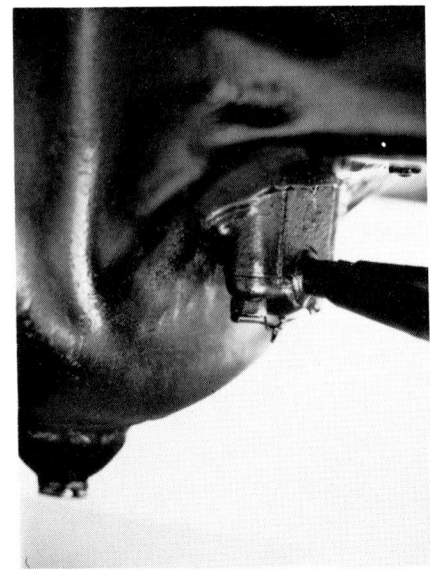

At what appears to be engine number 50,000, a major design change was instituted in the engine block. Although there appears to be some overlapping, possibly due to the manufacture of blocks at two or more foundries, it is evident that at about this time the enclosed-valve block was introduced.

Due to the relatively unsatisfactory nature of the open-valve arrangement with its leakage and the sticking valves caused by lack of lubrication, the block was redesigned to provide a chamber, actually two chambers, over which covers were placed and engine fumes encouraged to lube the valves. A clear photo of this arrangement on early block number 55988 is illustrated.

Casting dates are located above the water inlet and it appears that an insert was made in the mold to provide for date changes. Serial number is still located, on these early blocks, on the lower right front of the engine, just behind the bulge of the camshaft gear housing.

The timer is still of the two-piece brass style through June of 1911. Camshaft gears were straight-cut spur type.

The intake manifold, though cast of aluminum, is no longer of the "gooseneck" style, rather it is somewhat straighter. Carburetor is Holley and the hot air tube is cast.

The cylinder head has the familiar FORD script, but does not have the other identifications.

The exhaust pipe now fits the exhaust manifold with the flared lip and familiar pack nut.

75

Headlamps are Jno. Brown Model 19.

Horn, while still a double-twisted unit, now has its lip at an angle which appears more consistant with the contours of the body.

Sidelamps are Jno. Brown Model 85. Somewhat more square than the Jno. Brown Model 60 used in 1910, they appear more compact and less affluent.

Steering wheel, still installed on a brass spider, has been increased to 15 inches outside diameter, causing an increase in the size of the spider over the earlier style. Wheel itself is unpainted and appears to be of cherry wood.

Coil box is Heintz model 4600, although both Kingston and Jacobson-Brandon had provided somewhat similar coil boxes for 1911 cars. Speedometer is Stewart model 26. A rectangular patent plate is secured to the dashboard. Note the original floor mat with layout of FORD script.

The lower flange of the radiator is pierced to accept a carburetor choke pull rod. Earlier 1911 models employed either a five-ball Kingston or a Holley 4150 carburetor neither of which had a choke butterfly. Both were furnished however with a small priming plunger which served to displace the float and cause the gasoline level to rise above its normal level.

Note the unique design of the front fender irons which now provide an eye into which the leather strap holding the top is now hooked.

Gasoline tank is fitted with the cast brass spigot, riveted in place. Note that this spigot, when installed in the car, is outside the frame. Brackets on the gas tank are riveted in place, not soldered.

Front fenders in the 1911 model (right) differed from the earlier style (left). Note that the fender appears to be wider, principally due to the change in construction. The fender now curves in toward the hood and appears, therefore, to be substantially different than the earlier types.

(Ed. note: The accompanying pictures of the 1911 car were not necessarily of the same car, in fact there were several involved. This will explain the differences in some of the accessories. Pictures were selected that best illustrate the area under consideration and other features that may be shown in these pictures are not necessarily correct for all 1911 models.)

The rear fender of the 1911 (right and bottom) is modified with a flange that joins the body directly, and with this junction, the vertical lower "apron" is now omitted. The upper left picture illustrates the earlier style (1910).

The rear fender is secured to the body with the same two bolts at the rear edge of the running boards, but now the early "butterfly" brackets have been eliminated. In their place is a simple, single bracket, fastened to the body, with only one receptacle now needed on the fender. These receptacles, or fender "eyes," are secured to the sheet metal with 5/16" rivets.

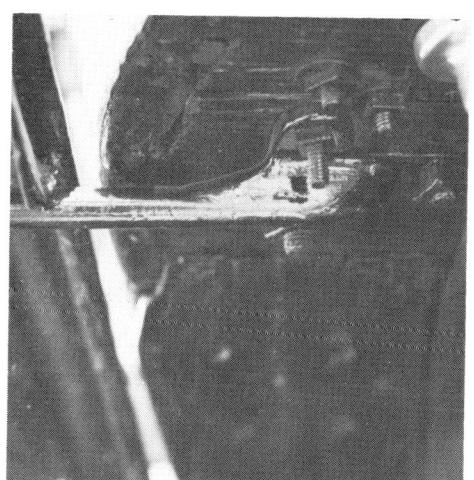
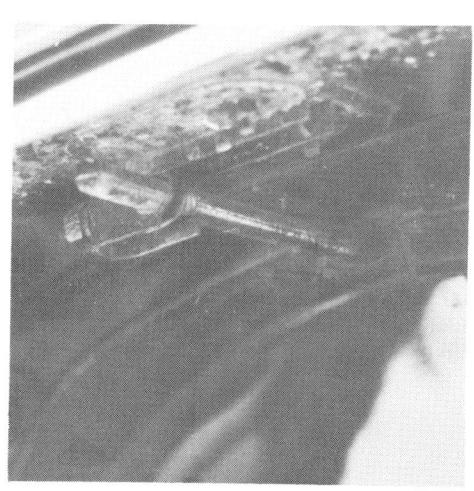

Running boards are of the lengthwise script style and are not interchangeable from one side of the car to the other.

The splash apron has an unusual bulge at the rear as well as a flatted section which adjoins the running boards. Diamond pattern of the running boards appears to be basic from now on although the placement and position of the FORD script will vary.

Door handles are changed in appearance although the door locking mechanism is identical with the earlier models. Hinges are castings and not stampings as previously. Striping appears not to be authentic (correctly, it appears inside the body highlights in the position shown on the photo of the door latching mechanism, a different car, incidentally).

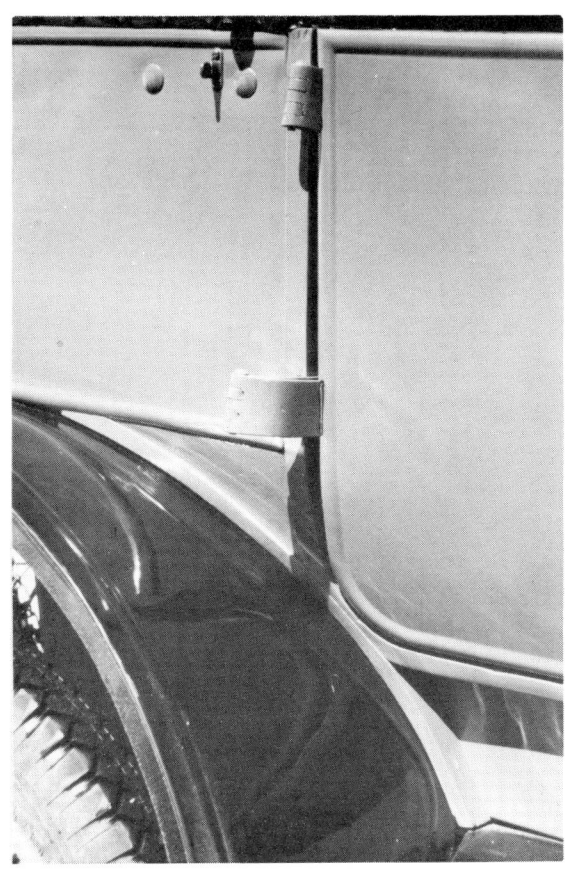

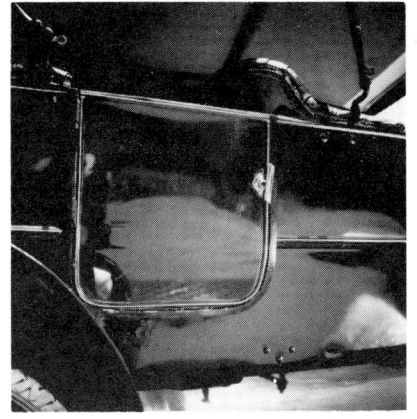

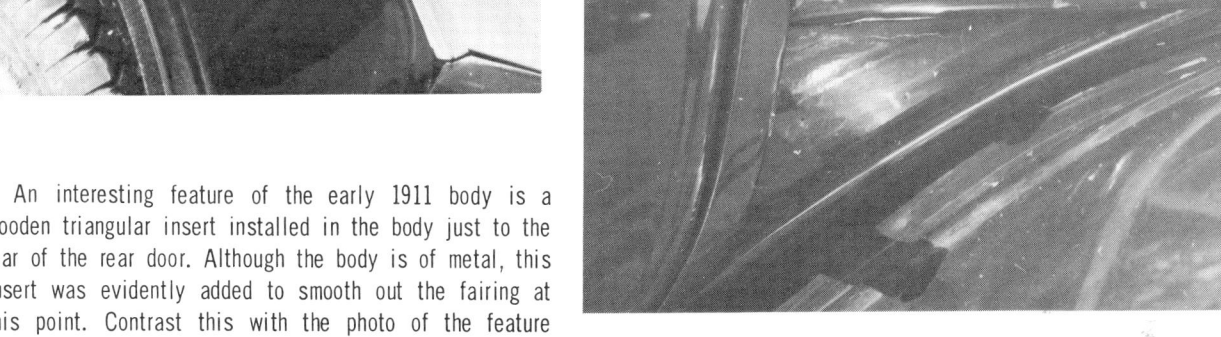

An interesting feature of the early 1911 body is a wooden triangular insert installed in the body just to the rear of the rear door. Although the body is of metal, this insert was evidently added to smooth out the fairing at this point. Contrast this with the photo of the feature car which more nearly represents the nature of the later 1911 metal body, and omits this wooden insert.

Hood latch is cast, slender, and a bit wider across the ring than earlier ones. Wooden sill boards are painted body color. Hood is of aluminum; contains no louvres.

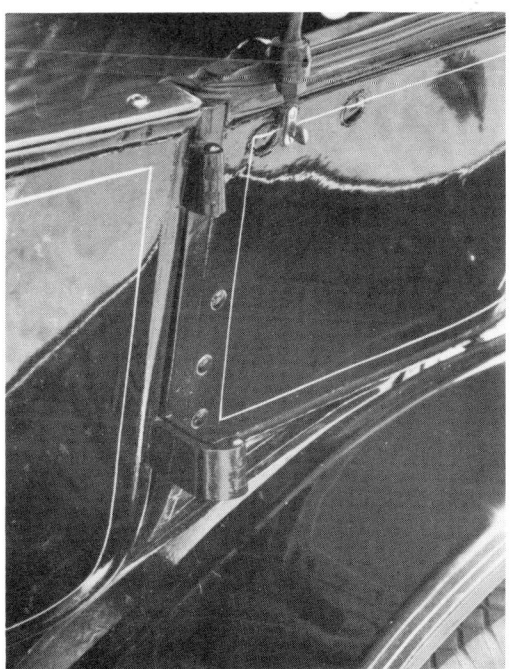

A brass trim plate was furnished, both front and rear, on the sill under the rear door and on the exposed portion of the front sill. Early front sills were considerably narrower than the later ones and followed the 1910 style, while the later ones were wider and similar to that shown here.

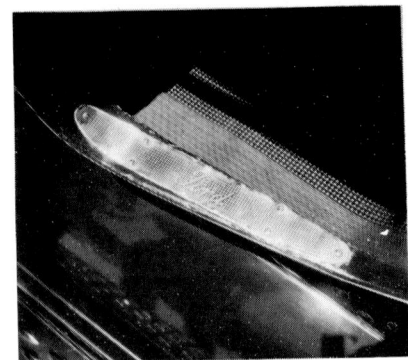

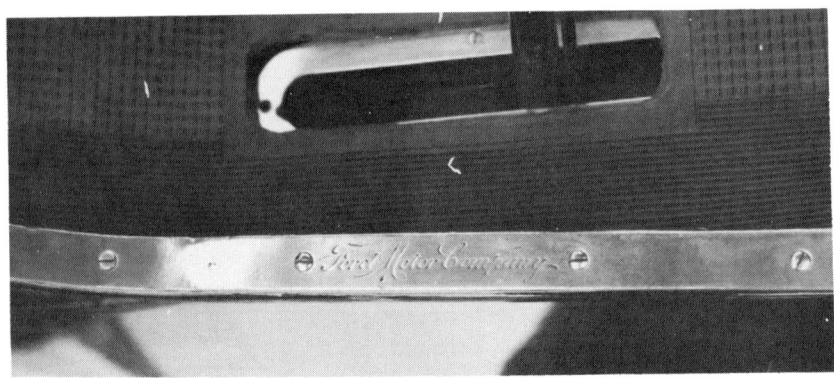

82

Detail of the hinge of the Rands Manufacturing Company's folding windshield. The windshield can be held in several positions by means of detents in the hinge.

The nameplate is installed in top center facing the rear of the car. It is secured with small brass drive pins.

View of original cast brass top fastener. "M" stands for Murphy, the original manufacturer whose name was lent to this style of fastener. These were used to secure the side curtains to the car, and were held in place by oval-headed screws.

"Were there any black Ts in 1911?" While we have been unable to find written evidence of any, there always seems to be an example. This view of one 1911, with what appears to be about eight coats of different colors applied over the years, shows, under one of the Murphy fasteners, what appears to be the original paint, complete with the stripe. The color: Black, with the stripe in gold!

The Two 1912 Model T Fords

By 1912, the Ford Motor Company had its finger on the pulse of the market and the Market, in turn, had now displayed an enthusiasm for Ford. In this calendar year were to be produced over 82,000 Model T Fords! Production numbers indicate:

    Jan. 1, 1912, no. 88,901
    Dec. 31, 1912, no. 171,300

Many relatively minor changes were made during the year, and some of them are chronicled here, but the most unusual discovery of our extensive research is the fact that there definitely were *two* models of the Model T Ford produced during the year, both to be known as the 1912 Model T Ford.

Illustrated are representatives of the two major categories. The earlier, apparently produced well into April of that year, greatly resembles the 1911 body style, but is characterized by the one-piece dash board. Note the "step" under the front seat assembly and the discontinuous lines of the sides. The top straps, on this model, are still fastened to the lower radiator area to an eye furnished for the purpose. The latest authentic car we have found with this style body is engine number 104,277.

Confirmed by the "Second Edition, April 1912" Sales Catalog, from which the illustrations on the next page have been taken, is the other, later, 1912 body style illustrated below. Characteristic of this model are the smooth sides, the lack of a "step" under the front seat, and the shorter top straps which now fasten to the center hinge area of the windshield. The earliest authentic such model which we have located, illustrated here, is number 110,369.

MODEL T TORPEDO The Model T Torpedo differs from the earlier model in several respects. Now furnished with a seat at the same height (not dropped, along with the steering column as earlier), it really differed little from the Roadster except that it was furnished with doors which were non-detachable, and on the rear deck, a sixteen gallon gas tank plus a metal tool box. Both doors opened, unlike the Touring car, and the top straps now fastened to the windshield support.

MODEL T ROADSTER The Roadster, cataloged as "Model T Commercial Roadster," was built with a removable rear single seat which afforded the owner an opportunity to convert from a three-passenger car to a two-passenger "pickup," as by removing the seat, he had a flat space 3½ by 2½ feet wide well suited for carrying extra loads.

DELIVERY CAR For the first time, a commercial vehicle, other than perhaps a taxi cab, was now offered as a standard part of the line of Model T Fords. Featuring its ability to turn in a 28 foot circle and to carry up to 750 pounds of cargo, the car has come to be known as the "pie wagon," although that description did not appear in the literature. Body was of wood and featured rear doors opening at the center.

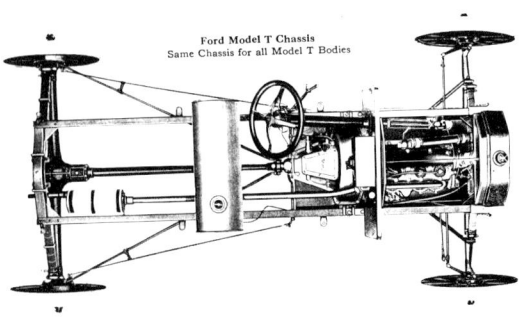

TOURING CAR Major feature was the appearance of the front doors (called "fore-doors"). These were standard, and detachable (Ford DID seem to straddle the issue) on the smooth-sided body introduced in April, and the fore-door assemblies were made available for owners of earlier, open models who wished to obtain and install same on their cars. In making these available, it is noted, they were still manufactured for right-hand opening only. Only the doors on the Torpedo model were made to open on both sides.

TOWN CAR Now furnished with detachable front doors, the Town Car was the model of elegance of the line. It was furnished with two small folding seats, thereby offering seating capacity for two extra passengers. Body on this model seems to have been similar to the 1911 style. Landau top was folding and could be laid back to open rear passenger compartment.

TWO UNUSUAL FORDS, owned by Paul Antonucci, Pittsburgh, Pa.

SPECIFICATIONS
For all Ford Model T Cars

Motor—Four (4) cylinder, four cycle. Cylinders are cast en-bloc with water jackets and upper half of crank case integral. Cylinder bore is 3¾ inches; piston stroke is 4 inches. The Ford Motor is rated at twenty (20) horsepower. Special Ford removable cylinder head permits easy access to pistons, cylinders and valves. Lower half of crank case, one-piece pressed steel extended so as to form bottom housing for entire power plant—air proof, oil proof, dust proof. All interior parts of motor may be reached by removing plate on bottom of crank case—no "tearing down" of motor to reach crank shaft, cam shaft, pistons, connecting rods, etc. Vanadium steel is used in all Ford crank and cam shafts and connecting rods.

Unit Construction—There are four (4) complete units in the construction of Ford Model T—the power plant, the front axle, the rear axle and the frame. Any of these may be removed or replaced as a single unit.

Three-Point Suspension—Each of the Ford Model T units is suspended at three points of the chassis. This method of suspension insures absolute freedom from strain on the parts and permits the most comfortable riding of the car body.

Transmission—Special Ford Spur Planetary type, combining ease of operation and smooth, silent running qualities. Clutch is so designed as to grip smoothly and positively and when disengaged to spring clear away from the drums, thus assuring positive action and maximum power. Transmission cover is of aluminum.

Magneto—Special Ford design, built in and made a part of the motor. Only two parts to the Ford Magneto, a rotary part attached to the flywheel and a stationary part attached to the cylinder casting. No brushes, no commutators, no moving wires to cause annoyance on the Ford Magneto.

Lubrication—Combination gravity and splash system. Oil is poured into the crank case through the breather pipe on the front cylinder cover. All moving parts of motor operate in oil and distribute it to all parts of the power plant.

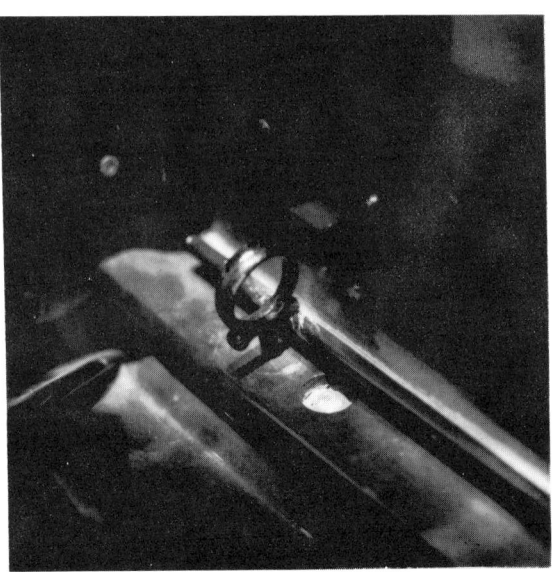

SPECIFICATIONS
(Continued)

Wheels and Tires—Wooden wheels of the artillery type with extra heavy hubs. Only tires of the highest grade are used on Ford cars. Front, 30 x 3 inches. Rear, 30 x 3½ inches.

Final Drive—Ford triangular drive system with all shaft, universal joint and driving gears enclosed in dust proof and oil proof housing. Direct shaft drive to the center of the chassis; only one universal joint is necessary. All shafts revolve on roller bearings; a ball and socket arrangement in the universal joint relieves the passengers of all shocks and strains caused by the unevenness of the road. The Final Drive of the Ford Model T is patented in all countries.

Axles—Front axle of I-beam construction, specially drop-forged from a single ingot of Vanadium steel, insuring the highest quality of axle strength obtainable. Rear axle also of Vanadium steel and enclosed in a tubular steel housing. The Ford Differential is of the three-pinion bevel type; all gears are drop-forgings made of Vanadium steel; all teeth are accurately planed and hardened.

Bodies and Capacity—Ford Model T cars are furnished with five styles of bodies—Fore-door Touring Car capable of carrying five (5) passengers; Torpedo Runabout for two (2) passengers; Commercial Roadster with rumble seat, three (3) passengers; Town Car, six (6) passengers; Delivery Car, two (2) passengers, 750 pounds merchandise capacity.

Prices—Fore-door Touring Car, f.o.b. Detroit . $690
    Torpedo Runabout   " " . 590
    Commercial Roadster   " " . 590
    Town Car   " " . 900
    Delivery Car   " " . 700

Equipment—All Ford Model T's are sold completely equipped—no Ford cars will be sold unequipped. Standard equipment includes Top, Windshield, Gas Lamps, Generator, Speedometer, Three Oil Lamps, Horn and Kit of Tools.

Weight—Touring Car, 1200 pounds. Others in proportion.

Wheel Base—100 inches; Standard tread 56 inches; 60 inches for Southern roads where ordered. All Ford Model T cars will turn in a twenty-eight (28) foot circle.

SPECIFICATIONS
(Continued)

Cooling—By Thermo Syphon water system. Extra large water jackets and a special Ford vertical tube radiator permit of a continuous flow of cool water and prevent excessive heating. A belt-driven fan is also used in connection with the cooling system.

Carburetor—New design, float feed automatic with dash adjustment.

Clutch—Multiple steel disc, operating in oil. There are 27 discs on the Ford Clutch.

Fenders—Large and graceful in design, enclosing the entire length of car.

Gasoline Capacity—Touring Car, Commercial Roadster, Town Car and Delivery Car, cylindrical gasoline tanks of 10 gallons capacity and mounted directly on frame under front seat. Torpedo Runabout, cylindrical tank of 16 gallons mounted back of seat.

Steering—By Ford reduction gear system. Steering knuckles and spindles are forged from special heat-treated Vanadium steel and are placed behind front axle.

Valves—Extra large, all on right side of motor and enclosed by two small steel plates, making their action absolutely noiseless. Enclosed valves are dust proof, thereby saving wear on valve stems and push rods and giving perfect valve setting.

Control—On the left side of car. Three foot-pedal controls, low and high speeds, reverse, and brake on the transmission. Hand lever for neutral and emergency brake on left side of car. Spark and throttle levers directly under steering wheel. Ford cars may be stopped or started without removing the hands from the wheel.

Brakes—Dual system on all Ford Model T cars. Service brake operates on the transmission and is controlled by foot pedal. Expanding brake in rear wheel drums serves as emergency brake. It is controlled by hand lever on left side of car.

Springs—Both front and rear springs are semi-elliptical transverse, all made of specially Ford heat-treated Vanadium steel. Ford Model T springs are the strongest and most flexible that can be made. Model T rear springs are extra large, giving easiest riding qualities to car body.

Note the machined filler, soldered to the tank, and the high "ears" on the radiator cap.

The brass molding around the dash is now flat and overlaps both sides of the panel. Dash is of one piece, and is square at the upper corners.

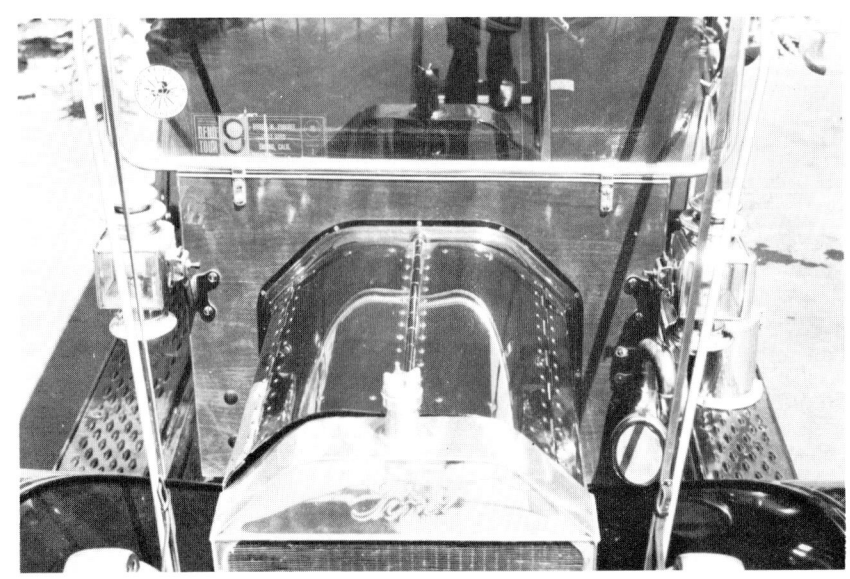

The Fore-Door was affixed to the dashboard with two bolts, and a bracket ran down to the lower frame rail through the floor board which was notched for this bracket.

The Fore-Door on the left side did not open, but that on the right was fitted with a latch and the sill was further modified to provide a metal strike-plate for the sliding latch which is clearly seen in the illustration on the facing page.

We have illustrated here the same car both with and without the Fore-Doors in order to show how the addition of same has altered the appearance of the early car.

Inside panels of the Fore-Doors were of leatherette, and the latches differed in that the rear latch knob was round and that in front was tapered. Note the change in latch from that employed on the earlier car where an external, brass handle was employed with a double-locking latch.

Number 104277, owned by Hy Pingree, Encino, Cal.

Number 110369, owned by Marty Fischer, Newhall, Calif.

Notable in the later 1912 body style was the hinging of the doors with the hinge installed so that both doors opened from the rear! Reminiscent of modern advertising claims, with this approach, it was possible for passengers to enter both the front and rear compartments at the same time from the same side of the car.

The upper illustration shows the rear door arrangement of the early 1912 car (and the preceeding years as well) with the hinge at the rear.

The center illustration is employed to show the rear-opening door on the later 1912 model. Note that it actually is a bit awkward to enter the rear seat due to the intrusion of the fender line on the access.

The left side picture illustrates the cocoa mat (30 by 28″) now installed in the rear compartment. The front mat was still of rubber.

The lower photo invites the entry of two passengers at the same time into the car, and from the same side!

96

Wheels are made with sturdy wooden spokes, 30 by 3" tires in front; 30 by 3½ in the rear. Hub caps are brass and now have the Ford script, but are otherwise plain. Front wheel bearings are ball type, both inner and outer race.

Running boards are of a non-symetrical design with the Ford script running lengthwise, requiring that a right and a left side pair be used.

Front end view: note the seven-leaf tapered end spring; aluminum crank handle; "Mae West" shackles; two piece spindles with tie-rod ends now fitted with oilers.

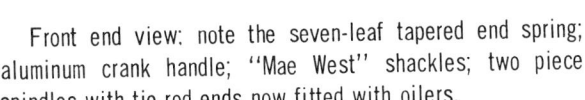

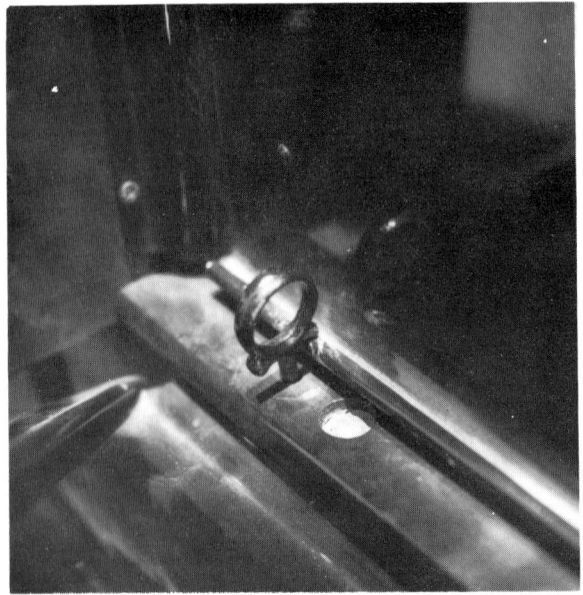

Engine hood, of aluminum, having no louvres, is secured by two-eared clamps against a wooden sill which is painted black. The steering wheel, incidentally, was also painted black.

Fundamentally unchanged, the engine looks about as it has since early in the series. The head has been raised slightly and the combustion chamber size increased, thereby lowering the compression ratio.

The crankcase is unchanged from that used in 1911, employing a three-dip removable inspection plate. The radius rods are still connected above the axle at the spring perch and secured at the rear end by cap screws on the ball joint cap.

A very unusual oil filler, integral with the timer, was used briefly in 1912 and is illustrated here. Expensive to produce and replace, and generally unsatisfactory because of so much oil in the timer, it was shortly discarded in favor of the more conventional style (which had been used since the later 1909 models).

Engine numbers have been relocated during this period. Earlier blocks had their serial numbers located on a boss at the lower right front immediately behind the timing gear housing. Casting dates were emplaced on a less clear boss over the water inlet. Such a block has been located at engine number 92270.

Later, the engine number was placed on a boss just aft of the water inlet, with the casting date shown on the block above the inlet. Note the screw heads apparently used to secure the casting date plate. Such an engine, number 116341, has been located and its photo is reproduced here. Casting is 1-30-12.

Still later, the engine number was again relocated to a boss located directly above the water inlet where the casting date used to appear, and this is where it remained through the balance of Model T production. Such an engine, number

127863, cast on 1-5-12, has been located, proving that changes in castings were made at different times in the different foundry lines!

The Dodge Brothers factory was manufacturing flywheels (along with many other parts) for the Ford Motor Company at this time as evidenced by the benchmark shown on the illustrated 1912 torpedo transmission. Note also the change in the shape and size of the magnets to the more conventional ones, from the illustration on Page 42.

Sidelamps are either Jno. Brown Model 100 as illustrated or could have been E&J "Pat. 1909."

Headlamps are either Jno. Brown Model 19, as illustrated, or could have been E&J No. 466.

Note the conversion by the owner to electric lighting. There were available lampholders such as is shown which would permit the dual electric wires to be inserted in place of the acetylene gas tube, and the bulbs illuminated by battery (the magnetos at this time were not able to supply both ignition and illumination power). Proper and original 1912 headlamp source was gas. Sidelights were oil (kerosene) as was the tail lamp.

Rear view of the 1912 Ford. Note "twelve-rivet" rear axle housings, tapered rear spring ends and three-tiered Jno. Brown oil tail lamp.

101

It is not the purpose or the intent of the Authors to establish inflexible rules regarding these identifications. Rather, we are describing a particular car in each chapter, one which represents to the Authors a car most nearly representative of the model year under consideration.

The 1913 Model T Ford

"To date, more than three hundred and seventy-five thousand FORD cars have been delivered! Practically every third car on the American highways is a FORD car."

"In the season just ended, the Ford Motor Company manufactured and sold more than seventy-five thousand new cars — a remarkable accomplishment for twelve short months — a record that represents even more than one-third of America's entire automobile output."

"In nearly six thousand cities and towns of the United States and Canada, FORD cars and FORD parts are for sale by responsible dealers."

. . . .*November 1912 Ford Motor Company catalog.*

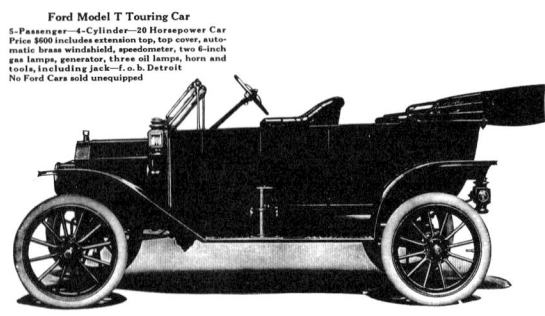

Ford Model T Touring Car
5-Passenger—4-Cylinder—20 Horsepower Car
Price $600 includes extension top, top cover, automatic brass windshield, speedometer, two 6-inch gas lamps, generator, three oil lamps, horn and tools, including jack—f. o. b. Detroit
No Ford Cars sold unequipped

The 1913 Model year brought a newer and different Ford than that produced even towards the latter half of 1912. Bodies were again changed to smooth out the contours; rear doors were again hung with the hinges at the rear, and windshields were relocated to give a somewhat more streamlined effect to the whole automobile.

Gone was the lavish use of brass in lamps with the 1913 style now being made of black-painted steel, trimmed with brass. Greatly resembling following cars, this model on study provides a definite line of demarcation from the earlier and more 'antique-looking' Fords.

Specifications
For all Ford Model T Cars

Motor—Four (4) cylinder, four cycle. Cylinders are cast en-bloc with water jackets and upper half of crank case integral. Cylinder bore is 3¾ inches; piston stroke is 4 inches. The *Ford* Motor is rated at twenty (20) horsepower. Special *Ford* removable cylinder head permits easy access to pistons, cylinders and valves. Lower half of crank case, one-piece pressed steel extended so as to form bottom housing for entire power plant—air proof, oil proof, dust proof. All interior parts of motor may be reached by removing plate on bottom of crank case—no "tearing down" of motor to reach crank shaft, cam shaft, pistons, connecting rods, etc. Vanadium steel is used in all *Ford* crank and cam shafts and connecting rods.

Unit Construction—There are four (4) complete units in the construction of *Ford Model T*—the power plant, the front axle, the rear axle and the frame.

Three-Point Suspension—Each of the *Ford Model T* units is suspended at three points of the chassis. This method of suspension insures absolute freedom from strain on the parts and permits the most comfortable riding of the car body.

Transmission—Special *Ford* spur planetary type, combining ease of operation and smooth, silent running qualities. Clutch is so designed as to grip smoothly and positively and when disengaged to spring clear away from the drums, thus assuring positive action and maximum power.

Clutch—Multiple steel disc, operating in oil.

Magneto—Special *Ford* design, built in and made a part of the motor. Only two parts to the *Ford* Magneto, a rotary part attached to the flywheel and a stationary part attached to the cylinder casting. No brushes, no commutators, no moving wires to cause annoyance on the *Ford* Magneto.

PRODUCTION FIGURES
Fiscal year, October 1, 1912 to September 30, 1913.

Motor No.	B1 to B12,247
Motor No.	169,452 to 370,147
Car No.	150,001 to 332,500

Ford Model T Runabout
2-Passenger—4-Cylinder—20 Horsepower Car
Price $525 includes top, top cover, automatic brass windshield, speedometer, two 6-inch gas lamps, generator, three oil lamps, horn and tools, including jack—f. o. b. Detroit
No Ford Cars sold unequipped

Although over 75,000 cars were produced last year, it took this, the *fifth*, fiscal year of production to provide Henry Ford with an over one-hundred thousand car production year! In the Ford Motor Company 1913 fiscal year, which ended on September 30, 1913, Ford produced 168,220 cars.*

Figures conflict as to the total number of cars actually produced. According to our records, Ford produced 212,943 engines (which may or may not have ended up in cars), and cars with serial numbers from 150,001 to 332,500 (182,499 cars). The 168,220 figure is from Ford's 1918 sales book.

Specifications
—Continued

Lubrication—Combination gravity and splash system. Oil is poured into the crank case through the breather pipe on the front cylinder cover. All moving parts of motor work in oil and distribute it to all parts of the power plant.

Cooling—By Thermo-Syphon water system. Extra large water jackets and a special *Ford* vertical tube radiator permit of a continuous flow of water and prevent excessive heating. A belt-driven fan is also used in connection with the cooling system.

Carburetor—Special design, float feed automatic with dash adjustment. No spring attachment on air valve.

Gasoline Capacity—Touring Car, Runabout and Town Car have cylindrical gasoline tanks of 10 gallons capacity mounted directly on frame under front seat.

Steering—By *Ford* planetary reduction gear system. Steering knuckles and spindles are forged from special heat-treated Vanadium steel, and are placed behind front axle.

Valves—Extra large, all on right side of motor and enclosed by two small steel plates, making their action noiseless.

Control—On the left side of car. Three foot-pedal controls, low and high speeds, reverse, and brake on the transmission. Hand lever for neutral and emergency brake on left side of car. Spark and throttle levers directly under steering wheel.

Brakes—Dual system on all Ford Model T cars. Service brake operates on the transmission and is controlled by foot pedal. Expanding brake in rear wheel drums serves as emergency brake. It is controlled by hand lever on left side of car.

Springs—Both front and rear springs are semi-elliptical transverse, all made of specially *Ford* heat-treated Vanadium steel. *Ford Model T* springs are the strongest and most flexible that can be made.

Specifications
—Continued

Wheels and Tires—Wooden wheels of the artillery type with extra heavy hubs. Only tires of the highest grade are used on *Ford* cars. Front 30x3 inches. Rear 30x3½ inches.

Final Drive—*Ford* triangular drive system with all shafts, universal joint and driving gears enclosed in dust proof and oil proof housing. Direct shaft drive to the center of the chassis; only one universal joint is necessary. All shafts revolve on roller bearings; a ball and socket arrangement in the universal joint relieves the passengers of all shocks and strains caused by the unevenness of the road. The Final Drive of the *Ford Model T* is patented in all countries.

Axles—Front Axle of I-beam construction, especially drop-forged from a single ingot of Vanadium steel, insuring the highest quality of axle strength obtainable. Rear axle also of Vanadium steel and enclosed in a tubular steel housing. The *Ford* Differential is of the three-pinion bevel type; all gears are drop-forgings made of Vanadium steel.

Bodies and Capacities—*Ford Model T* cars are furnished with three styles of bodies—Touring Car, capable of carrying five (5) passengers; Runabout for two (2) passengers; Town Car, six (6) passengers.

Prices—F. O. B. Detroit—Touring Car, $600; Runabout, $525; Town Car, $800.

Equipment—All *Ford Model T's* are sold completely equipped—no *Ford* cars will be sold unequipped. Standard equipment includes Top, Top Cover, Windshield, Gas Lamps, Generator, Speedometer, Three Oil Lamps, Horn and Kit of Tools, including Jack.

Wheel Base—100 inches; Standard tread 56 inches; 60 inches for Southern roads where ordered. All *Ford Model T* cars will turn in a twenty-eight (28) foot circle. This feature is of great advantage while operating in crowded thoroughfares.

Ford Model T Town Car
6-Passenger—4-Cylinder—20 Horsepower Car. Price $800 includes speedometer, two 6-inch gas lamps, generator, three oil lamps, horn and tools, including jack—f.o.b. Detroit. No Ford Cars sold unequipped

For this year there are only three body styles available. All three are illustrated.

Owner of the outstanding 1913 Model T Touring car used in the major illustrations in this coverage is John McInnis, President of The Model T Ford Club of America in 1967. This car is especially notable for the large number of original and authentic accessories with which it is equipped.

The 1913 Model T Touring car greatly resembled the late 1912 in body lines. However, the windshield was canted back at the lower half giving the impression of greater compartment closure. At the same time, the dashboard was reduced in size as the forward body sections were faired inward, adding to the effect.

1913 was the last model year in which color was available, for later the "all black" policy went into effect. Standard color choice seems to have been dark blue with black running gear, although green and even black "original" cars appear to have persisted.

Many of these will be seen in the photographs and, where possible, will be noted.

"Mac" drove this car to New York, from Los Angeles, several years ago, and confidently suggests that it is "just about the same as driving a modern car, only," he adds, "slower."

Curious in its nature was the Quantity Discount policy published in the 1913 catalog. Orders for single cars from commercial users were filled at "regular list prices according to our catalog." The standard discount for quantity was only 2/10ths of one percent per car! In other words, by buying *fifty* cars, the commercial user obtained a discount of only ten percent! Compare that with what we can do today to the "sticker price"! Incidentally this discount reached its maximum at fifty cars (10%) and was not increased for numbers over that!

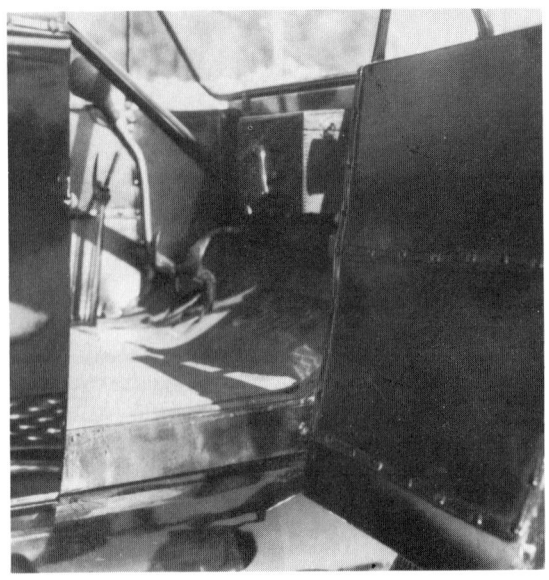

Unlike the late 1912 in which the doors were both hung with the hinges to the front, the 1913 body returns to the earlier style in which the rear door is hinged at the rear. Access to the rear seat is improved in this manner, and the style, generally, persists to the end of the production run in 1927.

Typical of the 1913 body style, the doors, both front and rear, extend below the longitudinal stringers. The square corners at the bottom are another distinguishing mark of the 1913 body. Note that the panel under the rear seat is of steel and does not open. Rear floor mat should be a cocoa mat; front is rubber.

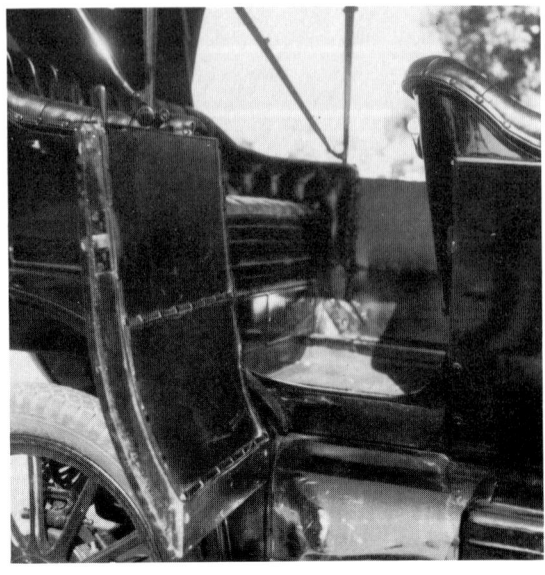

The 1913 body style, introduced in November of 1912, exhibited a serious problem in that the longitudinal stringers were not strong enough to properly support the rear seat assembly. As a result, the stringers often cracked, and in some rare cases, the entire rear seat assembly became disconnected from the rest of the body.

To correct this, the Company designed and built a re-inforcing steel plate of unusual contours, which was installed during production as well as being made available for field corrections. The illustration shows this re-inforcing gusset installed under the rear doors. Very early 1913 bodies had a stringer whose height was only 2-5/16 inches. Shortly after the problem was discovered, this stringer was increased to a height of 3-1/4 inches.

Door handles show clearly in this view. Gone are the outside brass handles, replaced by a type that protrudes through the top of the door. Also gone are the double-locking latches, and surviving is the sliding latch style used for many years thereafter.

Wheels are, as previously, 30 by 3 in the front; 30 by 3½ in the rear. Rims are clincher style. Hubs are secured with high-crowned carriage bolts. Front wheel bearings are ball. Brass hubcaps have, in addition to the script "Ford", the added "Made in USA."

Steering wheel is 15" O.D.; spider is of brass, as is the reduction gear casing. Spark and throttle levers have been flattened at their ends to provide suitable finger surface. The knobs used previously have been eliminated.

Bodies were upholstered in full leather, diamond tufted, and elaborate. Door panels were covered now in leatherette and later in the production, the seats, too, were of leatherette — an apparent economy measure.

The horn has been changed to an all-brass single-twist style which protrudes through the dashboard to the interior of the car. Made by "non-pareil," these horns are later found painted black except for the bell, but the all-brass construction persisted. Earlier horns were unpainted.

Bulb was mounted at the driver's left in an appropriate position. Flexible horn tubing was not restrained, but allowed to fall free to the horn.

The coil box is K-W, although Heinze and Kingston also furnished these units. During 1913, the wooden coil box was replaced with one of pressed steel and later the wooden box was no longer used.

Note, in the photo, the curved bracket under the coil box. This item, often overlooked in restoration, is the holder into which the sheet metal blanking plate which blocks off the engine compartment, is slipped for support.

The windshield was sloped backwards at the lower half. The top was secured with straps to the clip furnished at the hinge. Windshield frames were of steel (rather than brass), were black-painted and had a brass glass channel. The top half of the windshield folds forward.

111

Headlights on this car are E&J 666. The lamps are of familiar "black and brass" construction, meaning that they are manufactured of steel with brass trim. Lamps were painted black except for the brass portions. Other headlamps reported for the model year are manufactured by Jno. Brown, Victor and Corcoran.

Typical of the sidelamps for the model year are these, E&J. Note that they, too, are of "black and brass" construction and that the front lens has again become round, rather than square. As with the headlamps, Victor, Corcoran and Jno. Brown also supplied lamps.

The oil tail lamp features a red rear lens, a green left side and a clear right side lens (enabling the license plate to be illuminated). As with the other lamps, this is made of steel with brass trim.

The runningboard-mounted acetylene gas generator is made of steel, painted black, instead of brass. Latches and filler caps are of brass for trim effect. The inside compartment is a galvanized steel container for the calcium carbide. The caps are of brass for trim effect. The inside compartment has a galvanized steel container for the calcium carbide. The upper tank, in which water is placed, was also galvanized. Gas which resulted from the drip of water on the calcium carbide was piped through rubber hose and copper tubing to the headlights.

An interesting accessory on this car is the headlamp striker which is a flint and steel mechanism similar to a cigarette lighter. The mechanism is arranged so that the steel striking wheel can be rotated by a plunger which extends through the bottom of the lamp, and as a result, a spark is directed to the proper place at the burner. The door need not be opened to light the headlights, a very desirable convenience.

Horn is "non-pareil," single twist and protrudes through the dashboard. Smaller than earlier horns, it nevertheless gave adequate sound. The dashboard is bound in brass formed of flat stock to roll over the cherrywood dash both front and rear.

Radiator filler neck is riveted in place and is no longer a casting. The familiar Ford script is enhanced by the words "Made in USA" located below the script.

The frame for the 1913 models is similar to that used in the earlier cars. This is the last year in which the small cast body support brackets were used. During 1913 the frame was modified to include a longer rear cross member eliminating the need for these brackets. This remained standard until the 1926 models when the cross member was again altered. The fenders were secured to a bracket which extends from the body. The rear spring, as well as the front, has the tapered leaves with rounded ends.

Differential housing is still twelve-rivet, but is stockier than the 1912 style and features a cast inner section quite similar in shape to the more familiar later ones. The filler plug is a hex-headed screw for easier removal.

The intake manifold is of aluminum. The iron exhaust manifold has been modified so that now the tail pipe fits up to a flange at the rear of the mainfold and is held in place by the brass nut.

Standard carburetor is a Kingston "four ball." In this interesting device, the air inlet valves were stoppered by balls which dropped into appropriate seats in the body. As the demand increased, vacuum developed lifting one or more of the balls from its seat and allowing more air to flow. Generally quite satisfactory, these carburetors, like the five ball before them, exhibited wandering tendencies, especially at low speeds. A light choke rod extended through the radiator for use when cranking.

The serial number is located over the water inlet on the right side of the engine. The water pump (foreground) is an accessory.

Left side of engine showing the valve covers and manifold assembly. The odd system of levers and the rod extending through the dash is for the foot-operated choke which is used in conjunction with a pull-type of manual starter which enables the engine to be "cranked" from the driver's seat. This starting device was not too effective and is not installed on the car at this time. The cylinder head is a modern "Gemsa" patterned after the old "Giant" head.

The brass oil filler cap bears, in addition to the script 'Ford', the words "Made in USA".

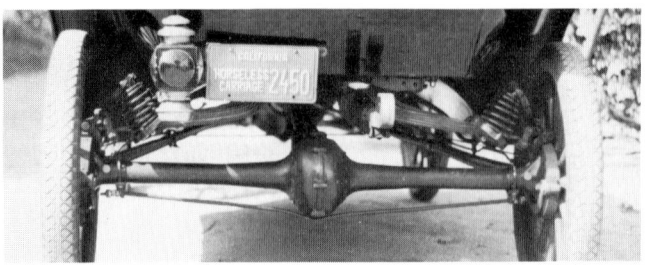

This particular car has a set of shock absorbers on the springs. Although Henry Ford is reputed to have said that "the passengers are the shock absorbers," many accessory devices were available for those owners who did want a smoother ride. The rear of this car is equipped with a common type known as "Hasslers" which were manufactured by the Robert H. Hassler Co., of Indianapolis, Indiana.

The front end of this car is equipped with another type of shock absorber, the K-W, which obtains its damping from the action of a dashpot and plunger, and an internal coil spring. Both types greatly improve the riding characteristics although, as accessories, do not represent the original factory-issue automobile. Note that both types provide their added springing by relocating the standard spring shackles to accommodate the shock absorber.

The 1914 Model T Ford

The 1914 Model T Ford was truly the start of the high production "peas in a pod" type of Model T. Conceived in 1913, the moving assembly line, incorporating an endless chain, was opened for operation on January 14, 1914, and as a consequence, radical innovations were made more difficult to incorporate.

Production figures for the 1914 model year show a substantial jump over those for any previous year and, although the number was to continue to grow for some years to come, Ford had a right to be excited about their first "quarter-million" year. The total actually approached 250,000 cars!

October 1, 1913	370,148
September 30, 1914	570,790

Profits for the 1914 model year are reported to have been $30,000,000, up $5,000,000 from the previous year. In the days when the Income Tax had not yet been imposed, Ford's position was becoming impenetrable. Note that at a production rate of 250,000 cars for the year, the profit was *over $120. per car* and this at a listed selling price of only $550. for the Touring model!

Differing only superficially from the 1913 body style, the 1914 represents the last year of "antique styling." Fenders were still flat and the front compartment still relatively unenclosed, but to many, the real significance of the style year is the fact that it introduced the one-color only policy which was to rule Ford production for years to come. No color choices were available to purchasers of the 1914 Ford, all being available only in black. But what a bargain that car was at only $550. for the Touring model!

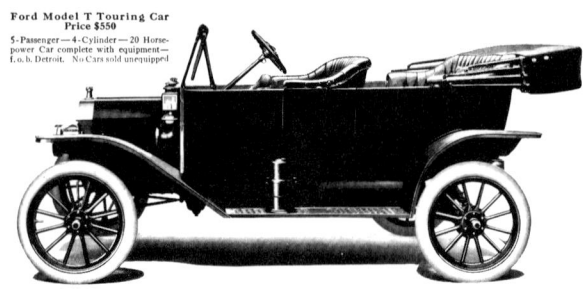

The Model T Touring car was considered a five passenger vehicle, and was sold completely equipped with lamps, top, etc. The car was an outstanding family car and, due to fundamental Ford manufacturing economies, was offered at the low price of $550., a real bargain for the day.

To make the deal even more interesting, Ford offered to refund $50. of the purchase price if he sold over a certain number of cars.* He made the quota, and made the refunds!

The Model T Runabout, often incorrectly called "roadster," was a lightweight, economical car for the two-passenger trade. It was offered at a price of only $500. and, as with all Ford cars, came completely equipped. Prices quoted were FOB Detroit.

*The exact figure is in doubt. Since Ford seems to have kept conflicting records on production, this number has been listed at between 200,000 and 300,000 cars. Figures as to the actual production vary, but Ford announced in later years that there were 248,307 cars built in 1914. The difference in 1914 serial numbers (engine) is 200,642. The difference in body numbers was 206,499. Part of the differences might be made by using a calendar year (which would then include some 1915 models) or by including foreign production.

Specifications

For All Ford Model T Cars

Motor—Four (4) cylinder, four cycle. Cylinders are cast en bloc with water jackets and upper half of crank case integral. Cylinder bore is 3¾ inches; piston stroke is 4 inches. The *Ford* motor is rated at twenty (20) horse-power. Special *Ford* removable cylinder head permits easy access to pistons, cylinders and valves. Lower half of crank case, one-piece pressed steel extended so as to form bottom housing for entire power plant—air-proof, oil-proof, dust-proof. All interior parts of motor may be reached by removing plate on bottom of crank case—no "tearing down" of motor to reach crank-shaft, cam-shaft, pistons, connecting rods, etc. Vanadium steel is used in all *Ford* crank and cam-shafts and connecting rods.

Unit Construction—There are four (4) complete units in the construction of *Ford Model T*—the power plant, the front axle, the rear axle and the frame.

Three-Point Suspension—Each of the *Ford Model T* units is suspended at three points of the chassis. This method of suspension insures absolute freedom from strain on the parts and permits the most comfortable riding of the car body.

Transmission—Special *Ford* spur planetary type, combining ease of operation and smooth, silent running qualities. Clutch is so designed as to grip smoothly and positively, and when disengaged to spring clear away from the drums, thus assuring positive action and maximum power.

Clutch—Multiple steel disc, operating in oil.

Magneto—Special *Ford* design built in and made a part of the motor. Only two parts to the *Ford* magneto, a rotary part attached to the flywheel and a stationary part attached to the cylinder casting. No brushes, no commutators, no moving wires to cause annoyance on the *Ford* magneto.

Lubrication—Combination gravity and splash system. Oil is poured into the crank case through the breather pipe on the front cylinder cover. All moving parts of motor work in oil and distribute it to all parts of the power plant.

Cooling—By Thermo-Syphon water system. Extra large water jackets and a special *Ford* vertical tube radiator permit of a continuous flow of water and prevent excessive heating. A belt-driven fan is also used in connection with the cooling system.

Carburetor—Special design, float feed automatic with dash adjustment. No spring attachment on air valve.

Gasoline Capacity—Touring Car, Runabout and Town Car have cylindrical gasoline tanks of 10 gallons' capacity mounted directly on frame under front seat.

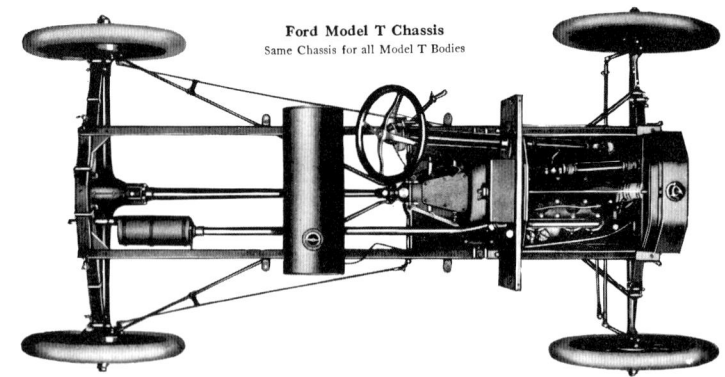

Steering—By *Ford* planetary reduction gear system. Steering knuckles and spindles are forged from special heat-treated Vanadium steel, and are placed behind front axle.

Valves—Extra large, all on right side of motor and enclosed by two small steel plates.

Control—On the left side of car. Three foot-pedal controls, low and high speeds, reverse, and brake on the transmission. Hand lever for neutral and emergency brake on left side of car. Spark and throttle levers directly under steering wheel.

Brakes—Dual system on all *Ford Model T* cars. Service brake operates on the transmission and is controlled by foot pedal. Expanding brake in rear wheel drums serves as emergency brake. It is controlled by hand lever on left side of car.

Springs—Both front and rear springs are semi-elliptical transverse, all made of specially *Ford* heat-treated Vanadium steel. *Ford Model T* springs are the strongest and most flexible that can be made.

Wheels and Tires—Wooden wheels of the artillery type with extra heavy hubs. Only tires of the highest grade are used on *Ford* cars. Front, 30x3 inches; rear, 30x3½ inches.

Final Drive—*Ford* triangular drive system with all shafts, universal joint and driving gears enclosed in dust-proof and oil-proof housing. Direct shaft drive to the center of the chassis; only one universal joint is necessary. All shafts evolve on roller bearings; a ball and socket arrangement in the universal joint relieves the passengers of all shocks and strains caused by the unevenness of the road. The final drive of the *Ford Model T* is patented in all countries.

Axles—Front axle of I-beam construction, especially drop-forged from a single ingot of Vanadium steel, insuring the highest quality of axle strength obtainable. Rear axle also of Vanadium steel and enclosed in a tubular steel housing. The *Ford* differential is of the three-pinion bevel type; all gears are drop forgings made of Vanadium steel.

Bodies and Capacities—*Ford Model T* cars are furnished with three styles of bodies—Touring Car, capable of carrying five (5) passengers; Runabout, for two (2) passengers; Town Car, six (6) passengers.

American Prices—F. O. B. Detroit—Touring Car, $550; Runabout, $500; Town Car, $750.

Equipment—All *Ford Model T's* are sold completely equipped—no *Ford* cars will be sold unequipped.

Wheel Base—100 inches; Standard tread, 56 inches; 60 inches for Southern roads where ordered. All *Ford Model T* cars will turn in a twenty-eight (28) foot circle. This feature is of great advantage while operating in crowded thoroughfares.

NOTICE

OWING to our inability to secure a satisfactory speedometer, our cars will not be equipped with them for the present.

An allowance of $6.00 will be made purchasers on Ford cars not equipped with speedometers.

(Signed)

Ford Motor Company

The "Luxury Car" of its day, the Model T Town Car was listed as a six passenger car and was delivered completely equipped at $750. This car found much favor with the taxicab industry which was then emerging, due to its low initial cost, its low operating costs, and the low cost of replacement parts.

Ford Model T Town Car—$750
6-Passenger — 4-Cylinder — 20 Horsepower complete with equipment—f.o.b. Detroit. No Cars sold unequipped

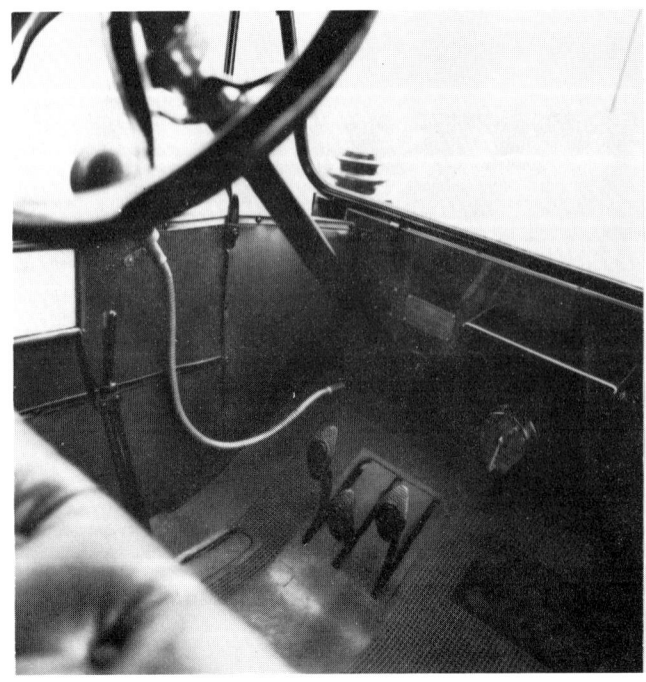

The Feature Car in this coverage is the beautiful 1914 Model T Touring owned by Rich Coors, of San Leandro, California. This car, excellently restored and maintained, won "best of class" over a dozen others at the H.C.C. 9th Biennial Reno Tour in 1966.

Engine number, 367,926, indicates a date of manufacture in late December 1913, supported by the casting date of 10-16-13 found on the block. The car appears to be largely correct and, although the fenders appear to have been replaced, the car seems to be a clear restoration of the original.

Noted in the following photographs will be the accessory outside rear-view brass mirror; other items seem to be standard, original.

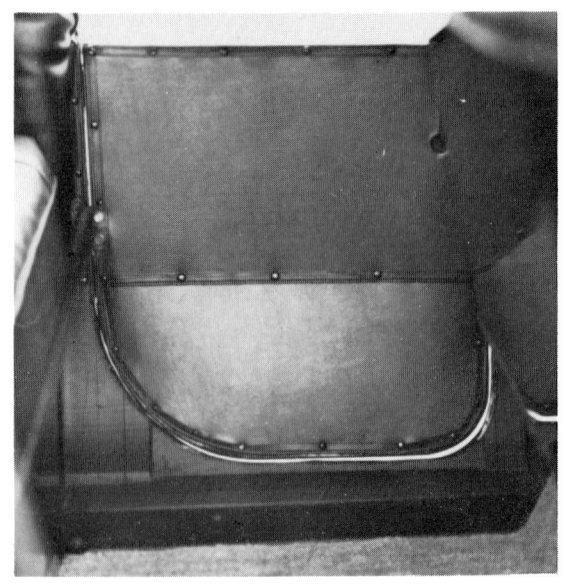

A mark for the 1914 body style is the door, whose lower edge is now rounded, rather than square as on the 1913. This improvement, or change, was probably dictated by the need of better support to the rear section of the body — a common problem with the 1913 style. By rounding the doors, the stringer could be increased in height. This, plus the extra body metal below the door sill, greatly added to the strength of the assembly.

The door latch was made so that the handle extended upwards on the inside. Single acting only, no hook latch added to the security offered by the sliding latch.

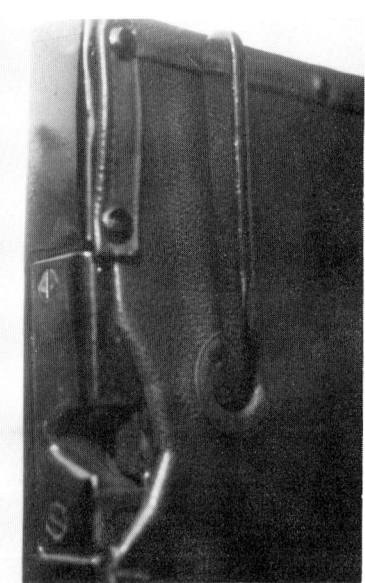

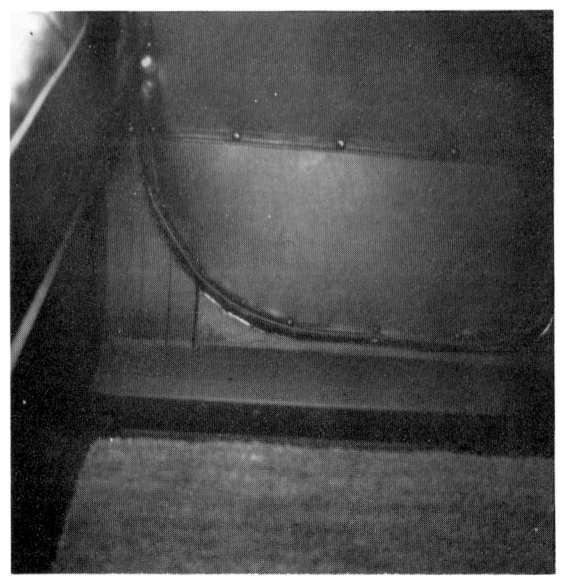

Note the wider section under the rear doors enabled by the rounded lower edge of the doors.

Very little outside difference exists between the 1913 and the 1914 Model T Ford Touring. Basic to the change in style is the rounded-bottom door. The 1913 had a "square" door (see 1913 coverage). Other changes are far more subtle, such as the reconfiguring of the windshield support brackets to permit the upper half to swing backwards (instead of forward as did the 1913).

Leatherette prevails on the 1914 Model T Ford. Seats, door panels and minor trim are all of leatherette. Seat cushions were of leather, although many cars were issued with leatherette throughout. Seat cushions continue to be diamond-tufted, although the seat backs no longer have the elaborate folds of the earlier cars.

Rear seat compartment sports a cocoa mat, part number 3676B, 30" by 28".

Front spring hanger is no longer of the "Mae West" type, and radii at both ends seems to be the same rather than as the earlier with the larger radius at one end. Still constructed of two "L" shaped halves, and furnished with a brass oiler, this general design was to be used for some years to come. Springs are still taper-leaved and appear unchanged from the earlier styles.

Fenders are flat. The running boards are diamond embossed, with the Ford script running crosswise at the center and are interchangeable from one side of the car to the other.

Front fenders were modified to include a strengthening rib across the widest portion.

Although standard issue called for the radius rod to be inserted above the axle in the spring perch, this car is embellished with an accessory strengthening support. This interesting unit is constructed to be attached to the perch below the axle and the rear end is welded to the rear section of the stock radius rod.

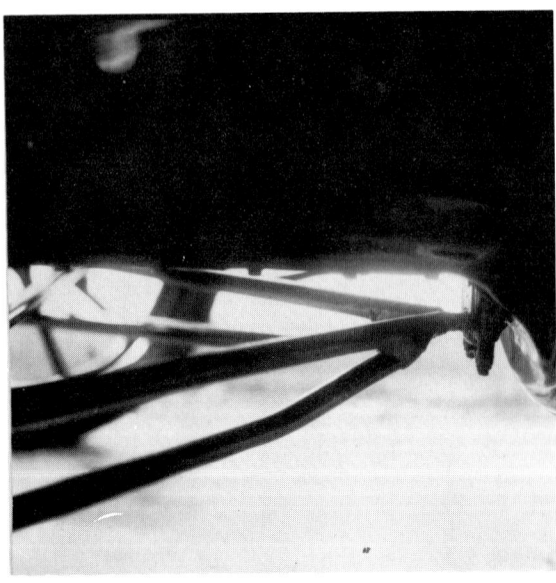

The front axle bears the factory part number, clearly read in the web. Part number, 202, is further enhanced, in this case, with the letter "T," hence T-202. Actually, the axle is cataloged as a "202-B" as it differs from the original axle which had the one-piece spindles.

128

Front wheels are 24" diameter (30 by 3" tire); rear wheels are 23" diameter (30 by 3½" tire), and still have the round felloes.

Brass hub caps, now embellished with the Ford script and the "Made in USA" designation, are further enhanced with a black-painted background for the lettering.

Illustrating a smaller-than-earlier speedometer drive gear. This part, made by Stewart, working through a reducer, drives a chain-link cable inside the brass flexible housing which runs up through the floorboards to the dash mounted speedometer.

In this unusual view, the rear axle housings are clearly seen. Note the cast center section, coupled with twelve rivets to the formed and drawn axle housings. The shape of this rear end is similar to the later styles and unlike the earlier "clam shell" twelve-rivet rear end. The pinion bearing spool (outer housing) is still cast, having the bolts enclosed. Although the picture does not indicate such, it is believed that a two-piece drive shaft is correct for the year.

The chassis, changed during the 1913 model year, now has the longer rear crossmember to support the body, eliminating the two castings used earlier. The rear springs are still taper-leaved. The muffler is wrapped with asbestos which is secured with three straps.

Headlamps on the feature car are Jno. Brown Model 16. In common with those of other manufacturers used during the model year, they are black with brass bonnet and rim only. Other manufacturers noted for the 1914 headlamps are E & J and Victor. Acetylene gas furnished the lighting source and and it was produced in a runningboard-mounted gas generator. Headlamps are not paired right and left, but are identical.

Sidelamps on the feature car are Jno. Brown Model 10, and like the headlamps, are austere. Painted black, they sported brass trim only. Sidelamps operated on kerosene stored in the font and required frequent cleaning to remove soot from the lenses.

Another manufacturer noted was E & J who produced their Model 32 with a round front lens and square side lenses. These were also black with modest brass trim.

The runningboard-mounted gas generator was made of steel and was painted black, but had small parts of brass. This interesting device contained water in the upper tank and calcium carbide in the lower section. Regulated water dripped down on the carbide producing acetylene gas which was then piped to the headlamps for a very workable light.

The tail lamp was an oil (kerosene) lamp and on the feature car is a Jno. Brown Model 115. Tail lamps featured a red rear-facing lens, a green lens on the right side of the car and a clear lens facing the center of the car to illuminate the license plate. Of black-painted steel, it too featured a minimal brass trim. An alternate tail lamp was the E & J Model 12.

The horn is black-painted with a brass trim. It is a single-twist and is mounted as shown so that the throat of the horn extends through the dashboard immediately above the floor-boards. A flexible brass tubing runs from the throat to the to the bulb and is allowed to fall free. The coil box, visible in this view, is of steel and has a flat lid.

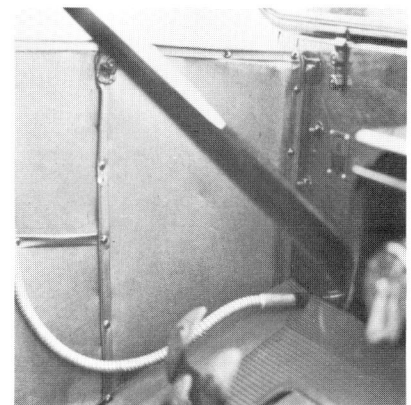

The radiator features the Ford script and the words "Made in USA."

The radiator filler neck is drawn and spun, not cast. It is riveted to the top tank with three brass rivets. The cap is stamped and has low "ears."

Radiators were made with five round tubes emplaced one behind the other, somewhat limiting the cooling effect. The lineup of these tubes is clearly illustrated.

Inside the radiator, right side of the upper tank, is an embossed nameplate bearing, in addition to the name Ford Motor Company, a number which is not considered significant. The number on this radiator is 1,223,503.

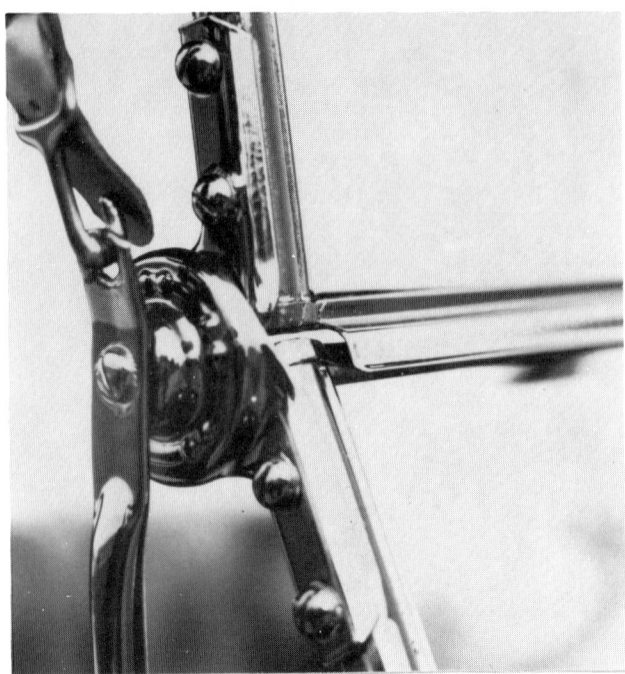

Top straps fasten to a hole in the upper end of the windshield support bracket. The windshield is black with a brass glass-setting channel. Changed from the 1913 style with which it is similar, is the manner in which the windshield folds. The top now folds to the rear (instead of forward), and the support bracket has been altered to clear.

The steering wheel is still fifteen inches in diameter, is of wood and is painted black. The spider is now black as are the flattened-end spark and throttle levers. But the acorn nut, the quadrant and the gear case are all of brass.

The speedometer, normally furnished with the car, is Stewart No. 26. Note that it has disc-shaped odometer dials rather than cylindrical as earlier. The speedometer head is brass.

The coil box is metal, the lid is flat, and the switch is round with black and brass plate. The key is lever shaped and is removable.

132

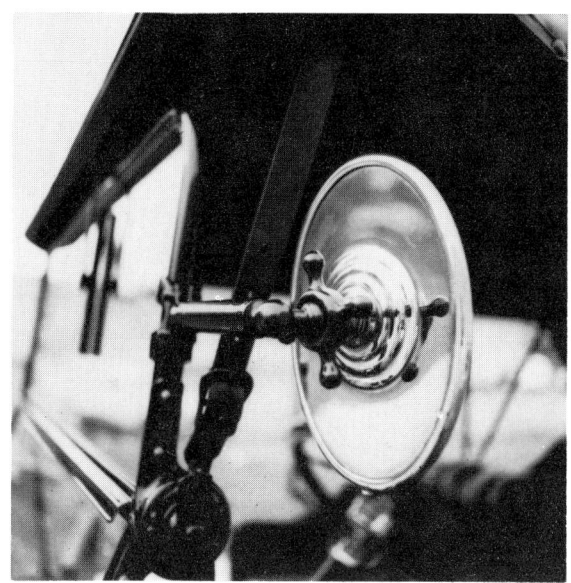

An unusual accessory rear-view mirror has an interesting adjustment lock. Note the knobbed locking ring which must be loosened to permit adjustment of the mirror. Note, too, the accessory windshield wiper.

The original aluminum hood, illustrating the correct hinge construction. Note that hinges are self-formed by folding back the flap which remains after piercing rectangular holes in the panels. Notice the insertion of leather strips which are held in place by tucking them under the lip of the reinforcing web.

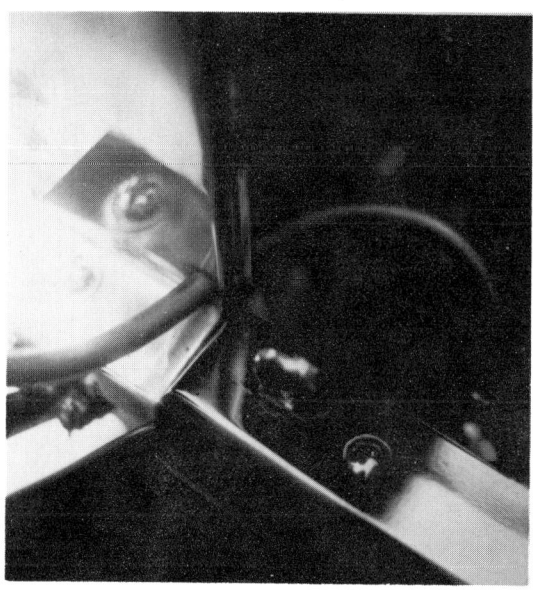

Illustrating a common, little noticed wiring fault. Coil leads to the spark plugs are interchanged from coil number four (the left-most coil) and number three. Lead from number three is connected to number four spark plug, necessitating a similar change at the timer or elsewhere. Correctly, the lead from number three coil should be connected to number three sparkplug.

Acetylene hosing from the headlights enters the engine compartment through an access hole in the side of the radiator. Wood sills are painted black. Hood latches are double eared.

A cast-iron intake manifold appears to be the major change inside the engine compartment. Engine head has Ford script and "Made in USA."

A brass Holley carburetor is fed hot air through a cast pipe that is secured around the exhaust manifold. A black rod, topped with a brass adjusting knob, controls the fuel mixture.

A brass choke rod protrudes forward through the radiator for use when cranking the engine.

New for the 1914 models was a less expensive plug for the water jacket holes. Up to this time, a ½-inch pipe plug had been used. After 1913, the more familiar steel disc became standard.

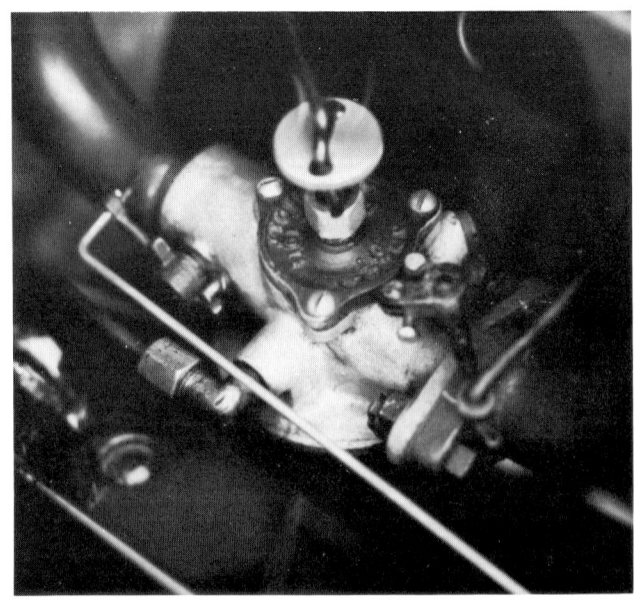

The 1915 Model T Ford

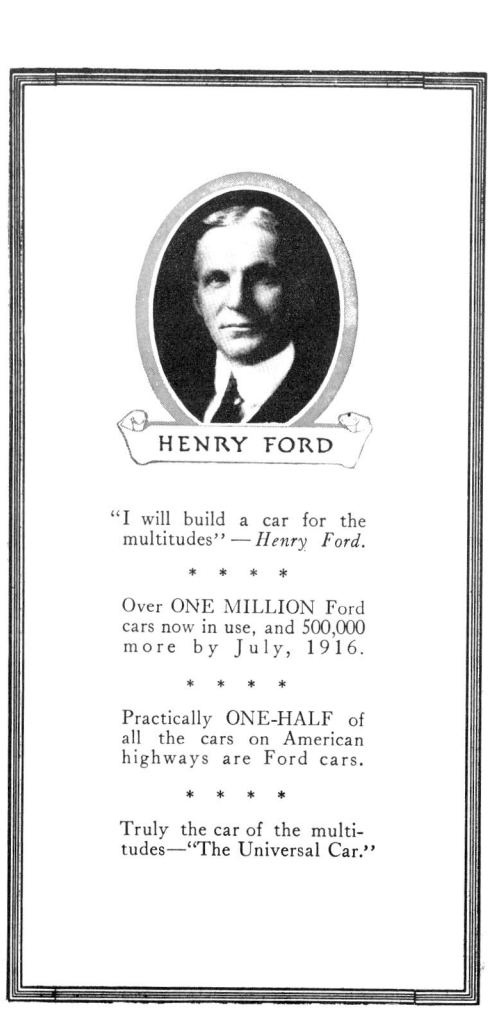

HENRY FORD

"I will build a car for the multitudes"—*Henry Ford.*

* * * *

Over ONE MILLION Ford cars now in use, and 500,000 more by July, 1916.

* * * *

Practically ONE-HALF of all the cars on American highways are Ford cars.

* * * *

Truly the car of the multitudes—"The Universal Car."

The New Ford Coupelet
Combines inviting trimness of appearance with the highest degree of utility

A new model in the 1915 catalog is the Coupelet, the forerunner of today's convertible. Featuring a soft leather top and windows which were pulled up out of the doors, the car became a cosy, enclosed all weather automobile. In appropriate weather the top could be lowered offering the driver a "handsome runabout."

The Coupelet is converted into a handsome runabout in two minutes by lowering the top

Also new this year is the Sedan which has become known as the "centerdoor", due to its placement of the doors between the front and the rear seats. This enclosed car offered five passengers a comfortable ride. Both front seats were hinged to allow easier access, and the right front seat was also hinged at the floor to allow it to fold forward, making it easier* for the driver to get in his seat.

* "Easier"—at best, entry to either front seat was difficult. The passenger seat was without any doubt, the most uncomfortable ever designed by man.

The New Ford Sedan
The convenience and comforts of the all-season enclosed car—at a new price

The 1915 Touring car, further described in this article.

The 1915 Runabout; a two passenger, lightweight, car favored by many over competitive heavier cars.

138

Specifications
For all Ford Cars

Axles—Front axle of I-beam construction, especially drop-forged from a single ingot of Vanadium steel, insuring the highest quality of axle strength obtainable. Rear axle also of Vanadium steel and enclosed in a tubular steel housing. The Ford differential is of the three-pinion bevel type; all gears are drop forgings made of Vanadium steel.

Bodies and Capacities—Ford cars are furnished with five styles of bodies—Sedan, five (5) passengers; Coupelet, two (2) passengers; Town Car, six (6) passengers; Touring Car, five (5) passengers; Runabout, two (2) passengers.

Brakes—Dual system on all Ford cars. Service brake operates on the transmission and is controlled by foot pedal. Expanding brake in rear wheel drums serves as emergency brake. It is controlled by hand lever on left side of car.

Carburetor—Float feed automatic with dash adjustment. Specially designed to give maximum power, flexibility and easy starting, with economy of fuel consumption.

Clutch—Multiple steel disc, operating in oil.

Control—On the left side of car. Three foot-pedal controls, low and high speeds, reverse, and brake on the transmission. Hand lever for neutral and emergency brake on left side of car. Spark and throttle levers directly under steering wheel.

Cooling—By Thermo-Syphon water system. Extra large water jackets and a special Ford vertical tube radiator permit of a continuous flow of water and prevent excessive heating. A belt-driven fan is also used in connection with the cooling system.

Equipment—All Ford cars are sold completely equipped, except speedometer—no cars will be sold unequipped.

Final Drive—Ford triangular drive system with all shafts, universal joint and driving gears enclosed in dust-proof and oil-proof housing. Direct shaft drive to the center of the chassis; only one universal joint is necessary. All shafts revolve on roller bearings; a ball and socket arrangement in the universal joint relieves the passengers of all shocks and strains caused by the unevenness of the road. The final drive of the Ford is patented in all countries.

Gasoline Capacity—All Ford cars have cylindrical gasoline tanks of 10 gallons capacity, mounted directly on frame under front seat.

Lubrication—Combination gravity and splash system. Oil is poured into the crank case through the breather pipe on the front cylinder cover. All moving parts of motor work in oil and distribute it to all parts of the power plant.

Magneto—Special Ford design built in and made a part of the motor. Only two parts to the Ford magneto, a rotary part attached to the flywheel and a stationary part attached to the cylinder casting. No brushes, no commutators, no moving wires to cause annoyance on the Ford magneto.

Specifications
—Continued

Motor—Four (4) cylinder, four cycle. Cylinders are cast en bloc with water jackets and upper half of crank case integral. Cylinder bore is 3¾ inches; piston stroke is 4 inches. The Ford motor develops full twenty (20) horsepower. Special Ford removable cylinder head permits easy access to pistons, cylinders and valves. Lower half of crank case, one-piece pressed steel extended so as to form bottom housing for entire power plant—air proof, oil proof, dust proof. All interior parts of motor may be reached by removing plate on bottom of crank case—no "tearing down" of motor to reach crank shaft, cam shaft, pistons, connecting rods, etc. Ford Vanadium steel is used on all Ford crank and cam shafts and connecting rods.

Prices—Ford cars are sold f. o. b. Detroit at the following prices for all points in the United States: Sedan $740; Coupelet $590; Town Car $640; Touring Car $440; Runabout $390.

Springs—Both front and rear springs are semi-elliptical transverse, all made of specially Ford heat-treated Vanadium steel. Ford springs are the strongest and most flexible that can be made.

Steering—By Ford planetary reduction gear system. Steering knuckles and spindles are forged from special Ford heat-treated Vanadium steel, and are placed behind front axle.

Three-Point Suspension—Each of the Ford units is suspended at three points of the chassis. This method of suspension insures absolute freedom from strain on the parts and permits the most comfortable riding of the car body.

Transmission—Special Ford spur planetary type, combining ease of operation and smooth, silent running qualities. Clutch is so designed as to grip smoothly and positively, and when disengaged to spring clear away from the drums, thus assuring positive action and maximum power.

Unit Construction—There are four (4) complete units in the construction of a Ford car—the power plant, the front running gear, the rear running gear and the frame.

Valves—Extra large, all on right side of motor and enclosed by two small steel plates.

Wheel Base—100 inches; Standard tread, 56 inches. All Ford cars will turn in a twenty-eight (28) foot circle. This feature is of great advantage while operating in crowded thoroughfares.

Wheels and Tires—Wooden wheels of the artillery type with extra heavy hubs. Only tires of the highest grade are used on Ford cars. Front, 30x3 inches; rear, 30x3½ inches.

Ford Town Car
Commodious, well upholstered, combining service and utility—the Ford Town Car fills the demand for a particular type of enclosed car

The Ford Town Car, the only six passenger Ford. The rear section of the top could be folded down in fair weather. Two foldaway jump seats were installed in the rear compartment. This model was a favorite of the heavy road-use taxicab companies and they were seen on the streets of the larger cities, such as New York, for years.

139

The year 1915 brought a newly-styled Model T Ford. Seeking to present a more nearly enclosed car, the dashboard was reduced in size and surrounded by a sheet metal cowl which faired smoothly into the body sides. By locating the windshield at the top-rear of the cowl, the illusion of further enclosure was clearly preserved. Rear fenders were curved apparently to modernize the appearance still further, and the hood was louvered to provide better engine cooling.

Someone once said, "There are now more 1915 Fords registered than Ford ever produced". He may have been right! This statement was prompted by the ever-increasing number of "1915" Fords which have been assembled using bodies and parts from later models. In general style, the 1915 body was used with minor changes until the 1921 model year and even the 1925 models had a similar appearance.

Yet, with all of this pre-dating, the 1915 Ford is unique, differing from those that preceeded it as well as those that followed. This was the last year for the aluminum hood, for example. Introduced this year were the louvres in the hood; the new style tail and side lights (with brass trim this year only); the standard rear axle housings which continued with minor changes until the end of the Model T production run. This was the first year for electric headlights, powered by a new magneto

140

which used larger magnets and a new coil. The hand klaxon horn, with a brass bell, was standard equipment this year (although some of the very early models had a bulb horn mounted under the hood, we have been told).

As in previous coverage we feature the Touring body – this being the most common – in this chapter. Yet, 1915 saw the introduction of two new body styles, the Coupelet and the Centerdoor Sedan. Continued from previous years were the Touring and the Runabout.

The Owner of the beautiful 1915 Touring featured in this article, is Hugo Richter, of Northridge, California, whose assistance in preparing this coverage is gratefully acknowledged.

Engine number 822598 indicates a date of manufacture of June, 1915, a date consistant with the block casting date of 5-23-15.

142

The hood former and dashboard cap are integral and are secured to a wooden dashboard. Note the manner in which the effect of the cowl is limited by the rather blunt surface above the hood former over the dashboard.

The hood itself is still of aluminum but now has six louvres on each side to aid in the cooling air flow through the radiator. The "boxy" look of the earlier models is retained.

The radiator is still of brass and typical of the earlier cars. It has the Ford script and the "Made in USA". The filler neck is riveted to the tank.

The general styling from the cowl back is similar in design and appearance to the 1914 Models. The bead along the body above the rear fender now curves to match the new fender lines. Later in the production run, the construction of the front seat area was changed and these cars had a "rivet" (actually the head of a carriage bolt) in the side panel between the front and rear doors. This bolt was used to secure the front seat frame to the body (or the other way around, if you prefer) and was a feature of Ford Touring car bodies for years afterward.

The wheels are similar to previous design; still 30 by 3 (tires) in the front and 30 by 3½ in the rear. Hub caps are brass.

The front fender is similar in design to the 1914 style except that now there are only three rivets holding the mounting clamp, instead of the four used before. The front fenders have the reinforcing beads introduced during 1914, and have lips on the front edges.

The rear fenders are now curved and similar in appearance to fenders used until 1926 models except that they had no crown (introduced in 1916 models).

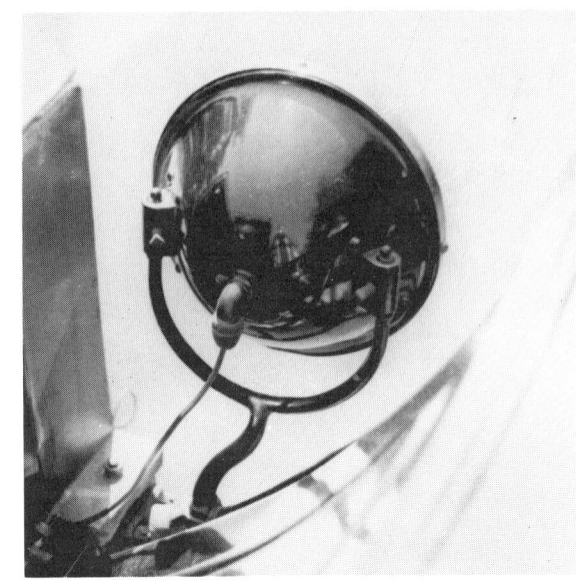

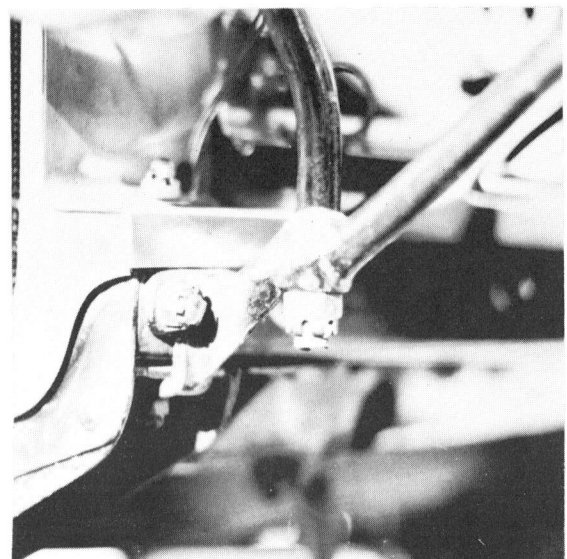

Note: Some of the pictures used in this article (such as the forked headlamps, windshield and driver's compartment) are of another, early, 1915 Touring, owned by Don Lawrence, of Encino, California. This car is one of the most authentic cars found. We are indebted to Don for his courtesy and cooperation in allowing us to photograph his car for these illustrations.

Early production 1915 Model T open cars were supplied with gas lamps similar to those used in 1914. Closed cars were supplied with electric lights which mounted on the same forked posts used with the gas lamps. About April of 1915, the gas lamps were discontinued and electrics were supplied on all cars. At this time, the forked posts were discontinued and the familiar flanged post used.

Bulbs for the electric lights were nine volts and were connected in series. Current was supplied by the magneto, which had been modified by using larger magnets and coils. Since the output of the magneto varied from around four volts at idle to over thirty volts at high speed, the lights also varied from very dim at a stop to burn outs at speed. Unsatisfactory as it was, Ford used the system in some of his cars (those without starters) until well into the 1926 model year.

The electric lamps were painted black except for the rim around the lens, which was brass. The lens itself was clear glass.

Sidelights were round and symetrical in order that they might be used on either side of the car. They were mounted by a threaded stud which secured them to a cast bracket on the windshield support. The lamps were painted black except for the top and rim around the lens, which were brass.

The oil taillight was similar to the sidelights except for the addition of a red lens and a smaller clear lens on the side to illuminate the license plate. Color and trim were the same as the sidelights.

The lamps illustrated are made by E&J (sidelamps are Model 8; taillight is Model 9). Lamps were also supplied by Jno. Brown (Model 560) and there may have been others.

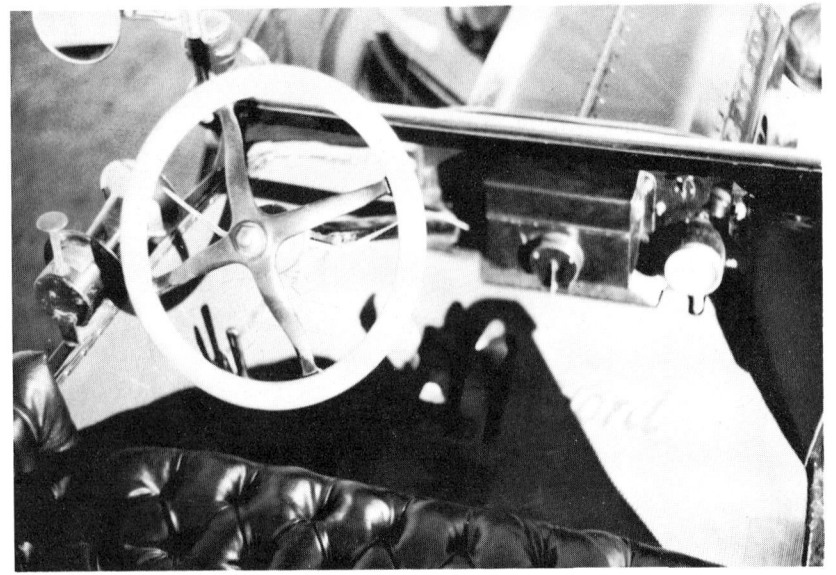

NOTE

The upholstery shown on the cars used in our Touring Car coverage is not strictly correct.

Factory production upholstery was not diamond tufted as is shown. Rather, the seat backs were folded and pleated, while the cushions were folded and pleated in a diamond pattern. Try as we did, we were unable to get a picture of this correct style in time to include it.

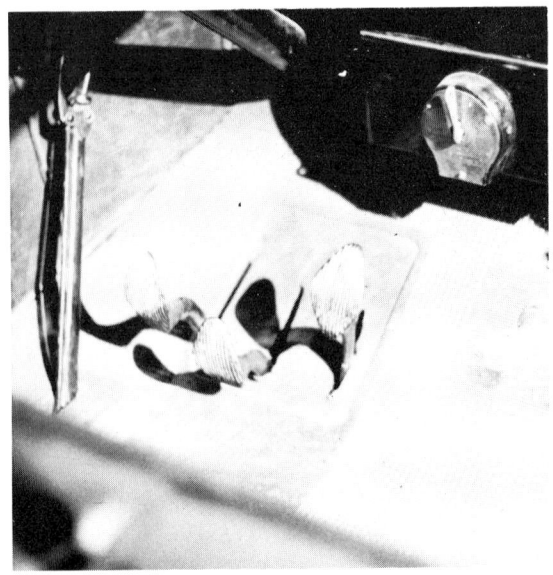

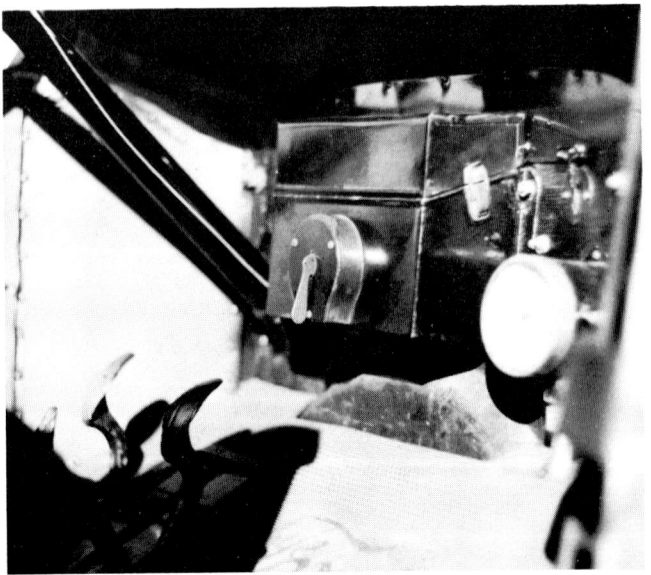

The steering wheel is 15" O.D. and should be painted black. The spider is cast steel, painted black. The quadrant is now of pressed steel; the spark and throttle levers now have the flattened ends that were to remain as standard for all Model T Fords to come.

The light switch is mounted on the dash, to the right of the coil box. It is a push pull type; out for "on".

The coil box is now designed with a sloping top opening which allows more clearance for removing the coils, needed because of the cowl construction. The box cover is of one-piece design (the top shown is incorrect) with rounded corners. The switch plate is black with brass lettering and trim. The key is removable; has ears to prevent its coming out when in the "on" position. The location is perfectly laid out so that the key will fall into the transmission hole if it is jarred while adjusting the bands of the transmission.

The familiar lettered pedals have now been discontinued and in their place are the unique ribbed ones used for this model year only.

The horn is now a hand-operated Klaxon, painted black with a brass end-bell. The first of the '15 cars had a bulb horn, similar to the '14s but mounted under the hood.

The windshield is two-piece and folds back at the center. The frame is iron, painted black, as are the hinges. The upper half of the windshield is positioned slightly ahead of the lower to allow the rain to run outside, rather than inside, the car. The hinge illustration shows the design of the hinge (left side is shown). Notice the detents designed to hold the top half in several positions.

The speedometer, manufactured by Sears Cross Co., of New York, has the familiar Ford insignia on the face. It has a black body and brass trim. Late in the year, the speedometer was discontinued as a standard item but was still available as an accessory. Other speedometers made by Stewart seem to have been used as well.

The door latches differ from later styles in that the bolt operates vertically rather than horizontally.

The front quarter panels are covered with a cardboard-like material. The framing is of wood, with no metal supports or coverings.

Electric headlamps had clear lenses and used eight-volt bulbs. The two lamps were connected in series and operated with current from the magneto. The light switch is located to the right of the coil box and is of the push-pull type. (Notice the correct, rounded-corner coil box cover.)

The seat frames are of wood. Late in 1915, presumably with the introduction of the 1916 models, the seat frames were made of metal, and continued with no significant changes until 1921 models.

The body number apparently was located in no standard spot. This car has a plate on the seat frame; others have the number on the door sill on the right side.

A wood panel covered both the gas tank and the rear-seat storage area. It is hinged at the rear.

Standard 1915 issue was the steering column quadrant of pressed steel which became regular equipment for the balance of Model T production. The spark and throttle levers have flattened ends. There is some evidence (at least in the closed cars) that these may have been brass plated on occasion.

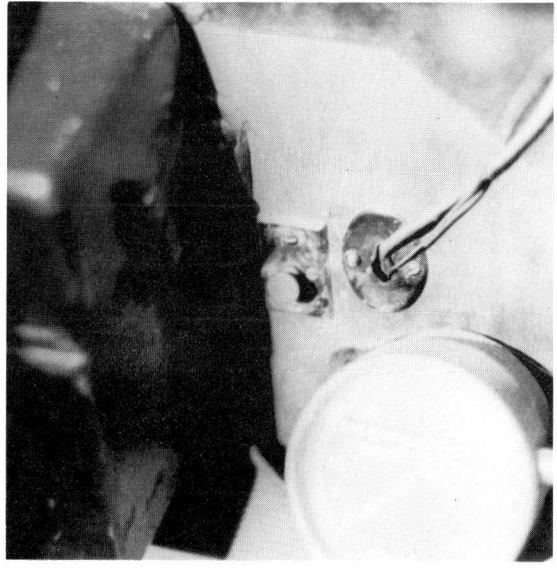

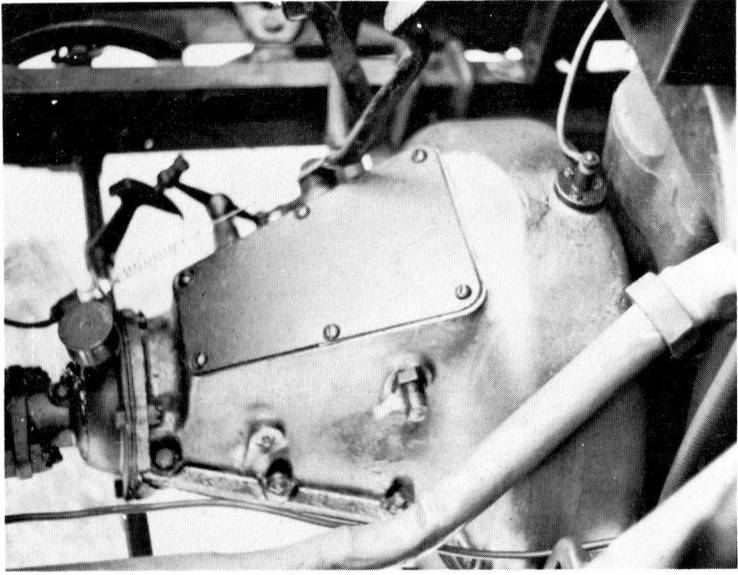

The aluminum transmission cover is now fitted with a flat steel access hole cover; no stamping or embossing appears. The head of the low speed clutch adjustment screw continues to be flat-sided rather than square as on the very early cars.

Small reinforcing webs have been added to the transmission cover at the bolt holes at the widest part of the cover. These were added to help prevent the corners from breaking off when the cover was installed, a common problem with the aluminum covers.

Note the manner in which the metal dash shield is embossed to permit it to clear the rear of the engine head. The magneto post is straight-sided and has a small brass knurled nut.

The tail pipe continues to be flared at the end to mate with the beveled exhaust manifold, and is secured with a large brass nut.

The forward end of the driveshaft is now the one-piece design which was used hereafter. The new design is stronger and cheaper than the old two-piece unit used before. Note the stop light switch. This is a modern addition, added not only for safety, but to comply with the California Vehicle Code.

The hood latches are cast. The hood cleats are still wooden and should be painted black.

The intake manifold is cast iron. At least two carburetors were used this year. The all-brass Holley with a 1914 patent date, using three screws to secure the cover and with the choke butterfly axis horizontal (the 1914 Holley had two screws and a vertical butterfly axis), and the Kingston all-brass with a single flapper valve.

The engine serial number is still located above the water inlet, where it remained throughout Model T production. In May of 1915, Ford discontinued the use of body numbers — they had little significance anyway — and the engine number was also called the car number from here on. The casting date is located just to the rear of the inlet.

The engine compartment is now embellished with a steel oil filler cap with the Ford script and the "Made in USA" stamped on the top. It, like just about everything else, was painted black.

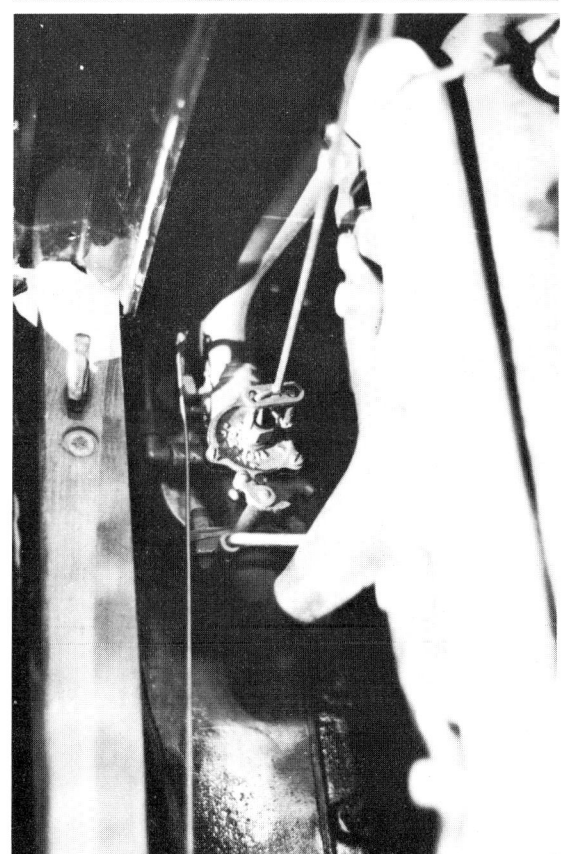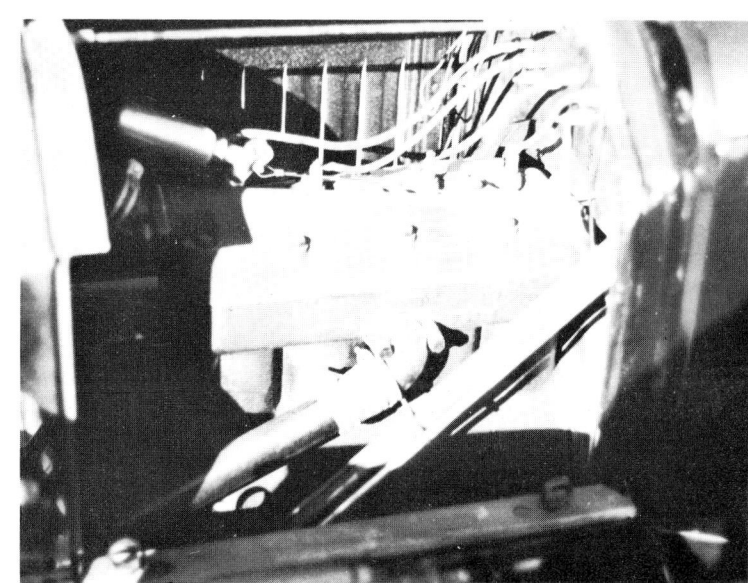

Springs, both front and rear, are still taper-leaved. The spring shackles are of a slenderized "Mae West" design and are furnished with oilers as in the earlier models. The spindle bolts, though, have been changed and now have the capped oilers that became so common. The spring shackles are "L" shaped; both halves are the same. The hangers on this car have been changed; should not have the oil hole on the top as is shown here.

Notice that the tie rod adjustment is still made on the left (driver's side) end of the rod. It was to be several years before someone at Ford thought of another way to save a few pennies and changed the design, putting the adjustment on the left and using the same nut that held the drag link ball to also lock the adjustment.

The front axle has the name and part number cast into it, a common practice which had been used and was to continued to this day. Many of the earlier Fords had the familiar "DB" on many parts, indicating that they were manufactured by the Dodge brothers. The Dodges began production of their own cars in 1914 and from here on out Ford used a declining amount of their services as a supplier.

The differential housings are cast and are the final design used in Model T production. The axle housings and brake backing plates were altered in later years, principally in the addition of strengthening ribs (in later 1915 production) and in the larger plates used in the 1926-7 models. The pinion bearing sleeve is of the enclosed bolt design as was used in the earlier models.

The muffler has cast ends incorporating integral mounting brackets and a straight, round tailpipe at the rear.

Floorboards are of three pieces, with metal plates around the brake and pedal cutouts.

The crank handle has again been simplified; now has a straight-sided steel sleeve. Parts lists issued by Ford at the time showed the aluminum handle as was used in 1914 but all '15 and later models we have seen had the style we have pictured here.

We have been fortunate in that many people have contributed photos of their cars. Of particular interest are the closed cars — there are not many of them around.

The Coupelet is owned by Edward Isele, Jr. of Ho-Ho-Kus, New Jersey.

Notice the side lights. Several styles appear to have been used during the year. These, the earlier type, have a larger lens and brass rim, and a lower font which is shaped quite differently from the later types.

The top and interior are of leather, and are original, according to the owner.

The Town car is owned by Bill Prous, of Minneapolis, Minnesota. Bill says that the upholstery in this car is of leatherette in the driver's compartment and cloth in the rear compartment. He mentions that other cars he has seen had leatherette throughout. Which is correct, we are not sure. Ford just says that "Upholstery of excellent quality is used throughout".

The front door on the driver's side of the car opens on this example. The illustration in the Ford catalog shows a door which does not open. No doubt, they either all opened and the catalog is wrong (the picture is an artist's drawing) or a change was made during production.

The most popular closed car in the Ford line was, however, the Sedan, commonly known as the center door sedan. For the first time, Ford offered the comfort of a closed car at a price which was within reach of the average man. While never reaching anyway near the sales of the less expensive open cars, the Sedan began the trend which in a little over a decade would see that body style the sales leader.

We are indeed fortunate to have the feature car available for this picture story. This 1915 Ford sedan has never been restored; is entirely original except for the exterior paint. The owner is Charles F. (Chuck) White of La Puente, Calif. Chuck purchased the car in 1952 for the outlandish price of $250.

The 1915 Centerdoor Sedan is as unlike those that followed as was the 1925 Sedan from the 1926. They are just a different car.

To mention just a few of the differences between this year's Sedan and the 1917 Sedan — the body sits lower on the frame. Notice that the splash aprons are narrower than all other cars in the line this year; they were unique to the 1915 Sedan. The rear fenders, too, are unique. They are screwed directly to the body rather than mounted on the normal fender iron. Notice that the rear body section has no seams; appears to be all one piece. And there is more —

155

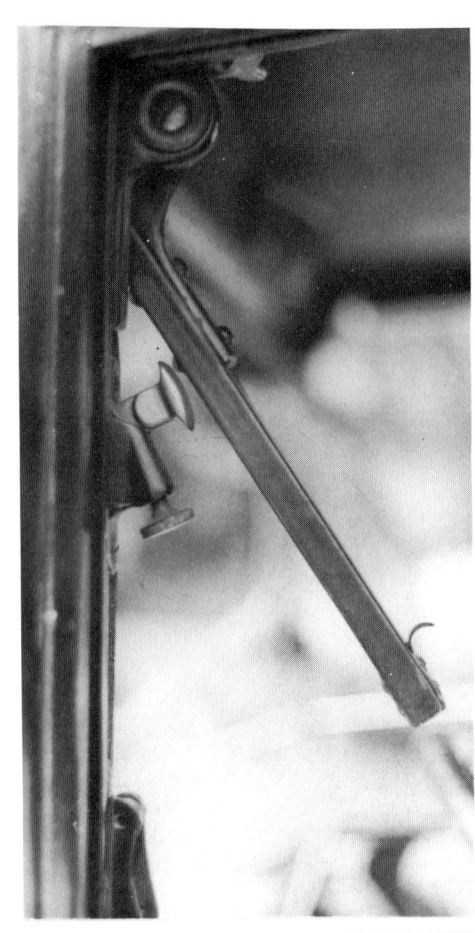

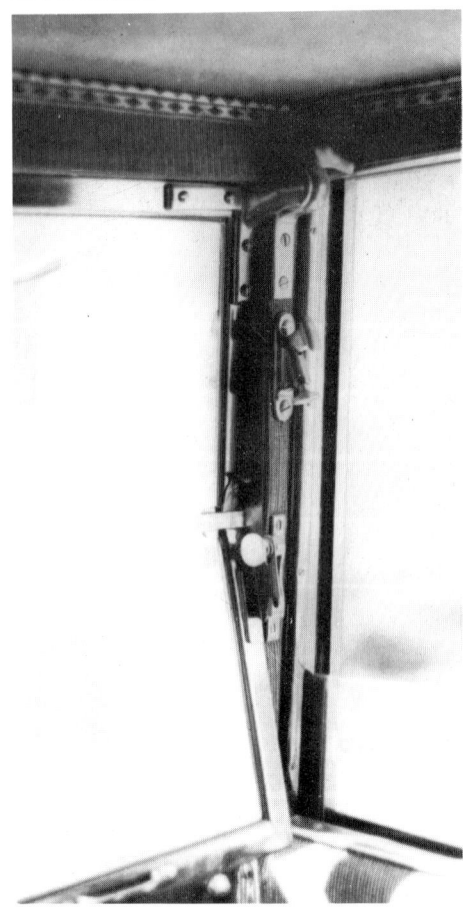

156

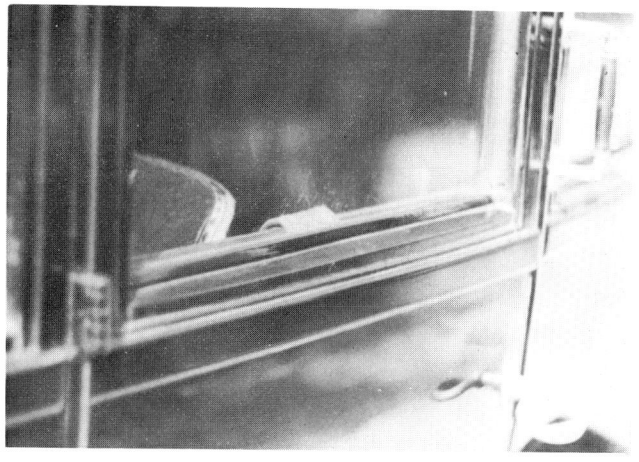 

One of the noticable differences between the 1915 and later Sedans is the shape of the window mouldings. Notice that they are not rounded off on this car.

One of the features of the '15 sedan is the three-piece windshield. A glass visor, hinged at the top, and held in any position by a quadrant on each side by means of a knurled set screw inside the car, is unique. The upper half of the windshield folds inward against the ceiling or any other position, and is locked with a wing screw in the hinge. The lower half, also locked with a knurled screw, can be raised slightly then pulled inward. This must be done to allow clearance for the upper half to be folded. Notice the lavish use of brass fittings.

The door handles were of the bail style, brass, and are turned to open the door. The latch is a sliding bolt affair similar to latches used for years. The door lock below the latch may have been added by one of the previous owners or may have come with the car — we are not sure.

The fuel tank is located under the rear seat this year. Shallow, it holds only about eight gallons. Due to its location, fuel flow was poor and it didn't take much of a hill to starve the engine. The following models moved the tank to under the driver's seat.

Early versions of the car still used the lettered pedals of the '14's (the brake pedal here has been changed).

Early versions of the Sedan used 1914-style fenders having four rivets to hold the bracket rather than three as was typical of the year (see illustration on the Touring car).

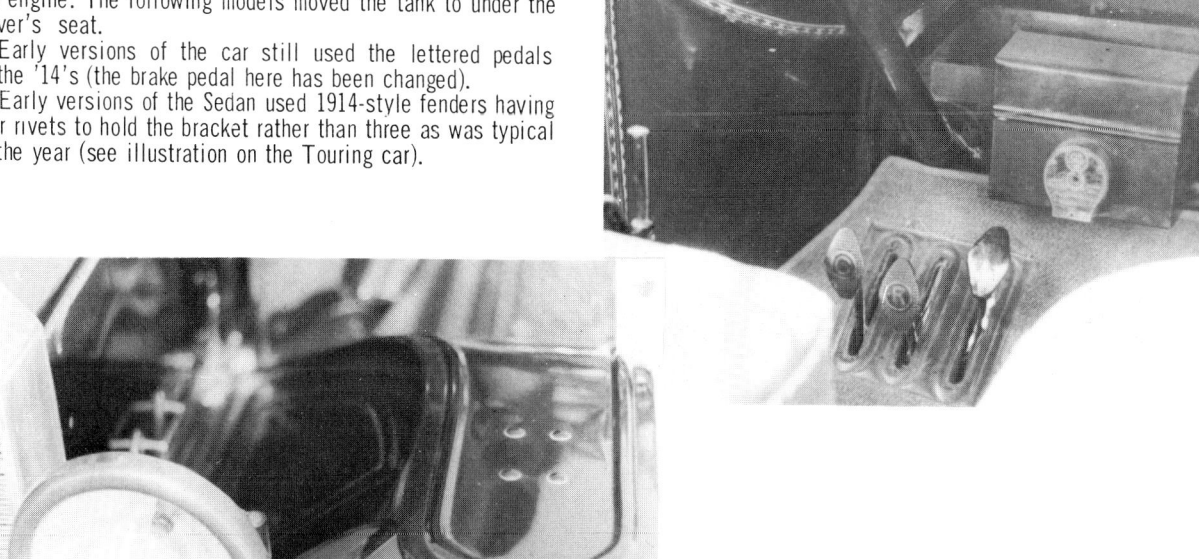

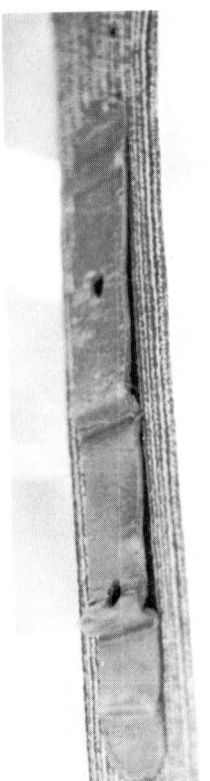

Ornate? It's hard to believe that a Model T could be this fancy! The door alone is a joy to behold. Just take a look at the window lifting strap. The window is lowered and raised with this strap. There is a small brass peg near the top of the door panel. On the back side of the strap is a leather reinforcement with holes punched through it. By pushing the leather part over the brass peg, several positions of the window could be held. Notice the tassle at the end of the strap, the fancy embroidery, the piping, the handles — there was nothing cheap or shoddy about this Model T!

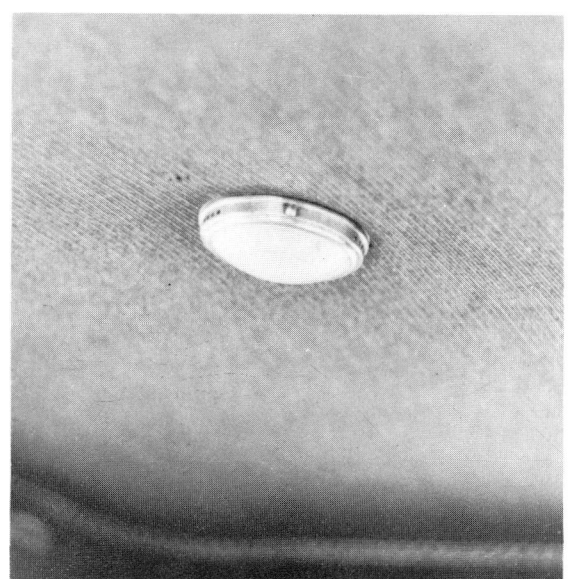 

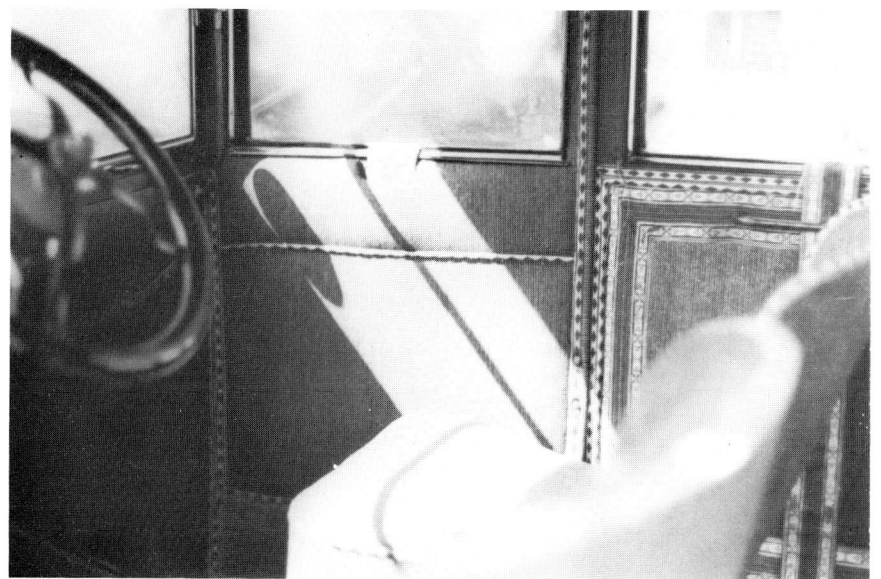

This particular car is equipped with a dome light. The unit appears to have been installed as original equipment. Wires run from the light to the right rear door post where the switch is located and then down the post and out under the car. Apparently there must have been a battery box somewhere but its location is in doubt. Reader's comment on this will be appreciated.

The interior is upholstered throughout with care and quality. Notice that even the area under the cowl is upholstered and trimmed with the same piping that is seen throughout the car. The straps for the front windows were not as ornate as those on the doors — they didn't have to be, they were stored inside the paneling through a slot in the upper edge. The rear windows (next page) were similar.

Both front seats folded forward for easier entrance. The passenger seat could be folded completely forward which made entrance to the driver's seat a little easier. (Loading passengers in any of the centerdoor sedans required planning and cooperation.) Notice that the upholstery on the driver's seat is diamond tufted, while the passenger's was rather plain. Both these seats are far from comfortable, the passenger's is downright uncomfortable. The rear seat? Just like a Pullman!

One must see the car in person to fully appreciate the beauty and finish. The rear seat area is truly regal! The seat is well padded and very comfortable. These photos, taken in far-from-ideal conditions, just don't do the car justice.

The Centerdoor Sedan illustrated here has a body number of 536 located near the right door sill. Since bodies were built by more than one firm, there may be a considerable variation between cars of the same body style. Owners of such cars are invited to comment.

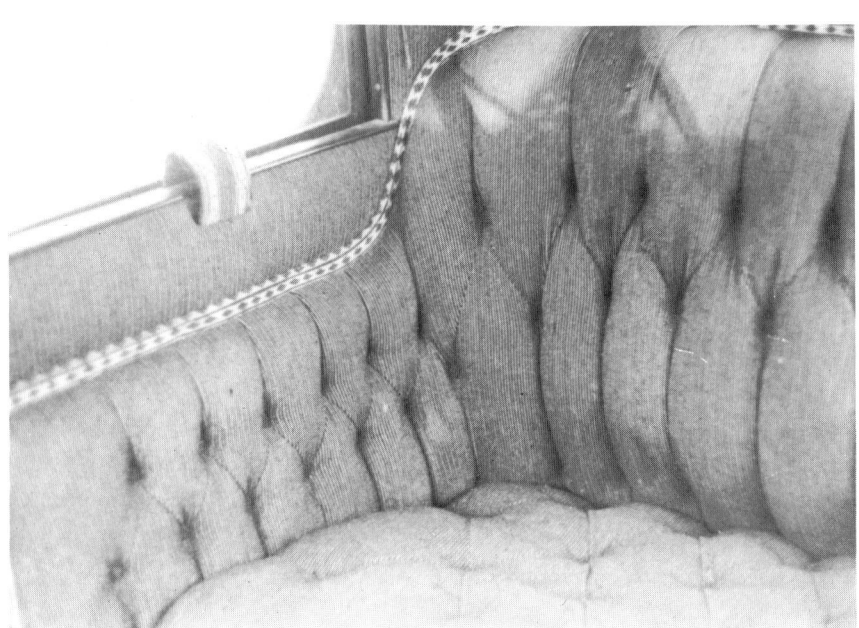

The Transitional Years
1916-17-18

1917 MODEL T TOURING

Photo courtesy Ford Archives, Henry Ford Museum, Dearborn, Michigan.

1918 MODEL T COUPE

We have grouped the year-model cars for 1916, 1917 and 1918, rather than treat each separately, because even though they appear quite different, they are much the same. During this period the Model T Ford assumed the style that was to become its hallmark.

The 1916 style Model T was but a carryover of the 1915 cars. During the calendar year 1915, the Touring bodies were modified to incorporate metal seat frames, replacing the wooden ones that had been used previously. This new body was used with little modification until the early twenties. The chief identification mark of this Touring body is the "rivet" or bolt head just forward of the rear door. This bolt held the seat frame to the body panel. Many later 1915 cars had it, and all the cars in this section of *the series* have it.

The 1916 style cars, then, looked just about like the 1915's — in fact they were probably just the continuing production '15's that evolved into the "iron" Fords of the 1917 style, which were introduced in August of 1916. The later "brass" 1916 cars were supplied with steel, rather than aluminum, hoods. The iron transmission cover made its appearance in 1916. The use of brass as a trim was discontinued on the headlamps, side and tail lights, and on the klaxon horn. These were all now "trimmed" in black. Front springs were supplied with either six or seven leaves, apparently due to differing sources of supply. The control pedals were smooth-surfaced; the lettering having been eliminated in the '15 style year, and the '15's ribbed style having been dropped for 1916. Top sockets remained oval in cross section. Later "brass" '16s appeared with the crowned rear fenders that were so typical of the "iron" cars.

In August of 1916, Ford announced price reductions ($80.00 on the Touring) and a "New" Model T! By changing just the front fenders, hood and radiator shell, the car was "modernized"!

The use of brass as a trim was now finished (although there may have been brass hubcaps on some of the early production '17-style cars) and nickel plating took its place. The iron radiator, while not as cute today as the brass, was a decided improvement in 1916. Few Ford owners bothered to polish the brass as we do today so it wasn't too long before a new car looked just like its ancestors. The higher hood and painted finish made for a better proportioned car, and required less polishing to keep it looking well.

Early production 1917 style cars carried a shroud around the fan which covered the rear side of the radiator except for the fan. This was discontinued during the year, probably because it hindered rather than helped the cooling.

No new body styles were introduced this year. The Sedan was redesigned allowing it to sit higher on the chassis, which in turn allowed the use of the standard rear fenders and splash aprons. The elaborate front window was simplified; it was now of two-piece design instead of the three-piece used in 1915. (There is no evidence of a 1916 Sedan, incidentally.)

This was the first year in which the magneto powered horn appeared. It was operated by a combination push button and rotary light switch which mounted on the steering column. The wood hood clash strips were now of pressed steel. The windshield hinges were redesigned and now, when folded, the two sections were not flush at the top. The rear windows in the open cars were now of three sections instead of the large single window with the rounded top.

1918 continued the '17 style except that the Coupelet was discontinued and replaced with the Coupe. Unique during the early years of its production, the Coupe had a removable post between the door and rear quarter window, making it one of the original hardtops. The Town Car was discontinued, never having been a good seller.

This year saw the introduction of the new-style top sockets, now rectangular in cross section, rather than oval.

Finding completely authentic examples of cars of this era seemed next to impossible. Here in California it seems that most of these cars have been converted to "1915's". The cars in this article are true 1916's and a true 1918. The brass models are styled to be '15 by the addition of the brass trim, which must be overlooked here. The 1918 is authentic except for the upholstery (which is more padded than the original), the top rear curtain (which can be folded or rolled up on this example) and the accessory demountable wheels.

The black '16 is owned by Vern Williams of Reseda, Calif. The light blue (!) one is owned by Donald Dupree of Sepulveda, Calif. The 1918 is owned by Ellis Gray of Van Nuys, Calif.

PRODUCTION FIGURES

As seems to have been typical of the Ford Motor Company in those days, there is no relation between the announced production figures and the serial numbers of the cars produced.

As an example:
August 1, 1914 to April 30, 1915
   570,791 to 773,487 (202,696 cars)
May 1, 1915 to July 31, 1915
   773,488 to 855,500 (82,012 cars)
or a total of 284,708 cars for the fiscal year 1915.

August 1, 1915 to July 31, 1916
   855,501 to 1,362,200 (506,699 cars)
for the fiscal year 1916.

August 1, 1916 to July 31, 1917
   1,362,201 to 2,113,500 (751,299 cars)
for the fiscal year 1917.

August 1, 1917 to July 31, 1918
   2,113,501 to 2,756,251 (642,750 cars)
for the fiscal year 1918.

OR

January 1, 1916 to December 31, 1916
   1,029,201 to 1,614,600 (585,399 cars)
for calendar year 1916

January 1, 1917 to December 31, 1917
   1,614,601 to 2,449,100 (834,499 cars)
for calendar year 1917.

January 1, 1918 to December 31, 1918
   2,449,101 to 2,831,400 (382,299 cars)
for calendar year 1918.

Ford announced that in 1915 they produced 308,213 cars; that in 1916 they produced 533,921 cars; and in 1917 they produced 785,432 cars. The difference in the figures may have been because of foreign production.

Production was down in 1918 because of the World War.

1917

Illustrated on the opposite page are cars typical of the 1916 model year. Our source, a catalog of early '16, shows illustrations of cars that appear to be '15s. Note the Coupelet lacks the side windows in the quarter panels, yet all '16s had them as shown in the phantom view from the same catalog.

Note, too, the lamps are shown in black with brass trim. Evidently, Ford didn't want to update his catalog in view of the soon-to-be-announced "new cars".

In August of 1916, the new Fords were shown. The new cars came in the same body types as the 1915 cars, although the Sedan was now altered, making it less expensive to produce.

This was the last year of the Coupelet and the Town Car.

Notice, too, that the illustration above, from the 1917 catalog, shows the Chassis still with the brass radiator, the flat rear fenders (no crown) and the earlier-style front fenders!

1918

Ford Touring Car

Ford Runabout

Ford Sedan

Ford Coupe

Ford Chassis

Enclosed car comfort and convenience for two passengers are disclosed in every feature of the new Ford Coupe.

FORD MODEL T ONE TON TRUCK

1918 saw the introduction of two new Fords, the Coupe and the Truck (TT) chassis. The Town Car has been discontinued.

The Coupe features a removable pillar which, when removed, gives the car the "hardtop" look. This feature lasted only for two years, was discontinued in the 1920 models.

The TT chassis was not "new" in 1918, having been tested in the field for a year or two before its introduction to the general public. The Truck featured a new, stronger frame, new worm-drive rear axle and generally heavier construction from the engine back. The engine and front axle were the same as used in the passenger cars.

Last seen in 1916, the small box-like hood is now made of steel but appears to be just like the 1915 hood which was aluminum. The hood is clamped against a wooden clash strip as in years past and is held down with two-eared, cast clamps.

The headlamps featured CLEAR lens; those shown are accessory type. Headlamps were the same on all cars from late 1915 through 1925, with the exception of the lenses which were altered in the early twenties.

1917, with the introduction of the iron radiator, saw the wooden clash strips replaced with these pressed steel ones. The clamps remained cast as in the 1916s.

The layout of the driver's compartment is similar in all cars of this era. The 1916 (left) has the headlamp switch located to the right of the coil box, as in the 1915 models. Note the smooth pedals, now standard.

Beginning with the 1917 style, the light switch was moved to the steering column where it was incorporated into the horn button. Lights were switched on or off by turning the knob; pushing the knob operated the magneto-powered electric horn, also new this year.

1917 compartment (below) and 1918 compartment (bottom) show the similarity. Speedometers, being options at the time, were not necessarily the types shown here. The floormats shown on the two earlier cars are home made. The 1918 style is correct.

The hand operated klaxon horn shown in the lower left picture is the style furnished on Don Dupree's '16.

The coil box cover on the 1915, 1916 and possibly later cars was of one-piece pressed steel design and had smoothly rounded corners.

Note that there is no rain gutter on the metal cowl strip on the early iron cars. As in the earlier models, water entering the seam between the body and the dash, or seeping under the hood, caused missing and difficult starting because of the coil box getting wet. Ford suggested that a sealer be used in the seams to prevent this problem, and later added a gutter on the engine side of the metal strip to catch the water.

Early 1917 cars had a metal shroud around the fan. No examples have been found of this part but we have reproduced the parts book illustration here. Apparently more of a hindrance than a help to cooling, it was discontinued during the year.

Standard wheels, as before, are 30 by 3 in the front; 30 by 3½ in the rear. Hub caps were brass until the 1917 style; nickel finish then became standard.

Our 1918 feature car has an unusual set of accessory demountable wheels. They have square wooden felloes and five mounting lugs. The name "Perlman" appears on each lug.

After late 1915, Touring bodies assumed a standard construction which was to continue (with minor detail changes) for several years. The major change occurred in the seat frames. No longer made of wood with metal cover, this new design was all metal. The identifying mark of these bodies is the bolt head, or "rivet" on the side of the body just ahead of the rear door.

In the earlier cars, using this body, both seat frames had metal covers which were hinged at the rear. Later, evidently, the cover for the rear seat frame was discontinued and later yet, the front cover was eliminated. All cars in this series had the front cover; only Dupree's late '16 had the rear.

The round gasoline tank remained standard; now rather enclosed by the metal toe-board at the bottom of the front seat-back.

The toe-board, now with pressed-in "beads" to add stiffness, extends from the rear floor and folds rearward to enclose the area below the front seat.

The rear seat compartment is similar to the older wooden style. The metal floor pan is riveted to the front panel and to the rear lip of the body. All these cars have the metal stringer across the compartment; earlier production had a wooden stringer under the metal, this being eliminated by 1918.

Many bodies were dated and numbered. The number and date on Dupree's car appears on the right-front body sill and reads "2 16 511" — the "511" being a little obscure due to wear and aging.

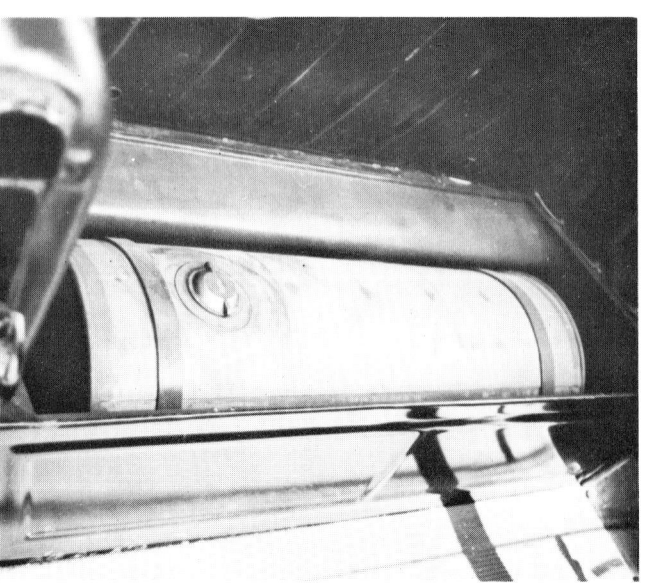

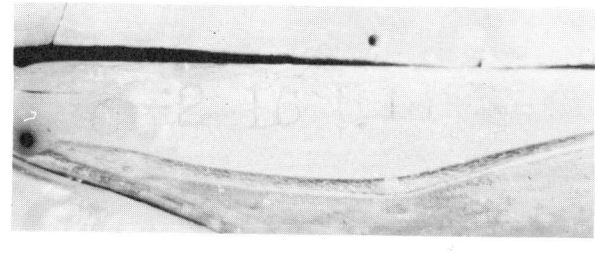

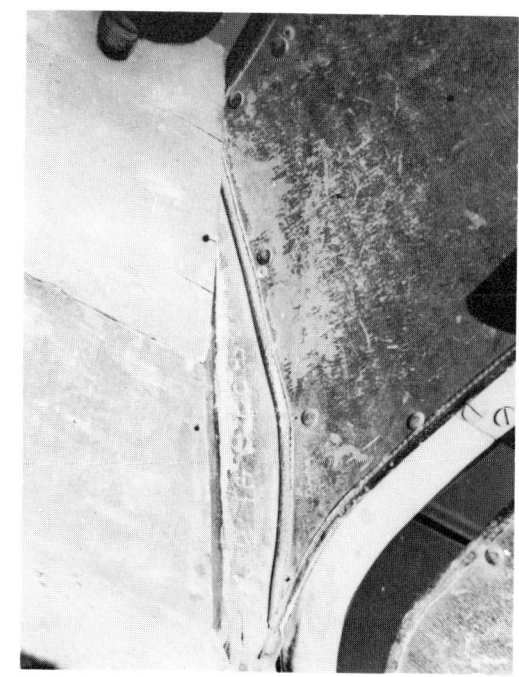

Excluding the new front-end design, one of the major differences between the last of the brass cars and the iron ones is in the windshield design. The 1915-6 design is shown above; the later, below. Note that the earlier windshield was riveted to the support brackets with the rivets through the front surface of the bracket, while the later design was held together with screws through the sides.

Note, too, the differences in the hinge design. The earlier hinges were mounted so that the hinge center was at the seam of the two windshield halves, while the later was about two inches above center. The earlier style has equal length arms, while the later has a longer lower arm. The reason for this change was probably to make the windshield a little higher when in the folded position (opposite page) giving a little more protection to the driver, without raising the seam in the line of vision when in the upright position.

174

The earlier type folded leaving the two sections at equal height at the top surface, while the new design has a considerable offset, as is shown.

Notice how the hook and eye have worn on the '16 shown in the upper illustration of the hinge, on the preceeding page — about half way through!

Headlights, not shown here, are the standard, flanged-post style, so typical for the Model T. They were all black and had clear glass lenses. Magneto powered, the bulbs were connected in series.

Side and tail lights were similar. Unlike the 1915 type, these were all steel and painted black. The style remained standard until 1926. The tail light had an additional window on one side to illuminate the license plate, and had, of course, a red lens at the rear.

Tail light mounting methods varied. Some had forged brackets, others pressed steel; some bolted under the body (on the Touring and closed models); others as shown here on the Roadster.

Typical of all roadster turtle backs from 1913 through this era and beyond, this '17 shows the locking handles used. This compartment was good for little other than a lunch box and a few tools — but it was cute.

The lower illustrations show the new crowned rear fenders used from the late '16s through the '25s. No longer do the rivets used to hold the fender clamp show on the upper surface. This clamp is now riveted to the lip under the bead on each edge of the fender. Front fenders had a similar construction.

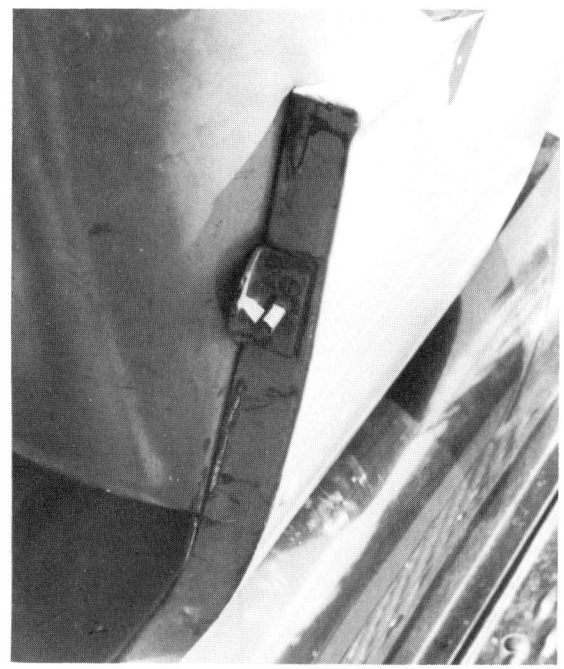

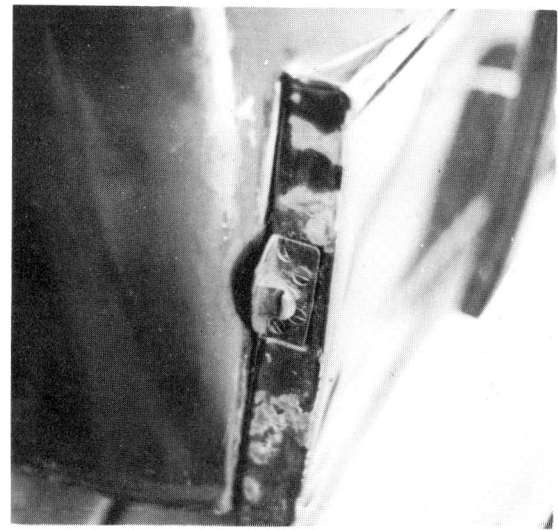

Touring bodies from 1914 through 1916 used a different type of latch than did the 1917 and later cars. The rear doors on these cars had the type illustrated in the top left picture. The bolt operated in a vertical plane, although the lever operation was similar to the later style to a person using it. This latch required a left and a right side so it didn't take too long for Ford to design one that would work on any door.

The new type used a bolt which operated horizontally. The 1916 here came with both styles; the earlier on the rear doors and the later on the front. In 1917 and later cars, the new style was used exclusively. The new type lever and bolt is used on the door shown here.

Engine and running gear remained much the same as it was in 1915. Note that reinforcing ribs have been added to the brake backing plates on the rear axle (1917) and the tapered-leaf springs. Front springs were also tapered; came in either six or seven leaves, apparently depending on the supply.

The crank is of the same design introduced in 1915. The Hassler shock absorbers are an accessory.

The front radius rod was still fastened to the spring perch above the axle (this car has an added support beneath the axle). Spring shackles remain of the L-shaped style.

The Ascending Years
1919 - 22

1919 through 1922 were truly the doldrum years in Model T Ford styling. One must be a real expert to differentiate between models of this period. Yet, while the outward appearance seemed to be the same, more changes were made during this era than had been made during any other similar period. The vast majority of these changes were in construction details and mechanical modifications. Some improved the car; others improved the profits.

Our coverage in this chapter will include these four years. Changes will be noted and illustrated where possible. It is important to remember that Ford's Model Years, his Fiscal Years and the calendar years did not coincide. Fiscal years began on August first and ended on July thirty-first, the following year. Model years ran approximately the same as fiscal years, but not necessarily coincidental. Thus, the 1919 Ford was produced from about August of 1918 through July of 1919.

To make matters even more confusing, there was no clean break from one Model Year to the next. As modifications were conceived, they were added without respect to Model Year or body style. Perhaps the most noticeable evidence of this policy occurred in 1922 when, in August, Ford issued a sales brochure showing the Touring with the 1923-style top and windshield, while the Runabout continued the 1922 (and earlier) style, *and the Centerdoor Sedan was continued!*

It is, therefore, impossible to say that all 1921's, for example, are this way and that all 1922's are that way, etc. We will indicate the years in which the changes were made, but these changes may not be typical of *all* cars of that Model Year.

The Touring in the top picture is typical of the 1917 to 1920 style. The two lower pictures are typical of the 1921-22 Fords.
While the appearance is similar, there are many differences. Perhaps the most obvious is the L-shaped top saddle bracket on the early cars, and the through-the-panel rod on the later ones. Other differences will be covered later in this article.

PRODUCTION FIGURES
Figures are for Ford's fiscal years.

1919
   2,756,252 through 3,277,851
     (521,599 cars)

1920
   3,277,852 through 4,233,350
     (955,498 cars)

1921
   4,233,351 through 5,223,135
     (989,784 cars)

1922
   5,223,136 through 6,334,196
     (1,111,060 cars)

1919

During the 1919 Model Year, many important changes were made in the Model T. No doubt the most significant of these was the addition of electrical starting equipment as an option on the *closed cars only*. Along with the starter and generator came the dashboard with the combination ignition and light switch and an ammeter. On cars furnished with this equipment, a choke pull rod was added, along with a bell crank on the firewall, so that the car could be choked from the driver's seat. Early production starter-equipped cars had the generator cutout mounted on the firewall but it was not long before it was moved to the familiar location on the generator. Early light switches were somewhat unique in that the handles were a casting rather than of the pressed steel style which was so common.

Front wheel bearings were changed from the ball type to Timken roller. The spindles were made longer to accommodate these new bearings
(Continued on Page 184)

The 1921 Sedan, shown here, is typical of this style throughout its production. The car was originally supplied with paint over the window frames, rather than the natural finish shown here. In 1922 the frames were covered with metal.

The Coupe, too, remained static in styling. The early 1919 models had a removable post at the door which made it like today's hardtops. Later production came with the fixed posts.

Demountable rims and 30 by 3½ tires, shown on all cars here, were an option. Standard production had the usual 30 by 3 in the front; 30 by 3½ tires in the rear, all mounted on non-demountable clincher rims.

The illustrations shown here are from the Ford catalog of 1920-21. The 1919-20 catalog was similar, using, apparently, the same illustrations. We have been unable to locate any catalog for 1922.

Apparently used by a dealer, the

182

price of each model is written under its picture. Prices here for the Touring are $644.20 with starter; $565.11 without starter. Roadster: $618.20 and $539.08. Sedan: $934.54 and $825.42. Coupe: $774.39 and $695.27. The area in which these prices were in effect was not indicated.

The charm of the new Ford Sedan as a family car and for all social purposes is apparent in this phantom photograph.

better but the roller bearings were offered as replacements on the earlier cars and could be used on the older spindles with no modifications.

This was the last year in which the tapered leaf rear springs were used; the tapered leaf front spring had been discontinued during 1916. Tapered leaf and square end leaf springs were both used in production as the supply lasted.

During the year, Ford tried a new timer brush which did not have a roller. It apparently was not too successful and was discontinued after a short time, in favor of the normal roller type. This new brush had a spring-loaded plunger which made contact with the regular outer case.

All cars were modified to use the new style front radius rods which fastened to the axle below the spring perches. This required a new perch which eliminated the hole formerly used to hold the radius rods, and which had a longer threaded section to allow for the new rod below the axle.

Ford discovered that money could be saved by combining the drag link fitting and toe-in adjustment at the right hand end of the steering tie rod, rather than having the adjustment on the left and the ball on the right as in earlier cars.

Along with the availability of starting equipment, all cars were furnished with helical timing gears. As the supply of engine castings in which no provision was made for the generator (i.e., the old-style) was used up, all cars were furnished with the new blocks. The open cars had cover plates over the starter holes, and a casting where the generator would mount.

Radiators were now mounted on springs, rather than on the leather pad which had been used. This modification required a new radiator shell and the hardware which held the springs. The old and the new shells were not interchangeable.

A rain gutter was added at the firewall to catch rain water and direct it away from the ignition coils This gutter was located on the engine side of the firewall and while it did keep the water away from *that* side, the problem of water dripping between the firewall and the cowl was still there. Ford recommended the use of a sealer at this point, to be installed by the dealer or owner, but not by the factory.

Demountable tires and rims, either Kelsey, Hayes or Ford, became available, again as an option on the closed cars only. They used 30 by 3½ tires all around.

Carburetors were either Ford "G" or L-2 Kingston.

The rear axle housings were modified to use a paper gasket between the two halves (of the differential housing). A new rear axle oil seal was now used, having a slightly larger diameter retaining cup.

1920

During 1919, presumably with the introduction of the 1920 models, electrical equipment was made available on all cars. For some time now, the engines had been cast with the necessary provisions and so the change became a natural.

During this year, the oval gasoline tank became standard. We have found no definite date as to when this change was made but it may have been during the spring of 1920 or with the introduction of the 1921 models, in August.

The fan was redesigned of pressed steel and replaced the riveted style that had been used for so many years.

The steering wheel spider was now of pressed steel and the wheel itself was sixteen inches in diameter.

Ford introduced the new "NH" carburetor during the year, and it was supplied in addition to the Ford "G" and the Kingston "L-2" carburetors.

1921

Up until now, Ford had supplied all cars with headlights with clear glass lens. Laws had been passed throughout the country which limited the amount of glare that would be acceptable. Rather than use the corrugated design which had been developed, Ford chose a lens with a green, pie-shaped insert at the top. This "visored" lens was not too satisfactory and in a short time it was replaced with the familiar Ford "H" lens. This lens was a great improvement as it directed the light in a pattern which gave a wider field of illumination.

Many modifications in general design became standard this year. A ten-tooth pinion gear was offered as an option in the differentials of cars that were to be used in mountainous areas. While this made the hill climbing ability greater, it also reduced the top speed. A new, lightweight engine connecting rod was now used which helped the engine to keep up with the ever-increasing speed on the highways. The retaining wire which threaded through the magneto magnet retaining bolts on the flywheel was discontinued. Tests had proven that it was not necessary if the bolts were drawn tight during assembly.

A new rear end pinion bearing housing was now used. This housing featured exposed mounting bolts and was of steel. The old style had the bolts enclosed and was a casting.

During this year, perhaps with the introduction of the 1922 models, the engine casting was again altered and the new engines featured a one-piece valve tappet cover. This improvement made it easier for the oil to leak out at this point.

The front motor mount/spring hanger was now of the style which used only two bolts. Ford claimed that this new design aided the riding

qualities by allowing more flexibility in the spring mounting!!!

The pressed steel muffler was new this year.

The general design of the Touring was changed. Changes included a new cowl and new rear quarter panel which did not have the vertical bead on the side and which had the top saddle brackets protruding through a hole in the panel. The running board brackets were now of pressed steel instead of the castings with the tie rods. Seats were lowered, giving the effect of higher backs and making them more comfortable.

The Kingston L-4 carburetor was used on some cars, in addition to the Ford "NH".

1922

1922 cars continued in the same style as the 1921 models with a few minor changes.

The centerdoor sedan was modified to use a latching device to hold the windows in position rather than the straps which had appeared. This latch consisted of a metal strip on each side of the window frame. The strips had a series of notches cut away and on the window there were two levers which would engage the notches and hold the window in a number of positions. The window frames were now covered with metal instead of being just painted wood as in the earlier sedans.

The little swivel at the lever end of the spark advance rod was eliminated and the cars were now supplied with the bent-wire rod.

Roadsters were given a new, larger, turtle back, which was continued through the 1925 cars.

The 1922 cars evolved into the 1923 style. In August, the new Touring was announced but all other body styles were continued well into the 1923 Model Year.

Again, remember that model changes were made during the calendar year and that a 1920 style car (for example) may have been made in 1919. Just as in today's cars, one which has a serial number after the model change time (July-August in Ford's case) should be called the next year's model.

The featured Touring is owned by George Romain of Tarzana, Calif. The Centerdoor Sedan is the pride and joy of Cliff Nordstrom, North Hollywood, Calif. The Coupe is owned by Dave Ayers, Santa Cruz, Calif., who also supplied many of the pictures used in this article. Other cars, or parts of cars, were numerous and will be credited where they appear, if possible.

The cars used in these illustrations are typical of the general style. All have accessories which should be discounted (such as the bumpers on the Sedan). The Touring is a 1921; the Coupe is a 1922; and the Sedan is a 1921.

This 1918 Touring, featured in our last article, is shown for comparison purposes only. It is nearly identical to all Ford Tourings until mid-1920.

Styling for the Ford cars of the period under study remained in the pattern of the 1917-8 models until mid-1920 and we refer you to the coverage of those models for styling details. During 1920, presumably with the introduction of the 1921 cars, the Touring bodies were redesigned. A new oval-shaped gasoline tank enabled the seats to be lowered, giving the effect of higher seat backs and adding to the seating comfort.

The rear quarter panel was now of one piece, eliminating the vertical bead in the side panel. The top saddle brackets which had been L-shaped, were now round rods which screwed into a metal bracket through a hole in the panel. Oddly, these posts were apparently offered as an option; most early photos show the hole but not the post. Saddles were new too. The new post was only one-half inch in diameter requiring a smaller hole in the saddle.

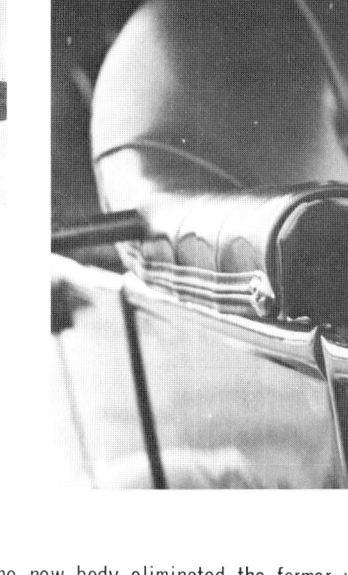

The new body eliminated the former wood tack strip which was secured over the metal panels; the new tack strip was inside the panels. This change eliminated the overhanging ridge which had been characteristic of the cars for years. The lack of the tack strip ridge allowed a newer, narrow metal cap to be used on the arm rests at the doors. The narrower arm rest was, perhaps, less comfortable but comfort was not one of Ford's best selling points anyway.

Windshields remained standard until 1922 when the 1923 style was introduced. Note the off-center hinge, allowing the lower glass panel to be higher and giving more protection to the passengers when the top section was folded.

All cars were now equipped with metal clash strips through which the pressed steel hood clamps passed. A rain gutter was added in 1919 to direct water away from the ignition coils. The firewall on all cars was wooden.

Standard wheels were non-demountable, using 30 by 3 tires in front; 30 by 3½ in the rear. Available as a factory-installed option in 1919 were the demountable rims, using 30 by 3½ tires all around. This option was initially available only on the closed cars but was made available on all models in 1920. Three makes were used; Ford, Kelsey and Hayes. All were mounted on square-metal-felloe, wooden-spoked, wheels. Front wheel bearings on all cars were now Timken roller.

Until 1921, Ford supplied all cars with clear glass headlight lens. For a short time in 1921, a green-visored lens was used but it was replaced with the familiar Ford "H" type shown here.

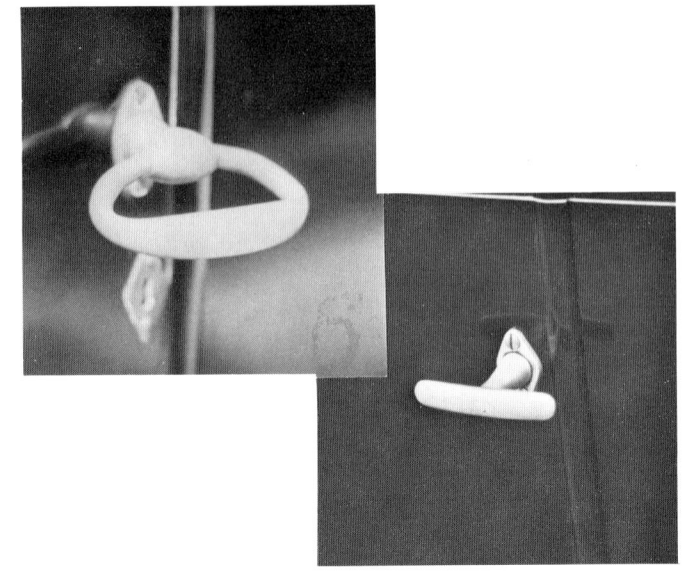
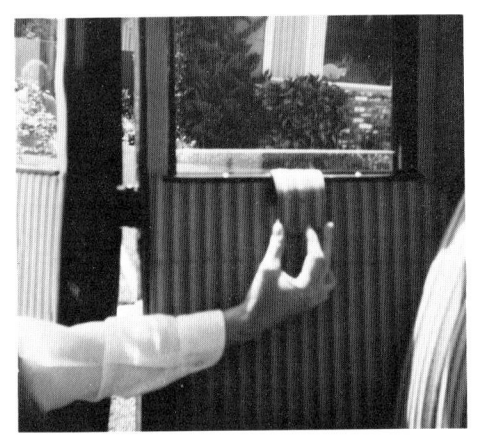

During the 1920's the closed cars became increasingly popular. Ford offered two; the Coupe and the Sedan. Both were similar in appointments and upholstery. Our samples do not have original upholstery; all reflect the whims of their owners. Correct upholstery was a broadcloth of contrasting shades of brown.

Windows on all closed cars were adjusted with pull straps until the 1922 models when a mechanical latch arrangement was installed. This latch consisted of two strips of notched metal, one on each side of the window, and two levers which engaged these notches, holding the window in a number of positions. The rear side windows were still adjusted with the straps as in the pre-1922 models.

The early cars had door handles of the bail type, as on the 1915 sedan. About 1920, a T-shaped handle was installed. The 1922 Sedan, owned by Howard Genrich, Long Beach, Calif., sports a fancy handle with nickel trim.

Note how the rear panels lap over the top covering, giving a smooth appearance to the rear, but making replacement of the material a real challenge.

The 1922 models had a metal overlay around the windows covering the wood framing, a real improvement because the painted wood finish soon checked and peeled.

The closed cars were unique in the line in that they both used a different gasoline tank than that used in the open cars. This square tank, part number 2900B, was placed under the driver's seat in the sedan, and inside the turtle deck on the Coupe.

The turtle deck on the coupe was separate from the body and could be removed. Conversion to a closed pickup was unlikely because of the location of the gasoline tank.

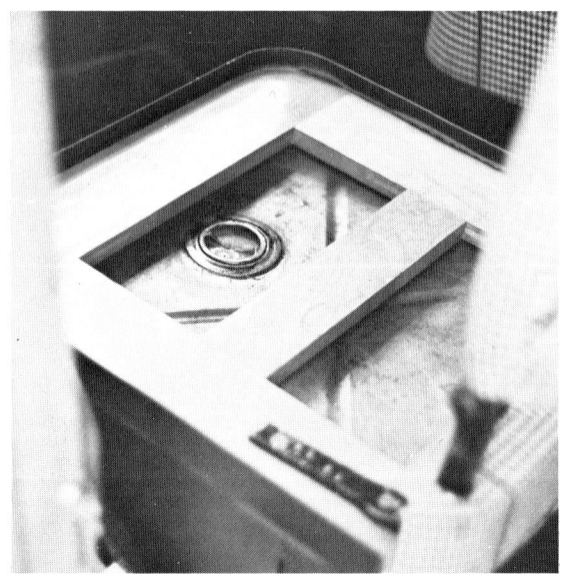

The Coupe and Sedan shared a similar windshield. Unlike the open cars, both sections were adjustable. The upper part could be opened to a horizontal position if desired; the lower could be lifted about an inch and then swung inward slightly, directing air downward into the passenger compartment. Details of the hinge and bracket assembly are shown here.

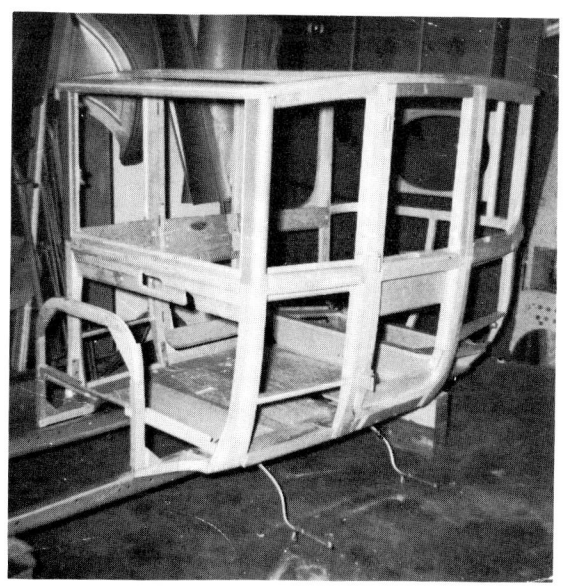

Framing for the Sedan was elaborate, making restoration a job for an expert. This photo of Cliff Nordstrom's 1920 Sedan, was taken in 1961. Using all new wood, and comparing to a fine piano in workmanship, it was really a shame to cover it with the body metal. Cliff said: "There's not a straight piece of wood in the whole car!"

The instrument panel on the starter equipped cars appeared similar to the one shown here. The first cars had a wood panel with a metal overlay. This was later discontinued and a metal only panel was used. While similar in appearance to the '23 and later panel, these were more vertical; had a straight bottom edge (from one side to the other); and had an exposed mounting nut on each side as seen at the right of our picture. The Stewart speedometer was an option.

A major change, common to all cars in this section of the series, is the new front radius rod, introduced in 1919. Of sturdier construction, it was now fastened below the axle at the spring perch. The new perches had a longer threaded section to allow for the radius rod and, of course, did not have the hole where the earlier rod was fastened.

Spring shackles were of the two-piece type; both sections being identical L-shaped units. The shackles shown are not correct.

Also introduced in '19, the toe-in adjustment and ball for the drag link were combined rather than being separate as on the earlier cars. The new assembly is shown on the left; the old on the right.

In 1922, the spark adjustment rod was changed to eliminate the little swivel (left picture) at the steering column end. Now just a bent wire, it seemed to work just as well (right picture).

1921 saw the introduction of the one-piece motor mount and spring hanger casting, using just two nuts instead of the previous four. Along with this came a one piece license plate bracket. A nickel here; a nickel there......!!

1921 was also the introductory year for the rear pinion bearing housing with the exposed bolts. Otherwise, the rear axle assembly was unchanged.

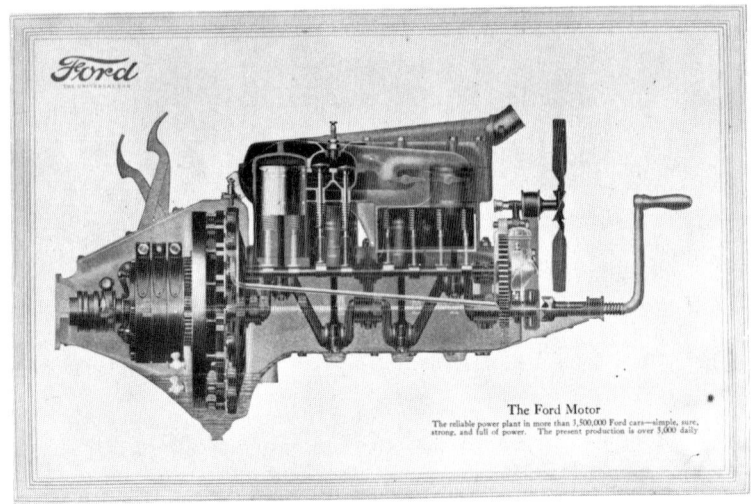

The engine illustration, taken from the same catalog as the models in the front of this article, clearly shows the "1920 Ford engine". Note the aluminum crank handle, the straight-cut gears, etc. Ford's use of such out of date pictures in his catalogs makes the use of these sources of information very confusing. By 1920 the engine had been altered in many respects from that engine shown in their catalog!

These changes included new timing gears, altered castings to allow the use of starting and generating equipment, a different crank handle, fan and so on. We have used the illustration just to prove that even catalogs can be wrong.

Major change in the engine compartment was the addition of the starter and generator. On those cars furnished without this equipment, a special casting was used over the timing gear which allowed the use of a front cover similar to the earlier cars. This casting bolted in place of the generator mounting type and made it possible to use the same engine block in all cars. Two cover plates were used on the transmission cover when no starter was supplied.

During 1921, the engine was altered to include a one-piece valve chamber cover and new light weight connecting rods. The new fan, no longer of riveted construction, had been added in 1920 as a running change.

Sometime during the 1920 to 1921 Ford production, a new starting crank appeared. No longer of the type with the separate handle, the new crank was of one piece; the handle being a sheet metal sleeve which was rolled on the inner edge to engage a groove in the crank, which held it in place. The earlier crank was far superior.

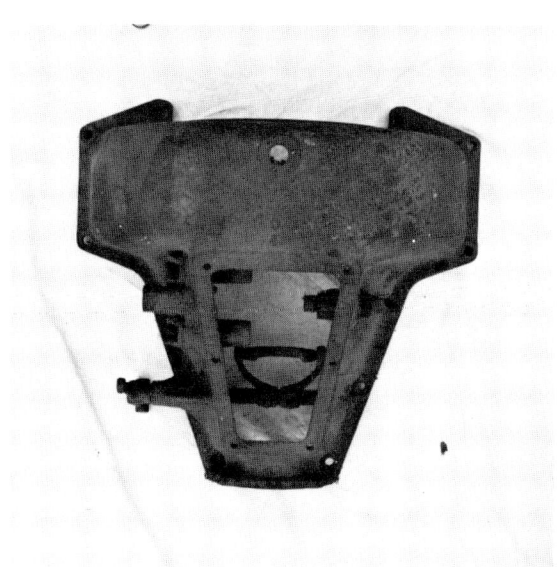 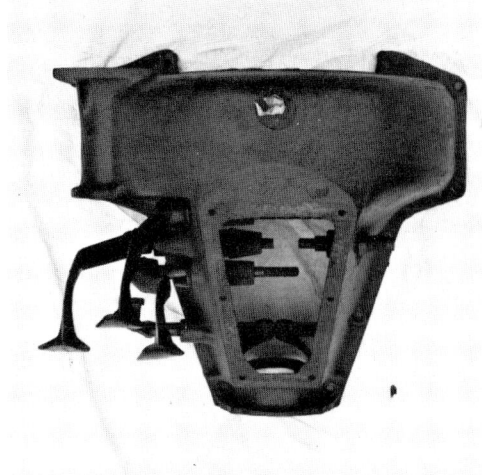

The standard transmission cover is shown at the right. Two plates were used to seal the starter holes in those cars which were supplied without electrical equipment. Earlier 1919 non-starter cars used the old style, iron cover until the supply was exhausted.

The Golden Era
1923-25

The 1923 Model T Fords as they appeared at the time of their introduction. These pictures were taken in late 1922.

Note that the Touring is the very early style (one of the first 100,000) with the straight-edged top assembly. The Roadster top is of the later style, as indicated by the gentle curve at the rear.

Photos courtesy The Ford Archives.

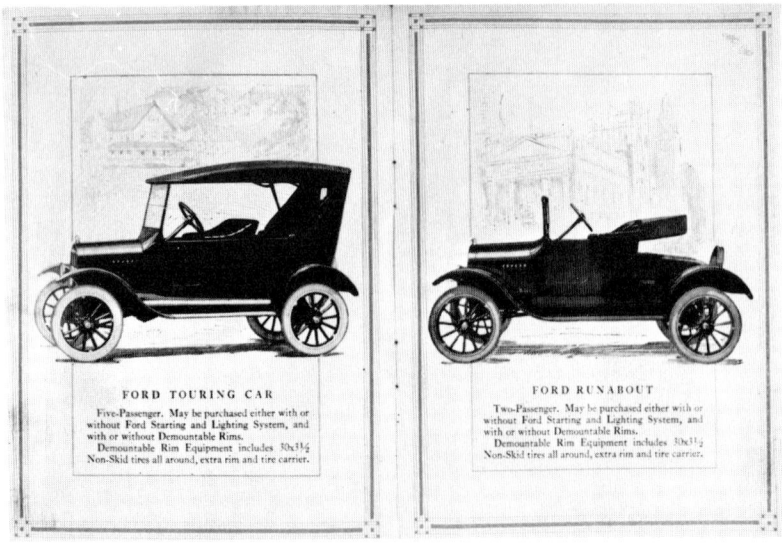

The illustrations on this and the opposite page are from Ford's catalogs of the early and late 1923 style year.

Notice that the early (left) catalog shows the Roadster with the earlier windshield, and also shows the Centerdoor Sedan. The Coupe continues in the 1919-22 style.

Later in the year the Catalog shows the Fordor, the Tudor, the new Coupe, and the two open cars, the Touring and the Runabout. Notice the unusual rear windows in the Touring. While the standard rear windows were two rectangles, a number of cars were furnished with the small oval windows.

Notice, too, that the cars in the later catalog now sport the higher radiator and the larger hood.

It is important to remember that these illustrations are artist's renditions and not actual photographs, and that artists, like the rest of us, can make errors. One example is in the picture of the late Touring — notice the early-style top lines. Touring cars built during the bulk of production had tops like that shown on Page 205.

TOURING CAR FEATURES

Immensely improved in appearance the Ford Touring Car also incorporates improved seating arrangements that add greatly to riding comfort.

Seats and seat backs have been set at a restful angle. Additional leg room has been provided by moving the front seat slightly to the rear and undercutting it on the back and enlarging the cowl.

The radiator has been made higher and a fender apron has been added which enhances the appearance of the car. A steering-post brace, riveted to the dash, reduces the possibility of vibration and contributes to the comfort of the driver.

Demountable rims are furnished as standard equipment.

The modern one-man top and snug-fitting side curtains ensure passengers thorough protection in all weathers.

With roomy accommodations for five passengers it is undoubtedly the most practical general utility car on the market.

THE TOURING CAR

FEATURES OF THE NEW COUPE

A completely re-designed body with higher hood and radiator and enlarged rear luggage compartment, gives the Ford Coupe a distinctly improved appearance as well as a higher utility value. As a personal car for the business or professional man, salesman or any other person requiring rapid, comfortable transportation for two the Coupe covers a wide range of usefulness.

The large carrying compartment at the rear provides ample space for a surprising number of grips and packages. A sun visor adds to the comfort of both driver and passenger.

The handy, recessed shelf at rear of seat, for packages, portfolios, etc., is a feature that appeals to every user.

The new Coupe is the lowest priced enclosed car on the market. Included among other features are: door handles, black with nickelled trimming. Yale locks on doors, revolving window regulators, anti-rattling device on doors, cowl ventilator and adjustable watertight windshield.

Starter and demountable rims are furnished as standard equipment.

A quality closed car at a lower price than any open car except a Ford.

Interior of Coupe

THE COUPE

TUDOR SEDAN ADVANTAGES

As the newest and most distinctive of Ford closed body types, the Tudor Sedan satisfies the demand for a 4-passenger coupe, as well as the call for a 5-passenger two-door car.

The individual front seats, deeply upholstered, are accessible from either side of the car. The left front seat is of the "bucket" design, the right front seat folds forward, giving a roomy entrance through the unusually wide door.

Large, well-proportioned windows and a straight roof line give the car an exceptionally pleasing appearance.

The Tudor Sedan features include: Yale lock on right door. Inside lock on other door, broad, rectangular rear window —clear vision, all side windows lower flush with window sills, cowl ventilator, adjustable watertight windshield and sun visor.

Starter and demountable rims are furnished as standard equipment.

Note the roomy comfort of the individual front seats.

THE TUDOR SEDAN

FORDOR SEDAN ADVANTAGES

For five adult passengers the Ford Fordor Sedan offers features of supreme comfort and convenience.

The wide door openings provide easy access to the commodious interior, and the exceptional depth and resiliency of the upholstery give restful support to the limbs.

The interior fittings compare with enclosed cars of much higher price. Revolving type window lifts, door locks, windshield visor, silk poplin shades, floor rugs, dome light, starter and demountable rims are furnished as standard equipment.

Wide doors permit easy access to front and rear compartments.

A few of the many features incorporated in the new Fordor Sedan are: body-work in heavy aluminum, cowl ventilator, bar type door handles, interior fittings nickel finished, adjustable watertight windshield, two-piece front seat cushion and sun visor.

Interior of the Fordor Sedan

THE FORDOR SEDAN

Ford RUNABOUT *Two-Passenger*

A practical business utility furnishing individual transportation at a minimum cost. Like the touring car, it may be purchased either with or without starting and lighting equipment and with or without demountable rims. Demountable rim equipment includes 30 x 3½" non-skid tires, all around, extra rim and tire carrier.

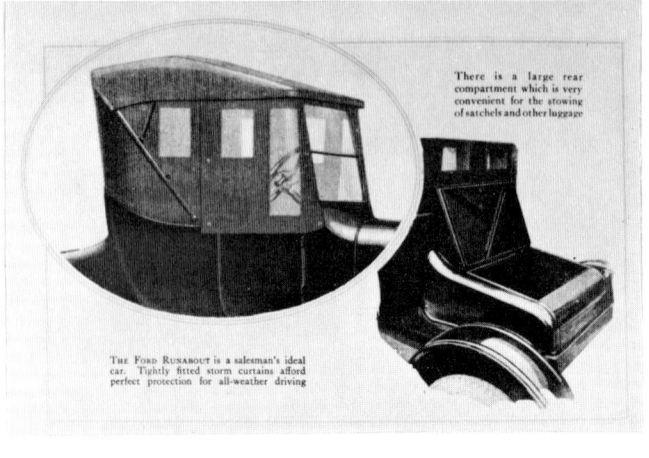

The Ford Runabout is a salesman's ideal car. Tightly fitted storm curtains afford perfect protection for all-weather driving

There is a large rear compartment which is very convenient for the stowing of satchels and other luggage

Ford TUDOR SEDAN *Five-Passenger*

The Tudor Sedan provides enclosed car comfort and utility for five passengers at exceptionally low cost. The straight roof line and well proportioned windows give this car a very pleasing appearance. Electric starting and lighting, demountable rims, non-skid tires, all around, extra rim and tire carrier are standard equipment.

All Ford enclosed cars are equipped with revolving type window regulators. The windows of the Tudor lower flush with the window sills

Both left and right front seats in the Tudor are broad and deeply cushioned. The driver's seat is of the bucket design accessible from either side of the car

The Tudor, a comparatively new Ford body type, has gained wide popularity. It is an ideal car for personal use yet affords ample seating capacity for five persons. The right front seat folds completely out of the way, making it extremely easy for rear seat passengers to enter and leave through the wide door

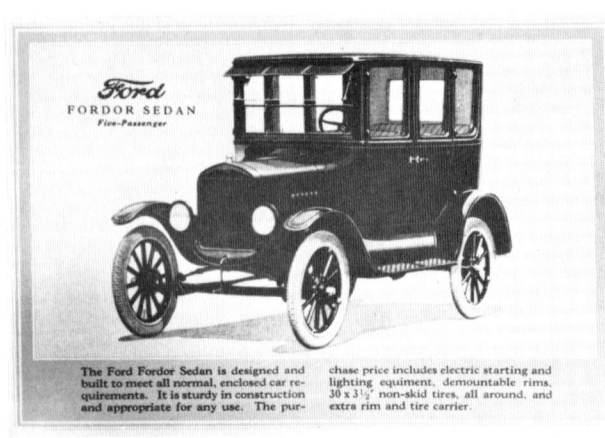

Ford FORDOR SEDAN *Five-Passenger*

The Ford Fordor Sedan is designed and built to meet all normal, enclosed car requirements. It is sturdy in construction and appropriate for any use. The purchase price includes electric starting and lighting equipment, demountable rims, 30 x 3½" non-skid tires, all around, and extra rim and tire carrier.

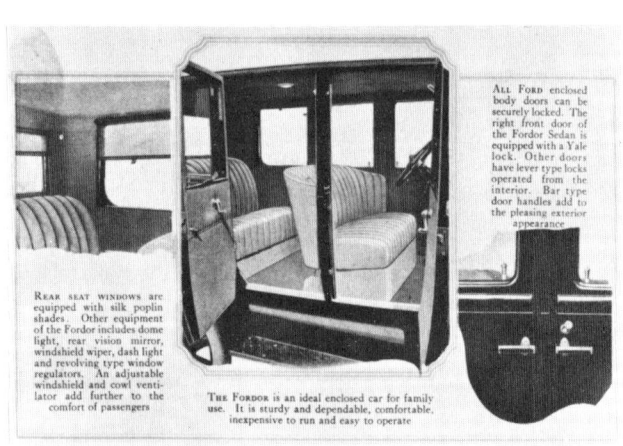

Rear seat windows are equipped with silk poplin shades. Other equipment of the Fordor includes dome light, rear vision mirror, windshield wiper, dash light and revolving type window regulators. An adjustable windshield and cowl ventilator add further to the comfort of passengers

All Ford enclosed body doors can be securely locked. The right front door of the Fordor Sedan is equipped with a Yale lock. Other doors have lever type locks operated from the interior. Bar type door handles add to the pleasing exterior appearance

The Fordor is an ideal enclosed car for family use. It is sturdy and dependable, comfortable, inexpensive to run and easy to operate

Ford COUPE *Two-Passenger*

The Ford Coupe covers a wide range of usefulness. It is well adapted for the personal or professional requirements of the business or professional man, salesman or any member of the family. Standard equipment includes starting and lighting system, demountable rims, non-skid tires, all around, extra rim and tire carrier.

A spacious rear compartment for baggage adds materially to the usefulness of the Coupe. This compartment is easily accessible through a large opening in the rear deck

A cowl ventilator, sun visor, and adjustable upper windshield glass are standard equipment on all Ford enclosed body types

The interior of the coupe is roomy and comfortable. A recess shelf back of the seat is convenient for carrying a brief case or small parcels

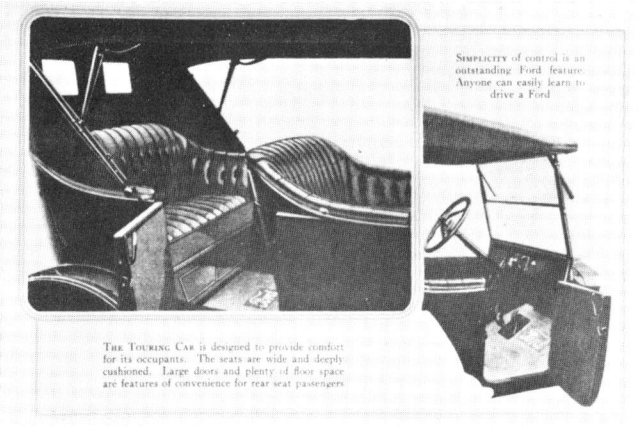

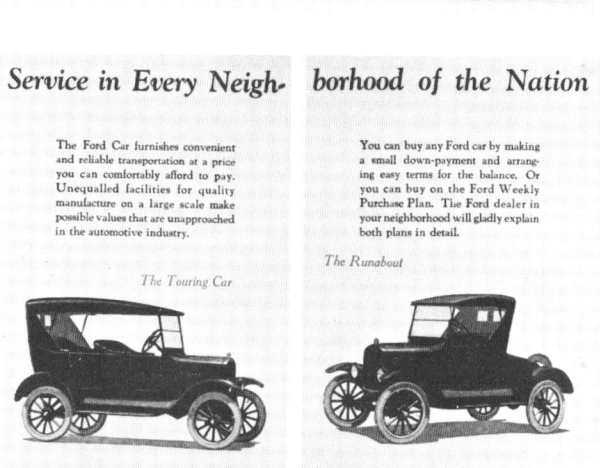

During the twenties, Fords sold and sold well, but as the middle of the decade neared, sales were requiring more selling effort. No longer just offered as dependable transportation, the words "Comfort" and "Style" began to appear.

"Ford Service" was one of the major sales pitches. "Easy Terms" was another. Who knows, why Ford may begin offering colors again before long.

The 1925 Model T Ford Fordor Sedan   Photo courtesy the Ford Archives

Truly, the "Golden Years" of Model T Ford history were the middle twenties. During the period from August, 1922, to the end of July, 1925, Ford built and sold almost as many cars as had been built during the previous fourteen years of production; 5,888,329 Model T Fords! (August, 1922, production began with serial number 6,334,197). The peak year was 1924 when production reached 2,143,796 cars.

PRODUCTION FIGURES

August, 1922 began with	6,334,197
July, 1923 ended with	8,122,674
Total 1923 production	1,788,477
August, 1923 began with	8,122,675
July, 1924 ended with	10,266,471
Total 1924 production	2,143,796
August, 1924 began with	10,664,472
July 1925 ended with	12,222,528
Total 1925 production	1,956,056

(The above figures represent production during Ford's fiscal years, which correspond with the model years. The figures for the 1925 period reflect some 1926 production.)

BY THE MILLION

Car number:	Date
1	October 1, 1908
1,000,000	December 10, 1915
2,000,000	June 14, 1917
3,000,000	April 2, 1919
4,000,000	May 11, 1920
5,000,000	May 28, 1921
6,000,000	May 18, 1922
7,000,000	January 12, 1923
8,000,000	July 11, 1923
9,000,000	December 26, 1923
10,000,000	June 4, 1924
11,000,000	January, 1925
12,000,000	June, 1925

The "new style" Ford was introduced in August of 1922 with the Touring leading off the trend. Featuring a "one man" top and a new windshield which sloped to the rear at the top, the car appeared lower and more streamlined (to

The 1925 Model T Ford Tudor Sedan. Photo courtesy the Ford Archives.

use *that* term in its broadest sense).

The "one man" top was the major change. The term, "one man" seems strange; the old style top could be raised or lowered by one man if he worked hard, and the new one required just as much effort. The first 100,000 (approximately) cars were furnished with a top which had a straight top edge (illustrated). The later tops curved down at the rear, giving a more enclosed appearance.

Continued in the 1922 style, until Fall of 1922, were the Roadster, Coupe and Sedan. The Touring body was identical to the 1922, except for the top and windshield.

All cars continued to use the "low" radiator. Firewalls were either wood or pressed steel, with either type appearing, apparently depending on the available supply.

The Roadster was restyled to include the new style top and windshield in the Fall of 1922.

Early in October, 1922, Ford announced (to the dealers) the new Fordor Sedan. A notice, dated October 10, said:

"A new four-door, five-passenger sedan body has been added to the line of standard Ford body styles. This body is an entirely new development in design and construction, and does not in any way displace the present two-door sedan, which will continue to come through.

"While this new four-door body will go into production within the next several weeks, the out-put will necessarily be limited for some time to come; therefore your sales effort on the present two-door type should be increased rather than relaxed. This present type still represents one of the best automobile values on the market, and the new type of body will simply broaden the field of sedan prospects, so far as Ford business is concerned.

"The price of the new four-door sedan is $725.00, F.O.B. Detroit, and the differential between it and the two-door type is large enough to prevent competition between the two models. There is no reason why you should lose a single sedan order because of inability to deliver the new type, WHICH SHOULD ONLY BE MENTIONED TO PROSPECTS WHO HAVE PREVIOUSLY

The 1925 Model T Ford Coupe.

The 1925 Model T Ford Runabout.

Photos courtesy the Ford Archives.

The 1924 Model T Ford Chassis. Photo courtesy the Ford Archives.

GIVEN CAREFUL CONSIDERATION TO THE PURCHASE OF A FOUR-DOOR SEDAN, AND WILL NOT BE SATISFIED WITH ANY OTHER TYPE.

"Continue pushing the sale of the two-door sedan, and only accept orders for the four-door type to prevent actual loss of business.

"VERY LITTLE PUBLICITY ON THE NEW SEDAN IS BEING GIVEN OUT. THEREFORE, FOR THE PRESENT, PREPARE NO ADVERTISING COPY ON IT, AND SEND OUT NO LITERATURE. IN THIS WAY YOUR SELLING PROBLEM WILL BE GREATLY SIMPLIFIED."

Enclosed with this notice to the dealers was the following description:

"The body is approximately three inches longer than the two-door type, the extra length providing additional leg room for the occupants of the rear seat.

"All body panels are of aluminum with embossed moulding, the metal extending up around the window sills and runways so that there are no wood parts exposed on the entire body. This feature insures a uniform finish and will largely prevent checking or other paint trouble.

"The body, though longer than the present design, weighs approximately eighty pounds less. The saving in weight is gained by the use of aluminum panels in place of steel and also a lighter roof construction.

"The roof is of the soft type with artificial leather reinforced and padded, making it as durable and substantial as the old fiber board type, and eliminating the possibility of vibration noises. The overall height of the body is one inch less than the present design. With the straighter roof line the car has the appearance of greatly increased length.

"A permanent leather visor above the windshield adds greatly to the appearance of the car while protecting the driver from the glare of the sun.

"The tire carrier is of a new and improved design which permits the spare tire to set at an angle that corresponds with the lines of the body.

"The front door openings are 23½ inches and the rear door openings 24 inches or the same width as on the present two-door sedan.

"Door handles are of the straight bar type made from hard black rubber with nickel tips and fittings. All doors are equipped with locks. Three of the locks are operated by levers from the interior of the body, while the right front door lock is operated by a key from the outside.

Ken Dunlap's 1924 Touring

"All doors are equipped with special Ford design double roller, dove tail guides at center as well as rubber bumpers top and bottom to prevent rattling.

"The upper sash of the windshield is adjustable either outwardly or inwardly to provide the proper degree of ventilation. An improved design of clamp permits it to be easily adjusted and securely fastened in any position. The lower section of the windshield is stationary which is a factor in preventing rain from leaking into the body.

"The windows in all four doors are operated by means of crank type window regulators, while the rear windows are operated by the present lever type used on the two-door Sedan.

"All interior body fittings, including window regulators, door pull handles, door latch levers, etc., are finished in oxidized silver.

"A dome light is operated by a button on the right rear body pillar.

"Upholstery material is of improved design with a fine dark stripe and a brown background of a shade that will not easily show dust and dirt. Silk window curtains to harmonize are provided for the three rear windows.

"The rear seat cushion is 46½ inches by 20 inches, or one inch wider than in the two-door Sedan. The front seat is 42½ inches by 19 inches and will accommodate a third person if necessary. The front seat cushion is divided in the center making it necessary to raise but one-half of the cushion to fill the gasoline tank. Therefore, the driver may have the tank filled without leaving his seat.

"Seat cushions are held in position by means of dowel pins in place of the covered binding

Don Beason's 1923 Runabout

strip used on our two-door Sedan.

"The price of the new Sedan is $750.00 F.O.B. Detroit."

The Centerdoor Sedan was (apparently) continued into early 1923, phased out, and replaced with a new-style two-door in the 1924 model year.

The 1923 Coupe continued in the 1922 style until the 1924 Models when it, too, was restyled to include an integral rear deck. Ford, in his literature, seems to make no distinction between the late 1923 cars and the 1924's. Apparently the changes were made and the new styles added as they were developed, without regard to model year.

During the 1923 model year, all cars were modified to include a higher radiator and shell, a new and larger hood, a new cowl section, a skirt under the radiator and lips on the front edge of the front fenders which matched with the radiator apron. This change gave the cars a more massive appearance.

Late in 1923, the new Coupe was announced. The following changes were noted by Ford:

"New rear fender curving outward at end with rear fender apron bolted to sill of body.

"Ventilator in cowl operated by quick action lever under the dash.

"Windshield visor supported to body by two steel rods. Has pull-to brackets on lower side of windshield frame.

"Bottom windshield does not open.

"Upper windshield is wider and lower windshield is narrower, bringing the division and the rubber strip below the vision of the driver.

"Seat divided. Gas tank opening under right

half of seat.

"Check straps on doors are rubber.

"Revolving door window regulators.

"Inside door latch and regulators nickeled.

"Pull rod on doors eliminated. New arrangements on window sill (embossed finishing strip).

"Turtle back rear deck with increased carrying capacity.

"Upholstery of soft brown cloth with mahogany stripe. Head lining plain brown mixed.

"Yale lock on right hand door.

"Inside lock on other door.

"Rear side curtains operated by rod and knob type.

"Silk curtain on rear window. No curtain on side windows.

"Curtain brackets nickeled.

"Broad, square back window, stationary.

"Battery held in bracket under rear deck and is accessible through trap in floor of rear compartment.

"Door handles black with nickeled trimmings.

"Top of body covered with leather.

"Anti-rattling device on both doors. Slot in frame with steel piece on door which fits in the slot.

"Heavy covered hinges on doors.

"Recess shelf at back of seat for carrying small parcels.

"Doors hinged at front."

1924 marked the first of the declining years for the Ford Motor Company. Competition was active with cars of only slightly higher price offering a more modern appearance, greater comfort and better performance. Sales of the Model T began to require real selling effort. Advertising, previously seldom used, became commonplace. Ford made many accessories available such as visors, rear-view mirrors, windshield wipers, dash lights, balloon tires, etc., none of which had been available *through the factory* before. Most of these were dealer-installed options, with the factory pushing their sale.

All models continued in the same style as the late '23 cars until the introduction of the "new Ford" in the Spring of 1925 — the 1926 models.

Construction of the cars did change, though, with the increased use of steel in the body framing and panels. A number of mechanical modifications were also made.

One running change, made during the 1924 model year, was the introduction of the four-dip pan, which now made it possible to adjust the rear main bearing without pulling the engine, and made the fourth rod bearing as accessible as the other three. Quick-change bands did not appear as factory-installed items until 1925, perhaps with the 1926 models. New pistons, a new oil tube and a new camshaft were some of the other refinements.

The wild ride was coming to an end. By 1925, sales had slipped instead of climbing. Dealers were hard pressed to meet the quotas set by the factory. The public, while loyal to Ford in great numbers, was no longer interested in the basic product produced by the Ford Motor Company. Pressed for years by his son, Edsel, and many of his other top men, Henry Ford reluctantly agreed to a new model. Nothing more than a rehash of the same old car, it, too, failed to turn the tide. The handwriting was on the wall; the end of the Model T was near.

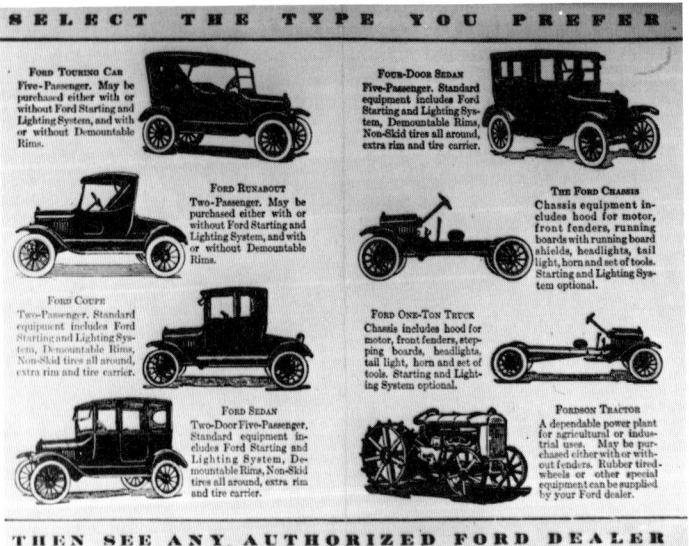

—From a December, 1922 catalog.

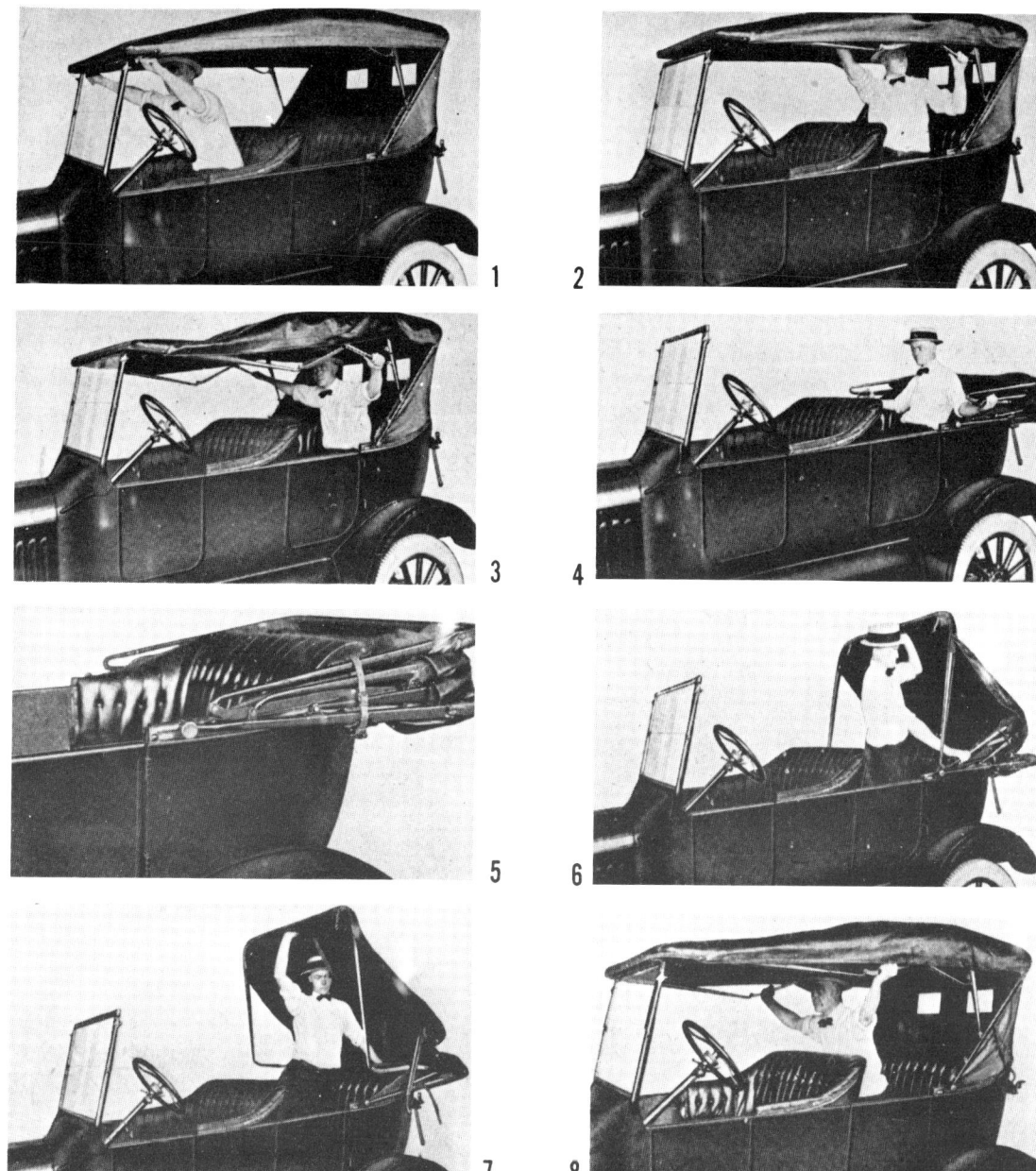

RAISING AND LOWERING THE ONE-MAN TOP

Those of you who may have tried lowering or raising the "one-man" top no doubt have wondered if the "one man" may need four arms. Here are Ford's instructions —

"The new design one-man top and slanting windshield which have recently been incorporated as standard equipment on all Ford touring cars, add greatly to the convenience and general appearance of the car. These improvements are in keeping with the policy of this Company to give purchasers of Ford cars the greatest car value per dollar on their investment.

"In order that dealers may correctly instruct owners as to the proper method of raising and lowering the new top, we are giving (above) detailed instructions regarding this procedure.

"First loosen wing screws which hold the front bow to the windshield as shown in Fig. 1, and the fasteners which hold the Gipsy Curtain to the rear bow. When this is done and the front bow is raised clear of the windshield, go into the rear of the body and remove the second bow from the clevis in the third bow by raising up on the second bow (see Fig. 2). This is done on each side. Next sit down and grasp second bow as shown in Fig. 3. A down and forward pressure throws the front bow over top center letting the top collapse as shown in Fig. 4. As on the old top it is important that the deck and pad are so arranged as to prevent chaffing. One end of the pin at lower end of the second bow should be fitted into the bracket on the rear bow, and the other end should be fitted into the hole in the second member of the front bow. The bows should then be strapped securely to the rests. Fig. 5 shows the top down and properly secured in position.

"To raise the top, undo the straps, and kneeling in the rear seat raise front and second bows sufficiently to disengage the pin from the rear bow and the second member of the front bow (see Fig. 6). This is done on each side. Next grasp first and third bows at the center and pull forward (see Fig. 7). Then facing forward take hold of front bow second member each side and raise top into position on windshield as shown in Fig. 8. Set ends of second bow in the clevis in the same manner in which they were removed (see Fig. 1). Draw down front end securing it to windshield and fasten Gipsy Curtains to the rear bow."

Yep....with two men it's easier!

During the 1923 model year, a change in the design of the front of the car was made. Sporting a slightly taller radiator and a wider (and higher) cowl section, the hood was enlarged, giving the engine compartment a more massive appearance.

Along with this change, the hood clash strip was widened by adding a 'dog leg' at the rear which allowed the hood clamp to be moved outward. The clamp now extended through the splash apron outside the frame.

Figure 1 shows the earlier hood-cowl section which was typical of the 1917 to 1923 cars. Figure 2 shows the late 1923 through 1925 style at the cowl section. (The lamps were optional equipment at this time, and are typical of the 1916 and later sidelamps.) Figure 3 shows the new clash strip.

Added, too, at this time was the skirt under the radiator, which covered the crank bearing, etc. To further dress up the front, a lip was added to the front edge of the fender apron which faired to blend with the radiator apron. Figure 4 shows the earlier radiator; Figure 5, the new style.

Standard equipment continued to be 30 by 3½ non-demountable wheels and tires but most cars were supplied with the demountable type shown in Figure 6. Featuring round spokes and a steel felloe, the rims were secured with four bolts and nuts. In 1925, Ford offered as another option, 4.40 by 21 "balloon" tires. Included with this option was a five-to-one steering ratio (which became standard on all cars later in the year).

Figure 7 shows the standard front fender, typical of all cars from 1917 on. Figure 8 shows a common, but different type. Note how the bead runs under the splash apron. This is believed to be the fender supplied with the commercial chassis. This fender, installed here on a car with the earlier hood, has the hole for the hood clamp mentioned earlier.

4

5

6

7

8

The dashboard (in the open cars) now has a more finished look. Sloping out at a slight angle and with the ends tapered, the new dash covers the mounting bolts at each end that were exposed in the previous design.

After the early production which used the wooden firewall, an all-metal pressing was used. The higher radiator change during the 1923 model year required a new fire wall (Figure 2) which was higher and wider. The lip at the bottom, which covers the rear of the engine, is now an integral part of the pressing, rather than the separate piece that formerly was screwed to the firewall (see Figure 3).

The use of wood as framing members in the bodies was declining. The 1925 open cars no longer had the wooden body sills where the toe boards rested, Now of pressed steel, these were lighter and stronger. The lack of wood, incidentally, made the cars a little noisier; the metal not insulating the engine noise as well. Figure 4 illustrates the new metal rail and front body member.

All closed cars used roll down side windows (after the centerdoor sedan was discontinued) except at the rear quarter windows, which used a latching arrangement similar to the one used in the late centerdoors. A number of regulators were used and are shown in Figure 5. The 17200A – 17201A shows two designs of the A type regulator. Either can be used in place of the other. There are rights and lefts of 17200A, B, and C, but 17200D is used interchangeably for either right or left side.

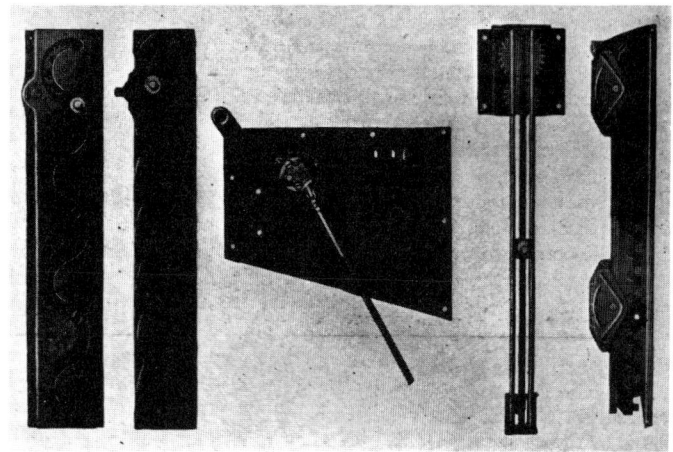

Three New Sales Opportunities

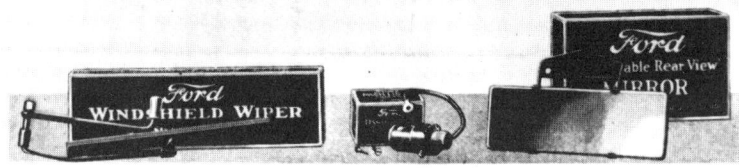

Ford began pushing accessories! Visors, at first standard equipment only on the Fordor Sedan, were pushed as options on the other closed body styles. Wipers, dash lights and mirrors were also supplied by the factory for dealer installation. Two mirrors were offered; one for the closed cars (top) and the other for the open cars. Visors became standard on all closed cars but were offered to owners of earlier models at a price of of only three dollars.

Running gear remained as it had been. The spring shackles were now of the U-shaped design; springs are square-ended; oil cups were everywhere.

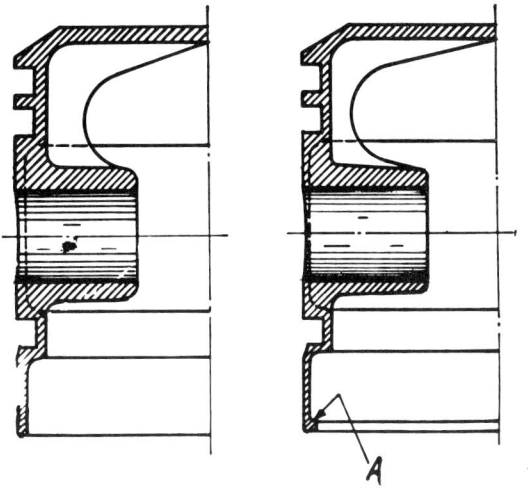

1

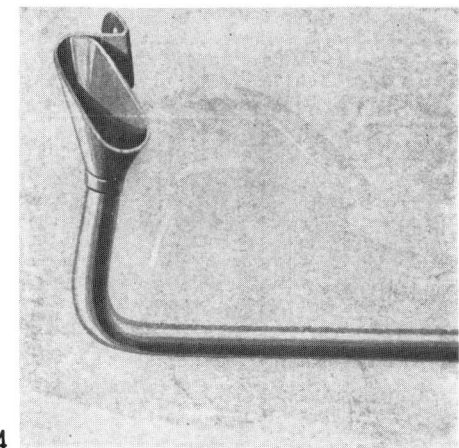

4

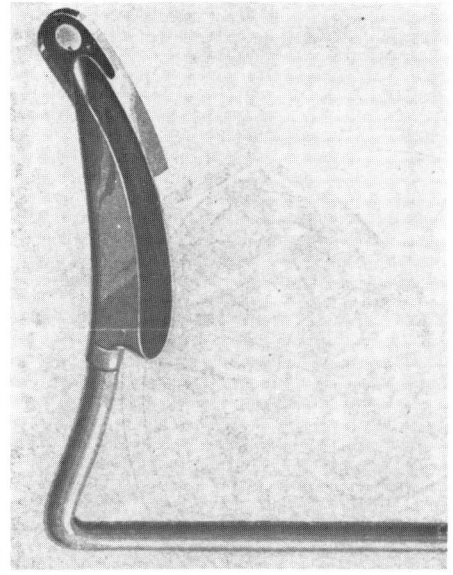

5

The engine and running gear remained in the pattern set in 1922. Many minor modifications were made, though, to either improve performance or reduce cost.

During 1924, a new piston was installed. Lighter in weight (1 lb., 12 oz.), the new design can be distinguished by the ridge ('A', Fig. 1) around the bottom.

Also changed during early 1924 was the camshaft front bearing. Now shorter, the new bearing did not have the chamfer ('A', Fig. 2) or the notch ('B') that had been necessary to clear the exhaust tappet. The new style is shown in Figure 3.

The four-dip pan appeared in 1924, a great improvement which every mechanic appreciated.

During this year, probably about the time that the 1925 models appeared, the new oil line with the larger funnel was installed. Figure 4 shows the old type; Figure 5, the new.

During the early part of the 1925 (perhaps even during the 1924 model year) a small rib was cast in the transmission cover ('A', Figure 6) which deflected oil towards the rear of the transmission cover.

Late in the 1925 model year, Ford finally did what owners had done for several years — installed transmission bands with removable ears so that bands could be exchanged without removing the transmission cover.

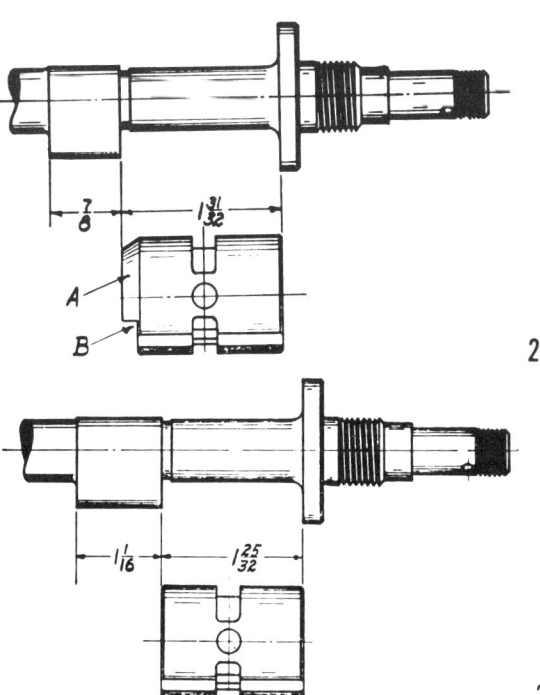

2

3

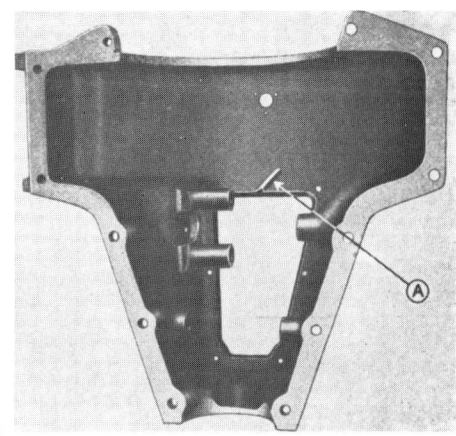

6

die Götterdämmerung*

The 1926-27 Model T Fords

The end of an era. Model T's days ended with the cars described in this article. Certainly, never before, and not likely ever again, will any product made by any manufacturer have the impact on our way of living as did this wonderful machine. With its passing, a way of life died too — a way of life that few would care to relive, but many would love to remember.

Photos courtesy The Ford Archives

The Model T Ford Touring Car for 1926

* *Wagner — The Twilight of the Gods.*

The Model T Ford Runabout for 1926

"Beauty of design is so conspicuously evident in the improved Ford cars that this improvement immediately impresses itself upon everyone who sees them. Open and closed body types have been redesigned with modern stream-line treatment. Many other important changes in bodies and chassis contribute to comfort and convenience as well. These changes include the following:

    Chassis frame lowered.
    Bodies lower and longer (except Fordor).
    Bodies redesigned (except Fordor).
    Closed cars in color.
    Improved upholstery with lower, deeper cushioned seats.
    Nickeled radiator shells on closed cars.
    One piece windshield on Tudor and Coupe.
    Larger, better looking fenders.
    Fuel tank under cowl (except Fordor).
    Added accessories on all cars.
    Coil box and sediment bulb more conveniently located.
    Improved brakes in rear axle and transmission.
    Two doors on Runabout; four doors on Touring Car.

It is of particular importance that the bodies of all closed and open cars are *all-steel throughout*, except the Fordor which has a composite body. All-steel bodies mean added strength and durability.

Note also that *Ford bodies have been entirely redesigned* for greater comfort, convenience and added beauty. Yet it is important to remember that these are in no true sense NEW cars. It is advisable to avoid using the word "NEW" in discussing them. The word "NEW" implies a redesigning of the chassis as well as the body. While it is true that certain refinements have been added to the chassis and that these are more radical and therefore more conspicuous than any which have heretofore been made, the Model T chassis (though lower) remains the same in design and construction as it has been since 1908. It is *the same Ford car*, now as always noted for economy, performance and reliability; only the bodies have been redesigned. Do not forget this point and do not fail to stress it in talking to prospective car owners. *It is a strong selling point.*

In telling your customer of these changes, it is not necessary to emphasize the details. Your prospect is more interested in the beauty of the

The Model T Coupe for 1926

car, to which especial thought has been directed, and in the added comfort and convenience than he is in how these improvements were achieved. However, the detailed information given in the following pages is intended to prepare you fully to answer any and all questions which are likely to be asked concerning the improved Ford Cars.

APPEARANCE

A pronounced stream-line treatment has been effected in all body types. The best way to appreciate this is to actually see the cars. If you can get your prospect into your showroom, you will find that little salesmanship is necessary as far as the beauty feature of these cars is concerned. They are so conspicuously different in design that they speak for themselves.

Many other factors contribute to appearance of the improved body designs. The chassis frame is lower. The bodies are longer and lower.

The actual figures are comparatively unimportant. The big fact is that the top of the body has been lowered and the seats too have been lowered.

The beauty of the bodies has been further enhanced by the slightly raised radiator, larger hood, nickeled head lamp rims and in the case of closed cars, nickeled radiator shells.

FENDERS — Changes in fender design are of particular importance. Like the bodies, Ford fenders have been completely redesigned to give added beauty to the cars. They are now of the crown type, wider, larger and more attractive. They extend lower both front and rear, affording maximum protection against splashing mud and water.

Running boards are also wider and nearer the ground.

CLOSED CARS in COLORS — Ford closed body types are now finished in attractive colors. The Tudor Sedan and Coupe are a deep Channel Green, and the Fordor Sedan is in rich Windsor Maroon. Open cars remain black.

ACCESSORIES — Standard equipment on all closed cars include windshield wiper, rear view mirror, windshield visor and dash light. The Fordor Sedan has, also, the dome-light, as before. Windshield wiper is standard on open cars.

WINDSHIELDS — On the Tudor Sedan and the Coupe, the plate glass windshield is of one piece opening forward. A passage way at the base of the windshield directs the ventilation downward into the front compartment when the windshield is slightly opened. Plate glass windshield in the open body types are of the double ventilating type; both halves opening. The windshield on the Fordor has been redesigned to conform with the improved cowl. Lower half is stationary and there is a cowl ventilator as before.

RADIATOR AND HOOD — The radiator is 5/8" higher and the hood larger, more louvres (side openings) in the hood permit freer circulation of air.

Radiator shells of bright nickel, polished and buffed are standard on closed cars.

WINDOWS — All windows in all closed body types are of Ford plate glass and lower flush with the moulding. They operate by lifters set conveniently within reach.

DOORS — All doors open forward on all body types except the rear doors on the Fordor Sedan.

SEATS — All seats in the Tudor Sedan, Coupe, Touring and Runabout have been lowered and set further back and with improved cushion effect, providing greater comfort.

TIRE CARRIER — A newly simplified design of arm type tire carrier accommodates either the Ford wire wheel or demountable rim. It is set at the most attractive angle to add to the appearance of the car.

TIRES — Standard equipment on all Ford cars includes *cord* tires in place of fabric as formerly.

HEADLIGHTS — The headlights have polished nickel rims, are set higher and further apart and are attached to pressed fender supports.

TAIL LIGHT AND LICENSE BRACKET — On all body types the tail light and license plate bracket are now located on the rear left fender.

CHASSIS CHANGES

CHASSIS FRAME — The chassis frame has been dropped one and one-half inches. This has been accomplished without materially effecting the road clearance by lowering the crown of the springs one inch. The spindle has been raised on the spindle body one-half inch.

COIL BOX — The coil box is now mounted on the left-hand side of the motor. This change is a

The Model T Ford Fordor Sedan for 1926

great convenience for servicing as access to the coil box may be had by simply raising the hood. The mechanic need no longer enter the car to make coil box adjustments.

FAN — The fan has been raised to add to its cooling efficiency. Fan belt adjustments are now more quickly and simply made. This is due to a special fan bracket with an eccentric adjustment. The bracket is designed as an integral part of the cylinder head outlet.

TRANSMISSION BRAKE BAND — The transmission has been increased from 1-1/8 inches to 1-3/4 inches wide, an improvement which contributes to the ease and smoothness of braking. In addition, the wider brake band lining requires infrequent adjustment and will last much longer than heretofore. All transmission bands now have removable ears to facilitate changing of band lining. Hardened steel shoes have been placed over clutch casing keys to prevent wear.

HAND BRAKES — Brake drums in the rear axle have been increased from eight inches in diameter to eleven inches in diameter and the width has been increased from 1-5/32 inches to 1-1/2 inches. Brake shoes are now covered with asbestos composition, eliminating the old method in which braking was effected by direct contact of cast iron shoes on the steel brake drum. Being of the self-energizing type, these new improved brakes render braking smooth and positive.

PEDALS — Brake and clutch pedals are farther apart and have wider surfaces with flange at the side to prevent the driver's foot from slipping.

STEERING WHEEL — The steering wheel on open and closed cars was recently increased from 16 to 17 inches in diameter. In all types except the Fordor Sedan the wheel has been set three inches lower for greater comfort and ease of driving as seats have been moved back and lowered. There is a 5 to 1 reduction in the steering mechanism to accommodate balloon tires.

GASOLINE TANK — In the Tudor Sedan, Coupe, Touring and Runabout the fuel tank is now placed beneath the cowl in front of the instrument board. This is a marked improvement, the importance of which cannot be over estimated. The gasoline now flows from the tank to the carburetor at an abrupt angle, *even when negotiating the steepest hills.* The tank can be readily filled from outside. The filler cap is located in the middle of the cowl under a rain proof cover, having the appearance of a cowl ventilator. A large trough and overflow pipe has been provided to carry any spillage directly to the ground.

There is a marked convenience in having the gas tank located under the cowl for it brings the sediment bulb, usually so difficult of access, to a convenient location under the hood where the water can be easily drained from the gasoline which is so necessary in freezing weather as all automobile owners already know. Any Ford salesman can readily see that the hazard has not been increased, for the ventilation and overflow provided has been a distinct improvement. The dash provides an adequate separation from the motor. Vacuum tanks containing a quart of gasoline and being suspended almost over the motors have not been considered dangerous, and the location of our gasoline tank is much improved over these.

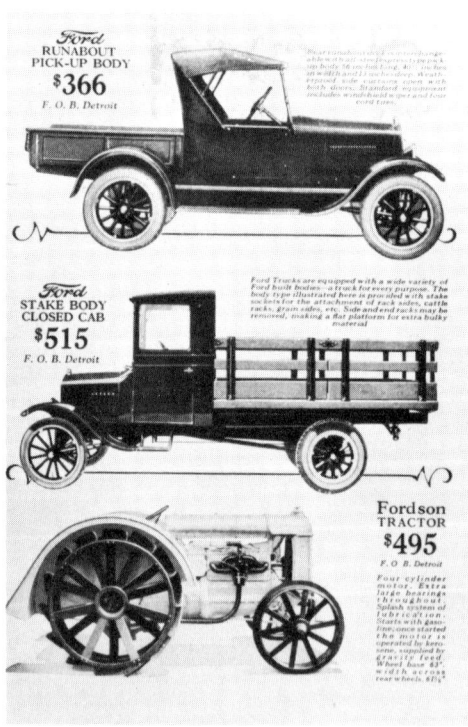

Still soliciting the commercial business, Ford offered a Roadster-Pickup, as well as a line of one-ton trucks with Ford-built bodies. Notice that the TT trucks continued in the style of the 1925 passenger cars.

FORDOR SEDAN

COLOR — The improved Fordor Sedan is finished in a rich Windsor Maroon.

NEW UPHOLSTERY — The upholstery fabric is especially strong and durable. It is of gray tone with a fine red stripe to harmonize with the exterior coloring of the car. The headlining is a fabric of gray mixture to harmonize with the upholstery cloth. Floor carpet is gray with a suggestion of red. The window curtains are gray silk.

SEATS — Same as in former Fordor Sedan.

GASOLINE TANK — Under front seat same as before.

CHANGES IN DIMENSIONS — Following are the approximate changes in dimensions between the former and the improved Ford Fordor Sedan:
 Body dropped 1-1/2 inches on the chassis.
 No other changes.

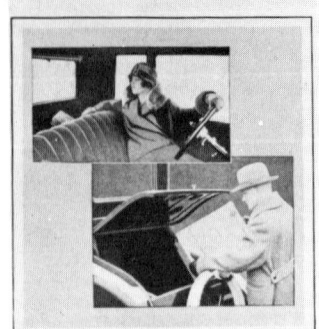

COUPE

COLOR — The improved Coupe is finished in a deep Channel Green.

NEW UPHOLSTERY FABRIC — The upholstery fabric in the Coupe is the same as in the Tudor Sedan. The back curtain is of gray silk.

BEAUTY — Improvements in the Coupe are most pronounced. The sweep of the body lines from the radiator cap back to the spare tire carrier is startling. By no means the least important feature is the rear deck which is full width of the body enclosure and extends well back over the rear spring with fenders bolted to the body. The rear deck compartment is not only wider and longer, but deeper as well. Rust-proof compartment lid hinges are concealed at the juncture of the rear deck and the body enclosure. The wide double steel panel lid sweeps backward and down almost to the floor level of the compartment. When opened, access to the compartment is extremely easy. An automatic catch fixes the lid firmly opened. This compartment is waterproof and dustproof. Hidden channels carry any rain or moisture leakages around the lid to the ground.

SEAT — Redesigned with deeper cushion and affording greater driving comfort.

RECESS SHELF — The shelf at back of seat is five inches wider than in the former coupe and affords more room to accommodate parcels or small luggage.

DRIVER VISIBILITY — Front pillars and windshield same as in Tudor Sedan.

DOOR — Door is wider, making it easier to enter and leave the car.

ACCESSORIES — Same as Tudor Sedan.

CHANGES IN DIMENSIONS — Following are the approximate changes in dimensions between former and improved Ford Coupe:

Body — 4-1/2 inches lower from top to road. 3-1/2 inches longer.

Seats — 2-1/2 inches lower from top of seat to floor. This with 1-1/2 inch drop of body on chassis brings seat four inches nearer the ground.

TUDOR SEDAN

BODY IN COLOR — The improved Tudor Sedan is finished in a deep Channel Green.

NEW UPHOLSTERY — The upholstery fabric is especially strong and durable. It is of a gray tone with a fine green stripe to harmonize with the exterior color of the car. The headlining is a fabric of gray mixture and the floor carpet is gray with a suggestion of green. The back curtain is of gray silk.

DRIVER'S SEAT TILTS — The driver's seat, in addition to the other front seat, is of the full bucket type, tilting forward, with much deeper cushioning, giving added comfort. When tilted forward, rear seat passengers may enter or leave the car without disturbing occupant of the other front seat, which is also deeper cushioned with higher back. Rear seat also is lowered and deeper cushioned. All occupants of the car have greater riding comfort, being seated nearer the road and having more leg room.

DRIVER VISIBILITY — Visibility for the driver has been materially increased by the new design front pillars on either side of the one-piece windshield. They are narrower, thus giving the driver better vision in every direction.

SUN VISOR — Another marked contribution to driving comfort is the redesigned leather cloth sun visor which is closed completely at both ends. It is of much better appearance.

ACCESSORIES — The Tudor Sedan now comes equipped with windshield wiper, rear view mirror and dash lamp. Starter and demountable rims are included in standard equipment.

CHANGES IN DIMENSIONS — Following are the approximate changes in dimensions between the former and the improved Ford Tudor Sedan:
    Body — 4 inches lower from top to road.
           3-1/2 inches longer.
    Seats — 2-1/2 inches lower from top of seat to floor. This with 1-1/2 inch drop in chassis brings the seat four inches nearer the ground.

Distance from back panel of front seats to front of rear seat increased two inches, affording more knee room. Foot room also is increased.

TOURING CAR

COLOR — The improved Touring Car is finished in black. The upholstery is of Ford leather cloth.

FOUR DOORS — An additional door is provided at the driver's left which is of genuine convenience both to the driver and passenger. All four doors open forward and are wider than before.

STORM CURTAINS are on uprights and open with the doors.

ONE MAN TOP — The top is a genuine one man top of Ford leather cloth. Improved design makes it extremely easy for one man to raise or lower the top.

COMPARTMENTS are provided under both front and rear seats for tools and curtains.

SEATS have been completely redesigned for increased comfort.

CHANGES IN DIMENSIONS — Following are the approximate changes in dimensions between the former and the Improved Ford Touring Car.

   BODY — 4-1/2 inches lower from top to road. 3-1/2 inches longer.

   SEATS — 2-1/2 inches lower from top of seat to floor. This with 1-1/2 inch drop in chassis brings the seats four inches nearer the ground.

Front seat is three inches wider.

Rear seat is five inches wider.

Distance between back panel of front seat and the rear seat is increased 3-1/2 inches, giving more room for passengers. This increased width also provides additional floor space between the seats to accommodate a bushel basket, an advantage for farmers.

228

RUNABOUT

COLOR – The improved Ford Runabout is finished in black. The upholstery is of Ford leather cloth.

APPEARANCE – **The sweep of the body lines from the radiator cap back to the spare tire carrier suggests the sport car more conspicuously perhaps than the other improved body types.** By no means the least important feature of the improved Runabout is the rear deck which is now the full width of the body and extends well back over the rear spring with fenders bolted to the body. The rear deck compartment is not only wider and longer, but deeper as well. Rustproof compartment lid hinges are concealed at the juncture of the rear deck and the body. The wide double steel panel lid sweeps backward and down almost to the floor level of the compartment. When opened, access to the compartment is extremely easy. An automatic catch fixes the lid firmly opened and it must be released by hand in order to close the lid which locks. This compartment is actually waterproof and dustproof. Hidden channels carry rain and moisture leakages around the lid to the ground.

TWO DOORS – An additional door is provided at the driver's left, a new convenience. Both doors open forward and are wider than before.

STORM CURTAINS are on uprights and open with the doors.

SEAT has been completely redesigned for increased comfort.

CHANGES IN DIMENSIONS – The following are the approximate changes in dimensions between the former and the Improved Runabout.

BODY – 4-1/2 inches lower from top to road. 7-3/4 inches longer.

SEAT – 2-1/2 inches lower from top of seat to floor. This with 1-1/2 inch drop in chassis brings the seat four inches nearer the ground. Seat is three inches wider.

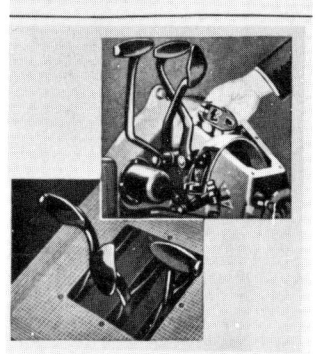

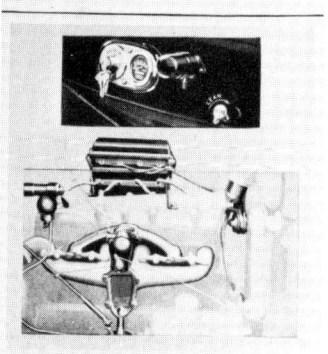

And there you have an exact quote of Ford's official announcement of the "New Improved 1926 Model T Fords". The bulletin was not dated but no doubt was issued in about June of 1925.

After the peak year of Model T production, 1924, sales began to decline. Now in its 17th year of production, the Model T was just an old car that had been around a long time. Competition was now snapping at the heels of The Ford Motor Company as it had never snapped before. Under the pressure of his son, Edsel, and many of the members of the Ford management team, Henry Ford finally relented and allowed the redesign of the Model T. A far cry from the changes that were really needed, the "New Ford" was, under the surface, another platter of the same old hash. Yet, its personality was changed. No longer the spindly-looking bare bones automobile of its predecessors, the 1926 Ford looked like an automobile.

Driving one of these new models was unlike any of the past. To be sure, the same three pedals were there — of a different shape, but still the same. The dash still came with only an ammeter (on the cars with electrical equipment), but the body was modern and what is more important, it was solid. The hood was made longer; the seats were pushed back a little; the windshield was moved back and a door installed on the left front of the Roadster and Touring for the first time since the open-front models of 1912. The new body, while being a great improvement in style, fell short in comfort—the front seat was cramped, and even shorter on performance. The old T engine just wasn't up to hauling all that weight.

All bodies, except the Fordor, were now all metal in construction. The Fordor was a continuation of the basic style introduced in 1923, with the addition of the new-style fenders, colors and a general refurbishing.

Fenders were now smoothly crowned, and bolted to the body, making them appear to be part of the car rather than looking like an afterthought as they had for so many years.

Bodies were lowered by not only reducing the the height of the body itself (except the Fordor), but also by lowering the frame by a redesign of the front spindles and a lowering of the crown of the springs.

Headlights were now mounted on flanged posts which bolted to the fenders. Later, a tie rod was installed between the two lights, and still later, the headlights were mounted on this tie rod.

Early production open cars were furnished with 30 by 3½ non-demountable wheels as standard equipment. Closed cars were furnished with the same size tires but demountable rims were standard. These were available as an option on the open cars. Balloon tires were optional on all cars. These were mounted on demountable-rim wooden wheels, available either in black or natural wood finish. A further option on all cars were the drop-center wire wheels which used the same size tire as the optional wooden wheels (21 by 4.50), and available in Casino Red, English Vermillion, Black, Green or Straw colors.

Wire wheels did not become standard until almost the end of Model T production. In February of 1927, the Louisville, Ky. Branch issued this announcement:

"Effective Monday, Feb. 14th, all Coupes driven from Branch or shipped to you will be equipped with black one piece all steel wire wheels, at no change in billing price.

"Effective Monday, Feb. 21st, black one piece all steel wire wheels on Coupes will be standard equipment, at no extra cost to customers.

"This gives you one week to dispose of your present stock of Coupes equipped with wood wheels.

"You should obtain all publicity possible on and after Monday, Feb. 21st, regarding this change, so the public in your territory will know that one piece all steel wire wheels are standard equipment on all Ford enclosed cars at no extra cost."

While we have no proof, it would seem that wire wheels were optional equipment on the open cars until the end of production — just three months later.

The frame was altered by the use of a longer rear cross member, needed to support the new bodies.

The rear brake drums were enlarged and the brake shoes were now lined, making them considerable more effective. Just why these brakes were not hooked up to serve as the service brakes is not clear; they could be used to stop the car. Otherwise, the driveline remained as in previous design.

The engine, while basically the same, had a number of modifications. The major change, of course, was the addition of the larger brake drum in the transmission. 5/8 inch wider, it aided greatly in the stopping of the new, heavier, car. The fan was now mounted on the water outlet fitting, rather than on the arm previously used. The transmission cover, in addition to being slightly wider to accommodate the larger brake drum, and having the new-style pedals, now bolted to the rear of the cylinder block, making the assembly quite a bit more rugged.

Initially supplied with a modified NH carburetor, during the 1926 model year the Holly hot plate carburetor became standard. This new carburetor featured a heating chamber in which the fuel was heated by the exhaust. Once started, the car would now run on kerosene. While not having the power of the old NH carburetor, this new one was more economical. The new carburetor required a new throttle linkage which now ran across the top of the engine instead of through the center. During late production, the hole between number two and three cylinders was sealed. The carburetor control rod at the dash was altered so that the same knob was used to choke the engine that was used to adjust the main jet. The choke wire still went out through the radiator — Ford still didn't have too much confidence in his electric starter.

With the introduction of the new cars in mid-1925, the open cars were offered in black only. The Coupe and Tudor were offered in Channel Green and the Fordor was offered in Windsor Maroon. After a short time, all closed cars could be had in either green or maroon. Still later, the closed cars were offered in a third color, Fawn Gray, giving the customer three choices of color for the first time in Model T history. Fenders and running gear were black on all cars. During 1926, the Runabout and Touring were offered in either Gunmetal Blue or Phoenix Brown; both with black fenders.

As mentioned earlier, wheels were available in a choice of colors. Standard wooden wheels came in black. A natural wood finish was offered as an option on all cars. Wire wheels could be had in five colors; Casino Red, Light Green, English Vermillion, Yellow or Black. Maroon cars used the red wheels; green cars, the light green wheels or the vermillion. Black cars used either black, yellow or vermillion.

Radiator shells were nickeled on all closed cars; came in black on the open models, with the nickel shell offered as an option. Headlight rims were nickeled on all cars.

Optional equipment abounded. Bumpers, nickel finished with black mounting hardware, were very popular. Stop lights were available, as were shock absorbers ("snubbers"), dash lights, windwings, top boots and automatic windshield wipers.

The 1926 models became 1927's with no fanfare, in fact we have been unable to locate any "new model" announcement of the '27's. It is assumed that production just continued until the end in May of 1927.

The heroic rejuvenation was, alas, a failure. Sales declined from 1,956,056 in 1925, to 1,826,500 in 1926, and slipped to 958,003 for the fiscal year from August of 1926 until May of 1927. Car production was halted by June and the changeover to the Model A was begun. Production of engines and replacement parts continued at the Highland Park plant through the better part of the year. The end of an era had come. The new Model A was an instant success, but it, too, was destined to an early demise. Ford had lost his position of leadership; it would be almost thirty years later, under the direction of another Henry Ford, that The Ford Motor Company would again be in the running for first place.

And so, the end of an era. Model T's days ended with the cars described in this article. Certainly, never before, and not likely ever again, will any product made by any manufacturer have the impact on our way of living as did this wonderful machine. With its passing, a way of life died too — a way of life that few would care to relive, but that many will never forget.

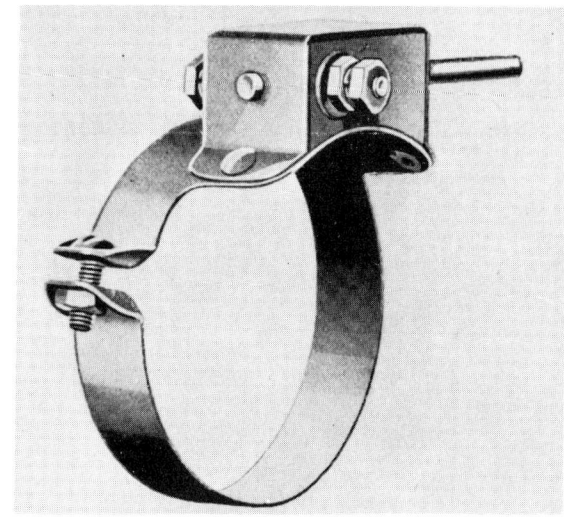

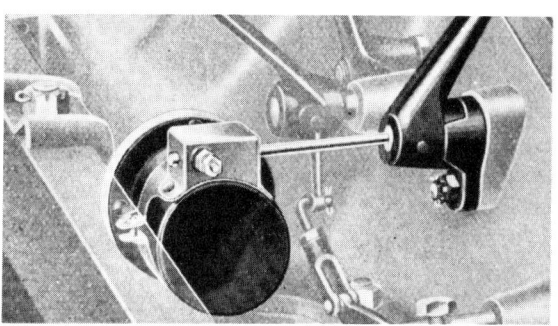

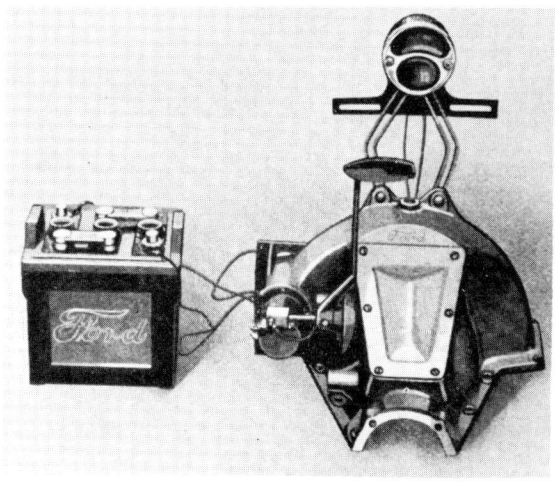

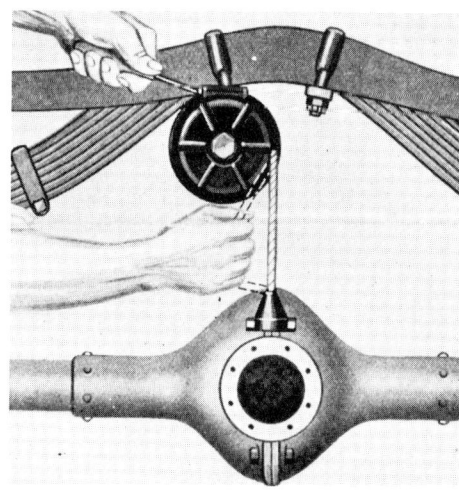

Two interesting pieces of optional equipment are the stop light switch and the "snubbers" or shock absorbers.
The right-hand top picture shows the switch which clamped over the starter motor and was operated by the outward movement of the brake pedal (second picture). The dealer display setup is shown with the license plate bracket mounted on the transmission cover.

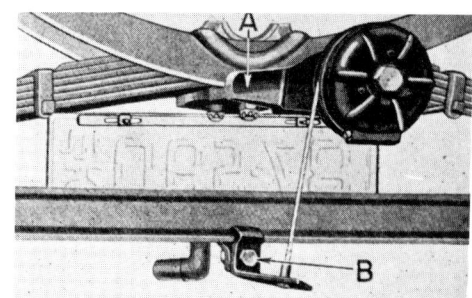

The dealer-installed snubbers helped reduce the bounce by resisting the downward movement of the axles. As the axle moved up, a spring reeled in the cord; a friction device resisted the release of the cord on the rebound.

233

Early production open cars, if purchased without electrical equipment, were supplied with 30 by 3½ tires mounted on non-demountable rim wheels. The bulk of Ford production, though, came with 4.40-21 tires mounted on demountable rims and wooden wheels. Standard production wheels were painted black but Ford offered them in natural wood as an option.

Wire wheels, available in a choice of colors (black, red, vermillion, yellow or green) were another option on all cars. There is no evidence that wire wheels ever became standard equipment on all cars. These wheels were of drop-center design and used the same size tires as the optional wooden wheels mentioned above. Featuring a nickel-plated hub cap which was crimped to the wheel, these wire wheels were a great improvement. Similar to the later Model A type, these have a smaller hub section and hub cap; the two are not interchangeable.

The spare is mounted on a tubular post with either the "Y" adaptor (pictured) for the demountable rim, or a flange with three studs for the wire wheel.

234

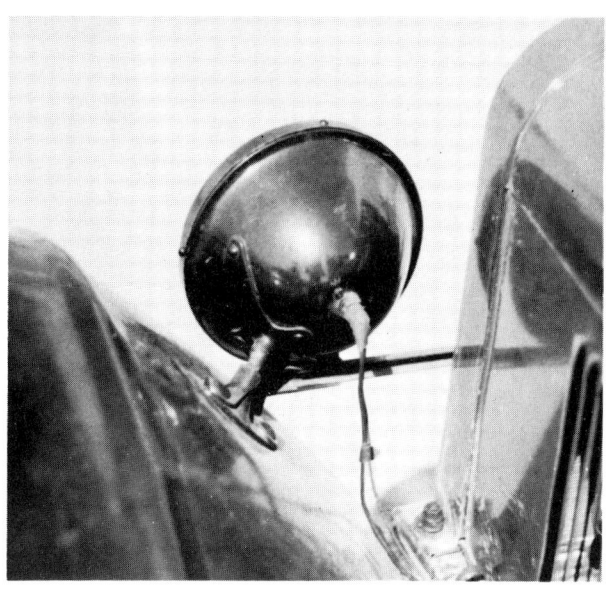
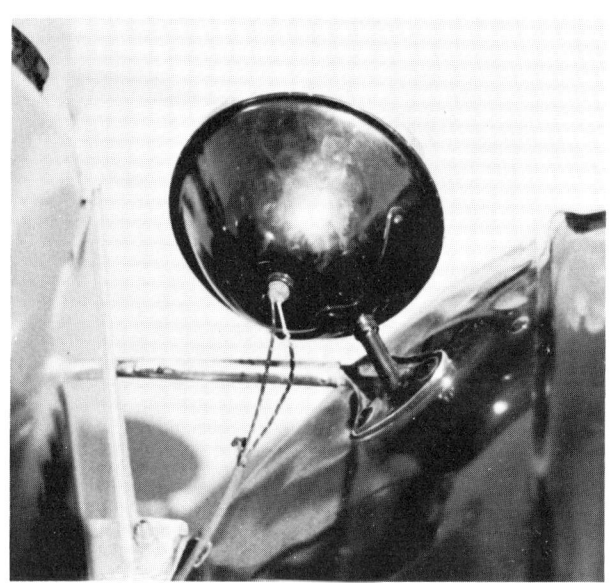

Headlights, similar to those previously used, were at first mounted on flanged posts which bolted to the fender (upper left). Later, a tie rod was added which ran from fender to fender in front of the radiator. Available in a number of styles, some of these tie rods were of channel section (upper right); others were tubular (center left). Later production used a tubular rod on which the lights were mounted (center right).

The radiator shell, similar to that previously used, was either nickel or painted black. On those cars furnished with the nickel shell, a nickeled trim strip was added on the splash apron under the radiator.

235

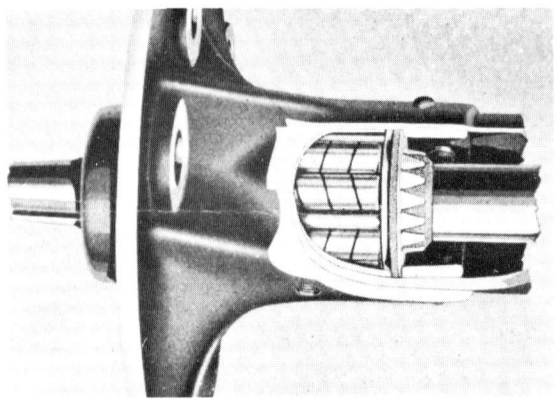

Many methods had been devised to eliminate the oil leak at the rear wheel bearings. Ford finally installed, as original equipment, an oil seal that fit inside the axle housing. The illustration, taken from the Ford Service Bulletins, shows an earlier axle, yet we have no evidence of it being used before the 1926 models.

Chassis design and running gear remained in the pattern of the previous seventeen years, with minor alterations.

The old spur type speedometer gears which became so noisy after a little wear were modified to a worm type drive. This arrangement was the one supplied by Stewart. Also seen in production was a modified spur type in which the drive gear was a pressed steel disk and the driven gear a small spur gear.

The rear brake drums were enlarged to eleven inches in diameter and were acted upon by asbestos lined, self-energizing brake shoes. While these brakes could be used to stop the car, the thin drums would heat rapidly and cause the brakes to fade.

The front axle continued in the same style as in previous models. The bearing spindle was raised one-half inch on the body, lowering the chassis a bit. Further lowering was achieved by reducing the crown in the springs, making the chassis one and one-half inches nearer the ground.

Running boards were now wider and featured smaller embossed diamonds. The Ford script appeared on each edge so that the boards could be used interchangeably on either side of the car.

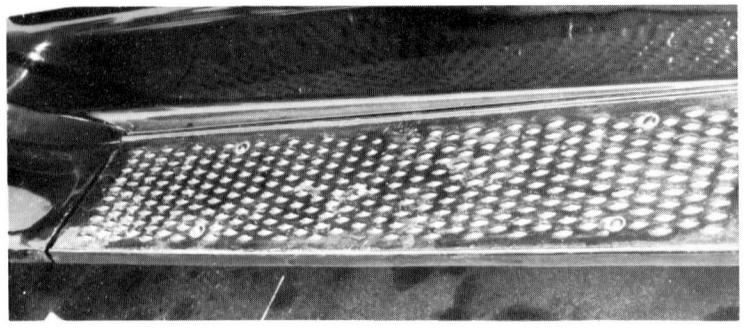

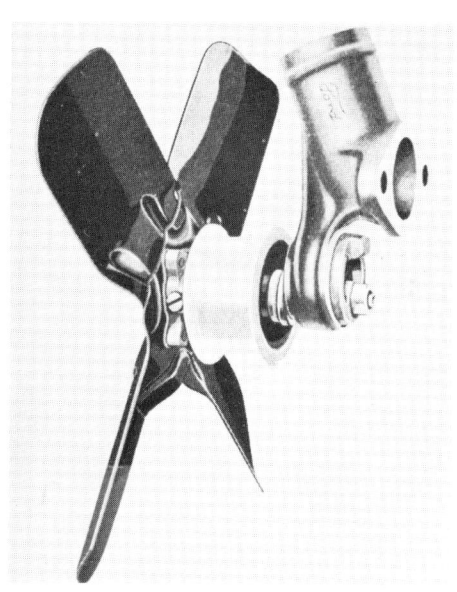

Many changes were made in the engine compartment. One of the more noticeable ones is the relocation of the fan to a projection on the water outlet. Early production fan brackets had an adjusting screw ("B", top left) which acted like a worm gear on the mounting ring "C". A nut on the other end of "B" locked it in position. The fan mounting bolt is mounted off center so that as "C" turns, the fan belt is adjusted.

Later, a less complicated and equally effective assembly was used. Similar in operation to the earlier type, this one is adjusted by loosening the one nut, rotating the mounting ring with a lever placed between the nut and the lug shown above it, and then tightening the nut.

Early production cars used a modified Ford "NH" carburetor. Similar to the '25 type, this one had a different needle valve, with a universal joint so that the same rod could be used to choke and to adjust the main jet.

Later, the hot plate carburetor became standard. The Holly was by far the most common but a few Kingston units apparently were used.

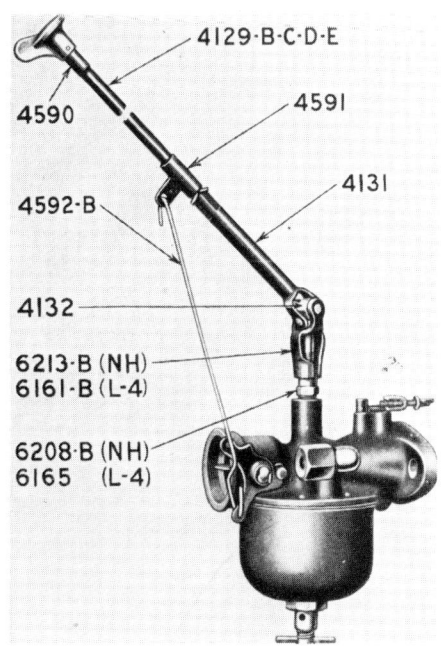

Kingston Vaporizer Parts

237

Another major change in Model T design was the move placing the ignition coils on the engine instead of on the firewall. Although easier to adjust, and certainly quieter in operation due to its new location, this ignition system was years out of date.

Engine color is not certain. Black, gray and green have been seen but we have no information which gives the original color. Among the last ditch steps to increase sales, was the addition of nickel plated head bolts. Having rounded heads, the use of these bolts was an attempt to make the engine appear a little more sophisticated.

The Holly hot plate carburetor is seen in the photo. The engine, incidentally, is part of the 1926 Touring owned by Henry Visser, from Holland.

A new transmission cover appeared. Featuring a wider rear section to accommodate the larger brake drum, and new, larger and better spaced pedals, it bolted to the rear of the engine block, making the assembly much more sturdy. The magneto contact now screwed into the cover (½ inch pipe thread) rather than being held with the three screws.

Aside from being larger (wider), the brake drum now had pressed-on steel caps on the clutch plate lugs. ("B" in the picture below.) Eliminating the tendency of the plates to wear the lugs, the clutch would now operate a little better after many miles of service.

The 1927 Tudor featured here is owned by Ken Santee of Portland, Oregon. One of the nicest cars we have seen, this one still has the original upholstery which is in almost new condition. Typical of the style and pattern used in all closed cars, this example may be of help to those of you who may be restoring a similar car.

The bumpers are correct, and still have the little medallion in the center, often lost because of the flexing of the bumper.

Notice the visor, leatherette-covered and ribbed, typical of all closed cars.

The
TUDOR SEDAN
$520
F. O. B. Detroit

Color Channel Green with interior upholstery to harmonize. All-steel body. Nickeled radiator and headlamp rims. Both front seats tilt forward. One-piece ventilating windshield. Plate glass windows with rotary lifts. Standard equipment includes starter, demountable rims, windshield wiper, hooded sun visor, rear view mirror, dash lamp and four cord tires. Balloon tires, $25 extra.

You can't help but appreciate the distinctiveness and individuality of the Tudor Sedan especially when it is equipped with natural wood wheels. Add to this the comfort of Balloon tires and you have a car of which you may be genuinely proud. Like all Ford cars, the Tudor Sedan is roomy inside but compact and readily parked in small space.

DISTINCTIVE features include nickeled radiator and headlamp rims, one-piece windshield, hooded sun-visor and a roomy luggage compartment. Standard equipment includes starter, windshield wiper, rear view mirror, dash lamp and 4 balloon tires.

THE COUPE

THE COUPE is one of the most popular of Ford cars, combining an unusually smart appearance with exceptional utility.

IT is extensively used by commercial and professional men who demand extraordinary closed car service at the lowest possible cost. The sturdy all-steel body is designed to afford the maximum riding and driving comfort, while many unusual features have been provided to increase the car's utility.

IN common with all Ford cars, the Coupe embodies those basic features of Ford design which have maintained Ford leadership throughout the years. And for those who want the dash and vigor of added color, the Coupe may be equipped with wire wheels in five optional colors, or natural wood wheels, and other special equipment shown. There is no other Coupe on the market that offers such value—as thousands of owners will testify.

[$485.00 F. O. B. DETROIT Special Equipment Extra]

TO the standard Coupe are sometimes added colored wire wheels contrasting with the rich green body, a lively touch which adds to the appearance of grace and fleetness. Bumpers front and rear are the final item of equipment, leaving nothing to be desired for comfort, convenience and driving safety.

ALWAYS a smart car, the Coupe assumes a new air of distinction when equipped with natural wood wheels. This forms a pleasant contrast with rich coloring of the body, a feature which people of good taste are among the first to recognize and appreciate. The spare tire and wheel mounted at the rear also add to the car's attractiveness.

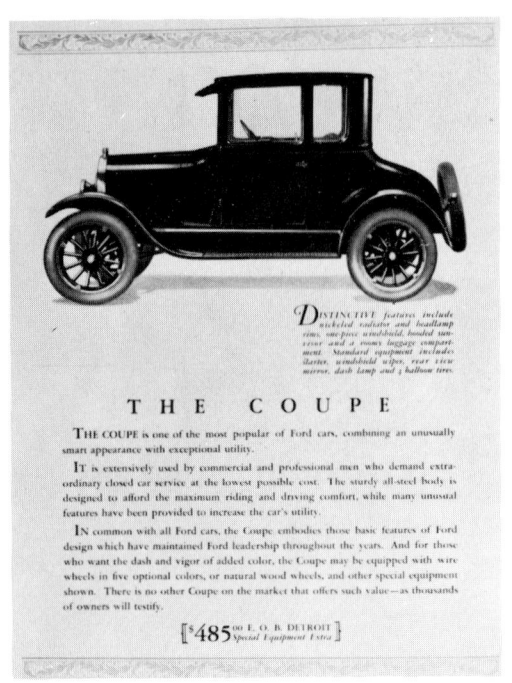

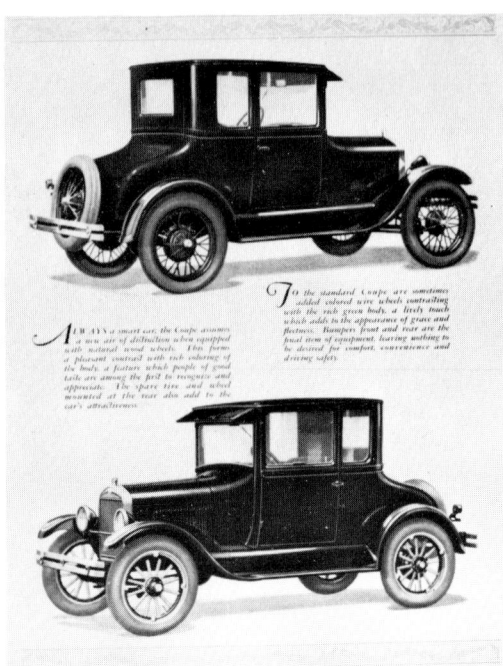

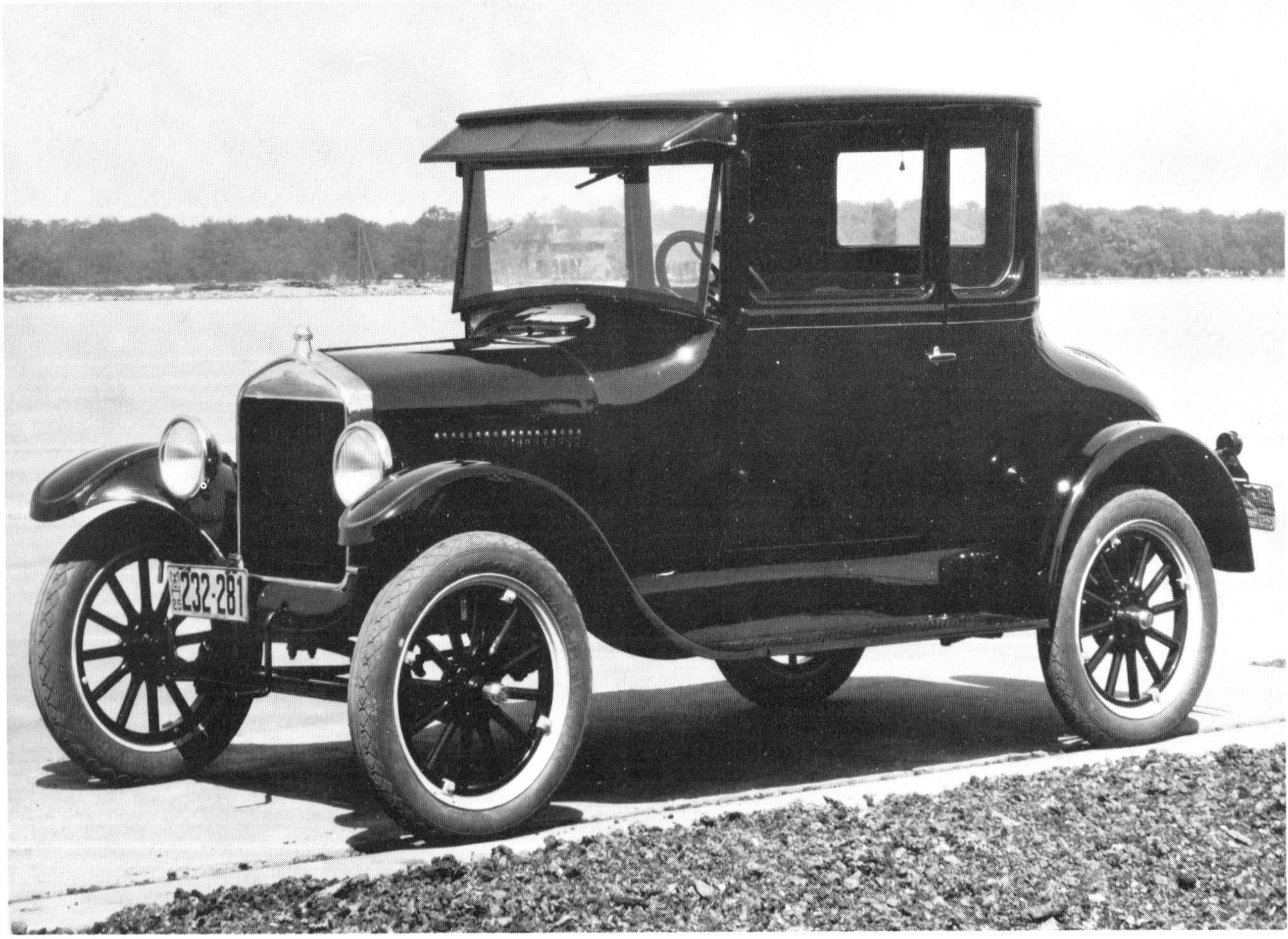

Another outstanding car of the period is this 1926 Coupe, owned by Jake Bergan, of Shafter, California.

The black radiator is contrary to the the information regarding closed cars as furnished by Ford at the time. All were supposed to have nickel shells. This would not be the first time there has been an exception.

"Let There Be Light"

A REVIEW OF MODEL T FORD HEADLIGHTS

The preceeding chapters have covered the many changes in the Model T Ford in a rather general manner. It would be next to impossible to go into great detail on each item, but there are a few on which we might elaborate. One of these should be headlamps.

In this coverage, we are not attempting to make inflexible rules regarding restoration standards; only do we seek to comment. We are told of various other styles that may be correct for a given year. Lamps were, it is true, made by other manufacturers from time to time. Victor, Corcoran and Atwood Castle were among these, and in addition, there were many accessory lamps made available for those who wanted their Fords to be just a bit different.

The earliest Model T's were not supplied with headlamps as standard equipment. Our coverage here will begin with the "Production 1909"; the earlier cars may have had any number of brands of "correct" headlamps installed.

If you think you've got trouble starting your Model T, consider the additional problems of the driver in bygone days who, in addition to starting a balky engine, also had to start a gas generator to obtain fuel for the headlamps.

The earliest headlamps burned acetylene gas which was generally obtained by dripping water on pieces of calcium carbide in a sealed container on the running board. The gas then formed was piped to the burners in the headlamps — which frequently either refused to burn, having become clogged with past use, or else flared wildly out of control with a frightening hiss.

Early electric headlamps, operated as they were from the magneto, varied in intensity as the engine speed changed. Many are those who report having read road signs in strange places by aiming the car at them and racing the engine to increase the brightness of the lamps. In addition, the increased magneto output would often burn out the filaments of the lights, making some caution necessary.

The latest of the electric lamps were operated from the starting battery which was part of the optional electrical equipment offered on Fords beginning in 1919. This rather constant supply of current proved very satisfactory and continues even today.

The "production" 1909 came equipped with the lamps as factory-installed "accessories." Generally speaking, these were E&J Model 466 and a curious situation has come out in our study of these lamps. In spite of the many sets we have studied, there seems to be a continuity of the situation. Lamps came in pairs; doors were right-hand and left-hand opening, but the two lamps *differed!* Note the elliptical bonnet holes on the left; the round ones on the right. In addition, the "466" on the bonnet had an imperfect "4" on left-hand lamp!

Later, in the 1910 model year, the more elaborate E&J's were replaced for a time with Jno. Brown Model 15, as is seen here. These lamps, still in pairs, were considerably less elaborate than the former. The "Ford" name was imprinted directly on the bonnet, and the screw used to lock the lamp on the fork was now on the front of the boss rather than on the rear.

The 1911 model sported the Jno. Brown Model 19 as seen here. Smaller yet than the Model 15, the main reason for the change seems to have been artistic rather than economical since weight, appearance, etc. is generally similar. This headlamp carried on through the 1912 models. At this time headlamps were no longer supplied in "pairs."

The E&J shown above was also used during the 1911-1912 production. Having no identification other than *"Made by E&J, Detroit, Mich."*, it may have been a secondary-source lamp used when the Jno. Brown Model 19 supply was low.

Appearing, too, in the 1911-12 production was the E&J Model 666. Similar to the "unmarked" E&J, this style came in pairs; had left and right doors. The 666 style continued through 1914 but was not of all-brass construction after 1912.

1913 brought about obvious and substantial change. Headlamps were now of the "Black and Brass" style, so called because, although the bonnet and rims remained brass, the bodies were steel and painted black. While still impressive in appearance, they nevertheless represented a production and cost economy.

A number of makes, all similar in general design, were used during 1913-14 production. Among them were the E&J Models 656, 666 and 66, the Brown Model 16, the Victor Model 2, and Corcoran.

The E&J Model 666 was similar to the earlier model of the same number, except for the steel shell. Later the "66" appeared; similar except for one of the "6's" being eliminated, leaving the number off-center on the label. Still later the lamp became the "656".

The E&J Model 666; similar to the 66.

The Jno. Brown Model 16.

The Victor Model 2.

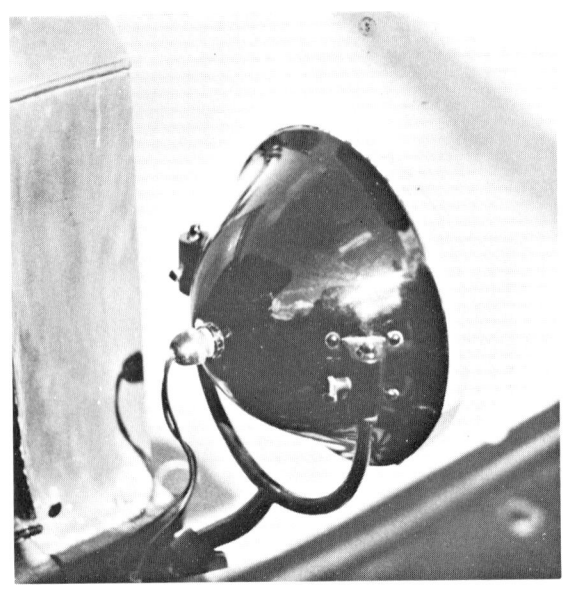

The 1915 Model T was the one on which the electric headlamp, with current supplied by the magneto, was introduced. Although the earliest 1915 cars still bore the black and brass gas lamp, changes made early in the model year introduced the lamp shown which mounted on the same forks used for the gas lamps. The rim was brass; the body steel and painted black.

Later in the year, a further economy permitted the introduction of the single post, flange-mounted headlamps which set the style for the next ten years. Similar in style to the earlier 1915 fork-mounted lamps, the rims remained brass until during the 1916 model year when the rims, too, became steel — and painted black. The lenses were of clear glass.

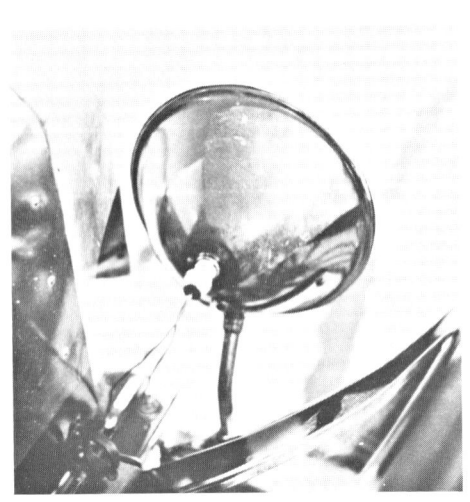

In 1921, Ford introduced — and shortly withdrew — a green-visored lens. This was replaced with the familiar Ford "H" lens. Prior to this period, all Ford headlamps featured a clear glass lens, although many accessory types were available.

The "H" lens, which had a series of molded-in ridges on the inside surface, aided in the distribution of the light pattern and was a marked improvement. It was continued through the balance of Model T production.

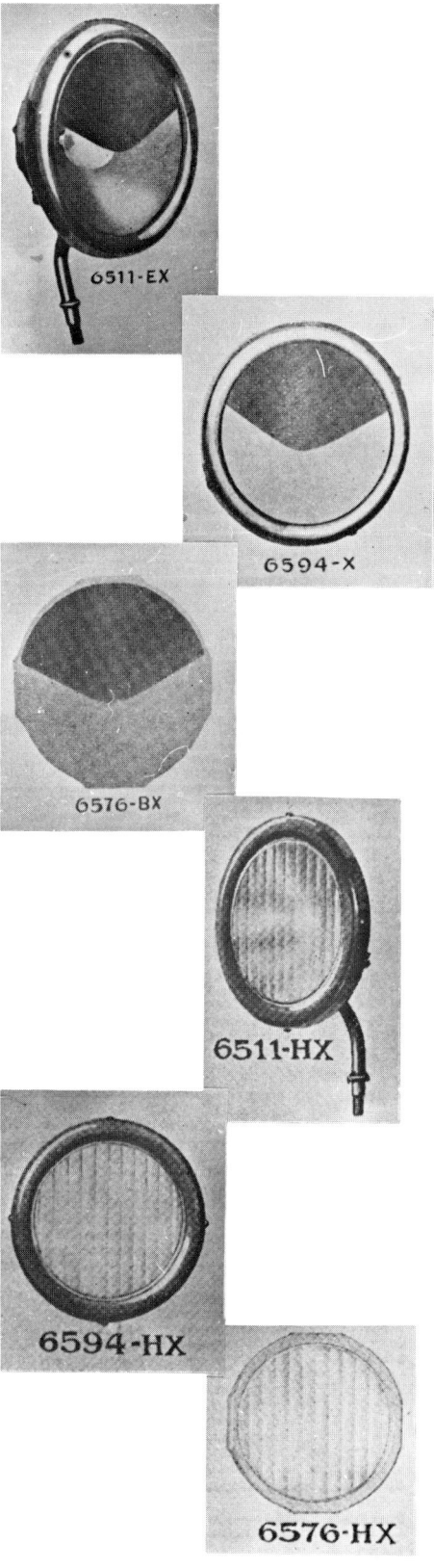

 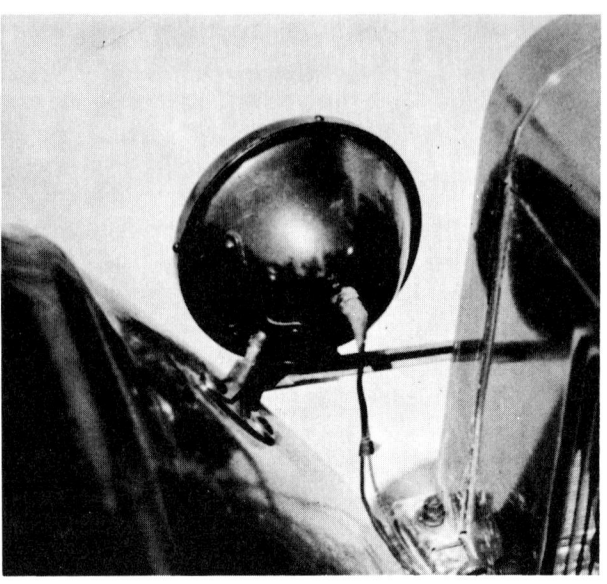

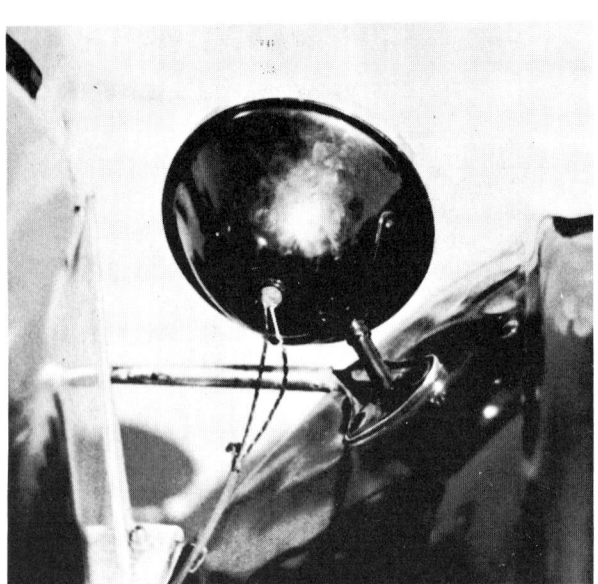 

With a final burst of creativity, the mounting arrangements of the 1926 and 1927 headlamps evolved through the steps shown. Introduced, too, with the deluxe 1926 models was the nickel plated brass rim — a feature which somehow failed to save the Model T from its rightful end.

A BAEDEKER OF MODEL T

To further illustrate the almost constant changes in the Model T during its nineteen year life span, let's take a look at just a part of the engine; the transmission cover.

To date we have been able to find *eleven* different types of covers. There may be more. Of this number we have been able to locate and photograph ten. The picture of the eleventh is taken from a Ford parts catalog (1909).

The earliest covers were of pressed steel and were in appearance much like the more familiar engine pans. We have heard stories that it is possible to rework the rear section of an early pan and make it into one of these early-type trans-

OCTOBER, 1908

Type 1. This cover is factory part number 826. Made of pressed steel, this two-lever assembly had a relatively "square" hole of approximately 5" by 5". The inspection hole cover was secured by a lever operated by turning the hex-head bolt in the center. The part number for the cover was 1546.

This particular unit is owned by the Los Angeles County Museum; engine number is 77.

LATE 1908 or EARLY 1909

Type 2 is similar in design to Type 1 but is now made of cast aluminum. Oddly, Type 1 had an external low speed adjustment screw; Type 2 did not. The external adjustment was reintroduced in Type 3 and was continued throughout production.

TRANSMISSION COVERS

mission covers. This design proved inadequate and after production of less than one hundred the cast aluminum type took its place. The aluminum covers were used until about 1916 when they were replaced with the cast iron type.

It appears that there were some relatively minor changes, possibly improvements, within the types shown here. For example, we have seen iron covers where the end of the clutch throw-out shaft assembly protruded through the side of the housing as in the style of the earlier covers, and others where it did not go through the side of the housing.

EARLY 1909
Type 3 cover is the elusive one. Factory number is 826B. Made of aluminum, it now included the three-pedal assembly and a more rectangular "square" hole roughly 4" by 5½". The inspection hole cover was still of pressed steel and was now secured with four screws. Part number for the door was 1546A.

JUNE, 1909
Type 4 cover is still of aluminum. Similar to Types 2 and 3, it appeared early in production — possibly at No. 2500; certainly by 5000. This cover, like the previous ones, had an external width of only about 17¼". Part number is 826C. The inspection hole cover is a casting now, not pressed steel, and has strengthening ribs on the underside. Part number for the door is 1546B. The cast inspection door was replaced with a pressed steel one, part number 1546C, at around engine number 10,000 and this remained unchanged through the life span of the "square hole" covers.

DECEMBER, 1910

Type 5 is quite similar to Type 4 except that the width of the cover was increased to about 18". This increase was made necessary at the time when the field coil was redesigned using thicker magnets in the magneto. Along with the change in the pan to provide the bearing inspection plate, its width was also increased to match the cover. The existence of this rare type of cover establishes that the pan was changed first (to the type with the removeable plate); the change to the cover with the tapered door (Type 6) came a little later.

FEBRUARY–MARCH, 1911

Type 6 came into general usage sometime early in 1911. This new cover, with its sloping, tapered inspection hole, for the first time offered a means of band changing and adjustment which did not require disassembly of the unit from the engine. (Changing bands without removing the cover was only possible if you had bands with the removable "ears", an accessory that was supplied by someone other than Ford. Even with the quick change bands, the job required strong hands and a few well-chosen words. In general, it was easier to remove the cover than fight the small clearances found with the aluminum covers.)

With the lettered pedals, this cover remained standard until sometime in late 1913 or 1914. The inspection hole doors were embossed with the Ford script at first. Later production used a flat plate with no script. Still later, perhaps in 1916, the familiar stamped cover became standard. Part number for this cover is 826D; the door is 1546D.

1914

Type 7 carries the same part number as Type 6 but now has reinforcing ribs cast around the bolt holes. In all other respects, it is identical to Type 6. Lettered pedals were continued until the 1915 models, at which time they were changed to the grooved style.

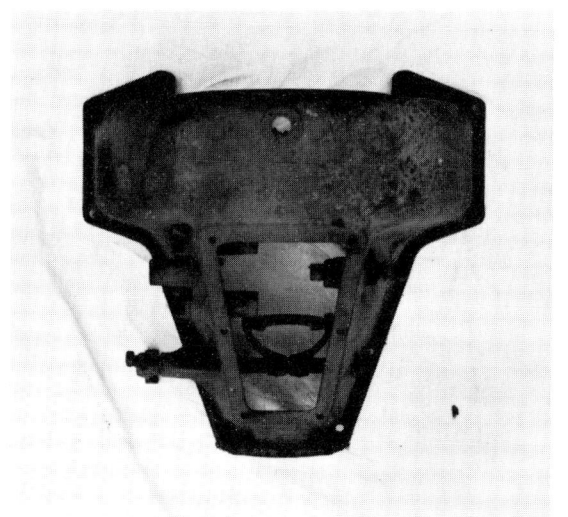

1916
Type 8 was made standard in 1916 and differs in that it is now cast iron, rather than aluminum.

A relatively minor change in the design of the neck of the tapered opening provided more clearance for band changing. This cover remained the standard until 1919, when starting equipment became available. Part number for this cover is 826E.

1919
Type 9 is the 1919 and on style which was modified to accept the starter. On those cars supplied without a starter, blanking plates were installed. This is the most common cover due to its extremely high production. Part number for this cover is 826ER. The door is still 1546D.

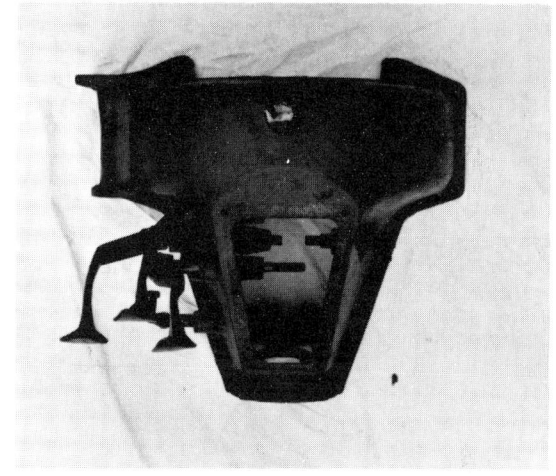

LATE 1924
Type 10 is identical to Type 9 except that a small rib was cast into the inside of the cover to deflect oil back to the transmission drums.

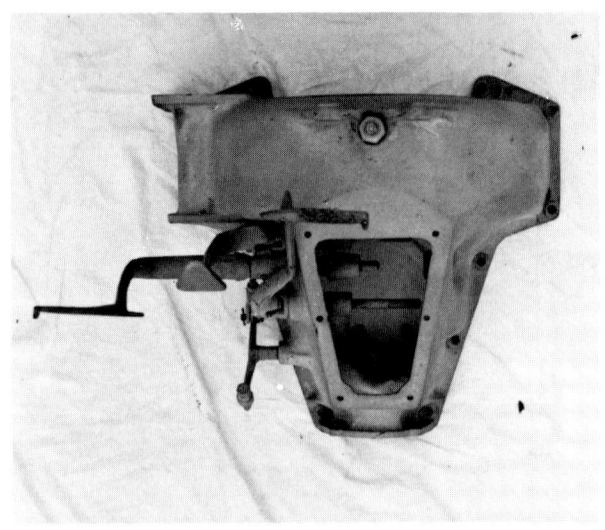

1926–1927

Type 11 is the last cover produced. It now includes "ears" for extra support when bolted to the top part of the cylinder block. Heaviest of all covers, this is also the most rugged. The rear portion was altered to provide more clearance for the larger brake drum. Part number for this cover is 826F.

In addition to the wider, more practical foot pedals, a new magneto post was installed. Rather than the three screws formerly used, the new post is threaded (½" pipe thread) into the housing.

Doors used on *Type 6 and later.* Left is the style used from 1911 until about late 1913. The center door, made of the same gauge metal but with no embossing, was used until about 1916. The right hand door became the standard used until the end of production in 1927.

Types 1, 2 and 3. The underside of the inspection door, showing the lever arrangement used to secure the door to the transmission cover. Note the dimples in each corner to hold the door when the locking nut is turned.

Types 4 and 5. Early in production, the inspection door was cast of aluminum. Later, it was stamped sheet metal. Illustrated (left) is the casting; on the right is the stamping. While externally about the same, the underside clearly shows the strengthening ribs in the casting which do not appear in the stamping.

Types 4 and 5 placed end to end to illustrate the difference in width.

MODEL "T" FORD

By HUGO H. RICHTER, JR.

1909 - 1914

HOLLEY
Ford Part No. 4150
1909-1911

HOLLEY
Ford Part No. 4550
1912

HOLLEY
Ford Part No. 4450
1913-1914

KINGSTON FIVE-BALL
Ford Part No. 4100
1909-1911

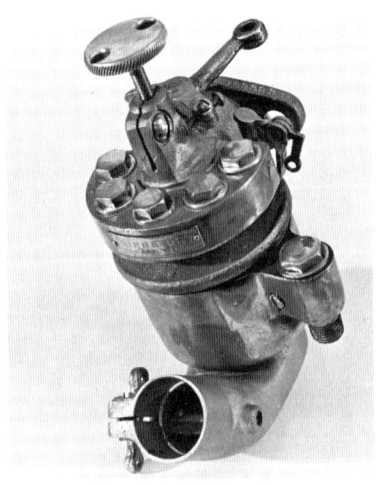

KINGSTON FIVE-BALL
(with choke on air inlet)
late 1909-1911

KINGSTON "Y"
Ford Part No. 4400
1913-1914

CARBURETORS

1914 - 1919

HOLLEY "G"
Ford Part No. 6040
1914

HOLLEY "G"

1915-1917

HOLLEY "G"

1918-1919

KINGSTON "L"

1915-1916

KINGSTON "L-2"
Ford Part No. 6100
1917-1919

1920 - 1927

HOLLEY "NH"
Ford Part No. 6200B
1924-1925

HOLLEY "NH"
Ford Part No. 6200
1920-1923

HOLLEY "NH"
Ford Part No. 6200C
1926

KINGSTON "L-4"
Ford Part No. 6150
1920-1923

KINGSTON "L-4"
Ford Part No. 6150B
1924-1926

Similar to above but with center bowl drain. New type adjuster in the 1926 model.

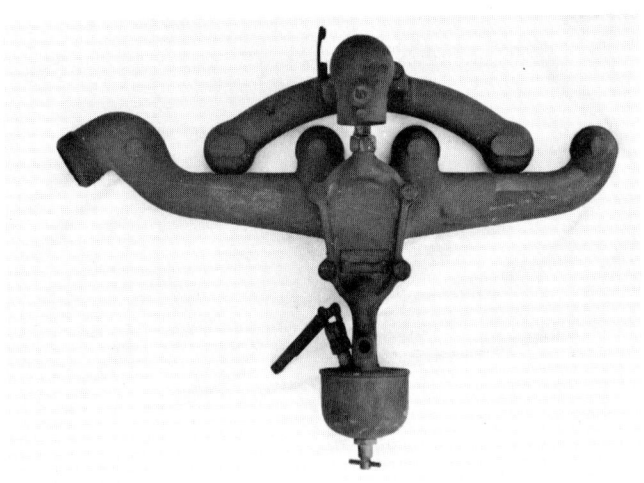

HOLLEY VAPORIZER
Ford Part No. 6250
1926-1927

KINGSTON VAPORIZER. Ford's catalogs show this unit but no examples have been found. (1926-7)

The following article represents the most accurate information that the authors could compile from available sources. While we believe it to be correct, dates of actual usage of the different units are nearly impossible to establish. Further information is desired; if any reader can offer assistance, please do so.

As a prelude, we might comment on the carburetion in the Model T Ford cars. Since the speed range of the engine was limited (as compared with modern engines), the carburetor could be quite simple. And, in general it was. Being of small bore, the air flow was such that no provision was necessary for an acceleration pump, power jets, and the many refinements found in today's carburetors.

Almost all Model T Ford carburetors were of the so-called "puddle" type. The exceptions were the first Holley and Kingston units, used on the 1909 to 1911 cars, and the "Hot Plate" units of 1926-7. In general, this means that the primary supply of fuel into the air stream came from a pool of gasoline over which the incoming air was directed. The amount of fuel in this pool, or puddle, was determined by the float adjustment (fuel level); the amount of fuel that could flow into the puddle was regulated by a dash-controlled needle valve. As the air passed over the puddle, gasoline was picked up and the resulting mixture directed to the intake valves of the engine.

Simple as it sounds, in order for the engine to idle slowly, some means had to be used to supply a richer mixture at low engine speeds. Most of the Kingston carburetors achieved this by means of an auxilliary valve which opened, allowing more air to flow, as the engine speed increased. This valve appeared as a weighted "lid" over a passage, or a series of small balls which acted as valves.

Holley, on the other hand (except in the 1926-7 "Hot-Plate, which is an altogether different story), used a venturi principle in which the air picked up its fuel from a richer source at low speeds and as the speed increased, the main jet (or pool) took over. The primary (idle) system took the form of a tube which dipped into the pool and discharged near the edge of the throttle valve where the air could "squeeze through". In the later models (the NH), this dip tube was discontinued; holes drilled in the casting of the carburetor body took its place.

The puddle carburetor is found only in the simplest of engines today. The wide speed range of modern engines doomed it to the lawnmower.

How many different carburetors were used on the "changeless" Model T? Which one goes with a particular model year? The search for answers to these questions has led to a good many uncertainties, and some seemingly reliable information.

The evidence shows that Ford bought Model T carburetors from only two firms; the Byrne Kingston Company of Kokomo, Indiana, and Holley Brothers, Detroit, Michigan.

The KINGSTON Five-Ball carburetor, used in the 1909 to 1911 production. This is a jet type carburetor (rather than the puddle type). Air is drawn in through a venturi which surrounds the jet ("C" in picture). As engine speed increases, air is drawn in through the five inlets ("X") controlled by the five balls ("B"). Additional air is necessary because of the jet's characteristic of allowing a greater proportion of fuel to flow as the air through the venturi increases, making the mixture too rich.

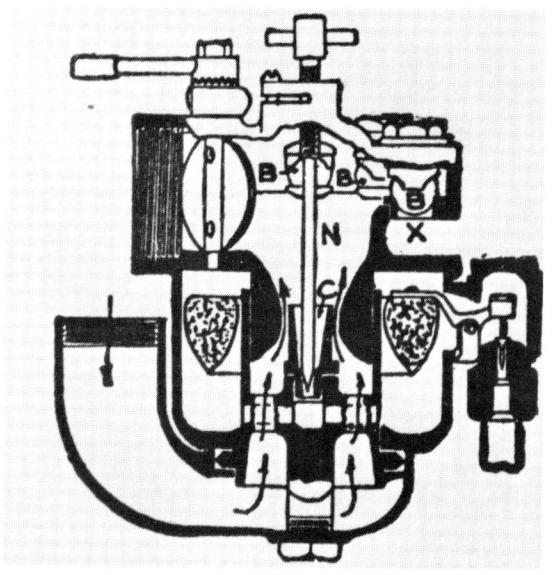

The first Model T's were equipped with a Kingston carburetor. This was a five-ball air valve type, and it was continued through the 1912 model year. The first of this model used a bellcrank arrangement to depress the float for starting enrichment. Some time prior to 1911, a butterfly type choke was installed in the air intake pipe. The air inlet for this carburetor passes vertically through the body casting in the center of the float chamber. Characteristic of the carburetors of this period is the extensive use of brass. This one is no exception. Only those parts whose function was better served by the use of steel were made of steel. The float is of cork.

During 1909 (apparently) a Holley carburetor was also installed. This one had the bottom air inlet, similar to the Kingston, and used the float-depressing device for priming such as appeared on the Kingston.

The Holley used in early production Model T Fords is of the air valve type, unlike the Holleys that followed. Used in 1909 to 1911 Fords, this unit was apparently not as popular as the Kingston Five-Ball.

The 1912 Holley appears similar in construction to the Model G used in the 1914 and later Fords. The most obvious identifying feature is a cylindrical projection cast integral with the body. This houses the gasoline inlet needle valve, and is topped by a slotted-head brass screw.

The mixing chamber cover was held with either two or three screws. This cover has an integral stop for the idling adjustment screw. The choke butterfly shaft is horizontal. Both choke and throttle levers are of cast brass; less massive than those used on the Kingston. Holley continued the use of brass levers until about 1917.

The 1912 HOLLEY carburetor. The identifying feature is the cast extension for the fuel inlet. Internal construction is similar to the drawing below; typical of all Holleys until the "NH" model of 1920.

Internally, the 1912 Holley appears to use parts which are interchangeable with the 1914 and later Model "G". When the mixing chamber cover is removed, the idling dip tube may be seen. This tube is attached by a "B" nut to a passage in the body. It extends down into the fuel puddle, through the venturi throat. The fuel nozzle or jet is placed just under the throat and screws directly into the carburetor body. When the float bowl is removed, the relatively slender cork float and hinge are exposed. The float hinge attachment of the float extends further around the circumference of the float than any others we have seen. The needle valve for fuel is placed in the body projection beyond the edge of the bowl. This is the last Holley used on Fords to utilize this configuration.

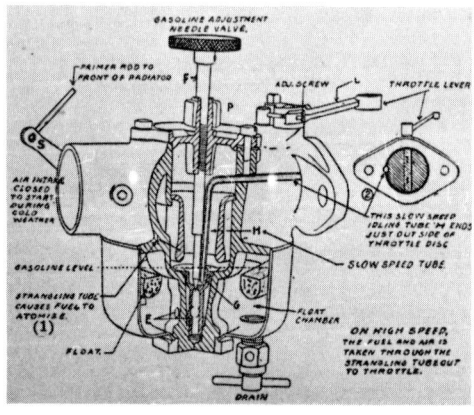

The Kingston Model Y, used in 1913 and 1914, retained a family resemblance to the earlier model. This one used four ball type air valves. The air inlet is in the carburetor body, in line with the outlet. All parts except the gasoline inlet needle and the float are of brass. The relatively massive cast brass choke and throttle levers are continued from the previous model, and are seen on all Kingstons until 1920. Also characteristic of this (and the succeeding) model is a cast brass float bowl with the integral gasoline inlet and needle valve seat.

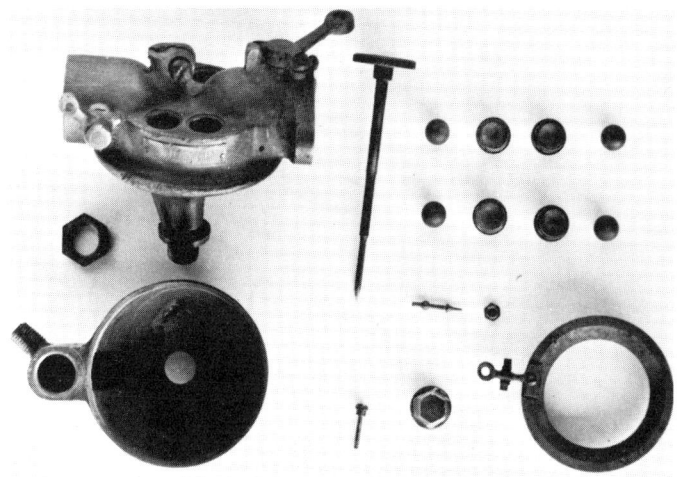

The Kingston "Y" disassembled.

This carburetor, and all Kingstons supplied on Fords until 1917, used the air bleed, or auxiliary air valve principle to achieve automatic mixture control throughout the speed range. This carburetor, when properly adjusted, provides a very slow, smooth idle, and a sharp acceleration response when the throttle is opened suddenly. The Model Y, and the prior five ball models, have one flaw, which probably led to their replacement by the Model L, late in 1914. After the air valve balls and seats became worn, the balls would stick in place and spoil the performance. A sharp tap on top of the carburetor body will provide a temporary cure for this condition.

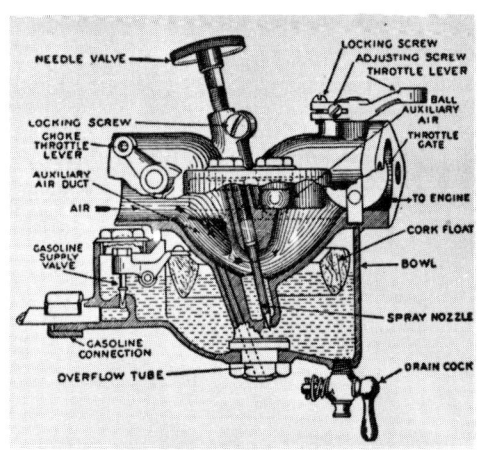

The KINGSTON Model "Y", or Four-Ball carburetor. While similar in appearance to the earlier Five-Ball, the principle of operation is entirely different. Rather than drawing fuel from a jet, this one is of the "puddle" type. Air is directed across the fuel puddle above the needle valve, where a certain amount is "scooped up". The balls act at higher speeds to add air to the fuel mixture, similar to the previous design.

The 1913 Holley. While similar to the 1912 model, in this one the idling dip tube is soldered to the mixing chamber cover. A cross drilled passage in the mixing cover provides for idling fuel flow into a matching drilled passage in the carburetor body. The throat, which is of spun brass, is retained by a wire snap ring. The fuel jet, or nozzle, has a cylindrical extension which surrounds the mixture adjustment screw. This cylinder extends approximately one half inch above the needle tip. The float chamber houses a relatively small diameter, but massive cork float. The gasoline inlet valve seats directly into the body (no replaceable seat) within the confines of the float bowl. This model has more brass components than any other Holley.

The 1913 Holley can be identified by the vertical placement of the choke butterfly shaft. The gasoline inlet elbow is short and screws directly into the side of the body, above the float chamber. The mixing chamber cover is secured with two screws and retains the integral idle adjustment screw stop of the previous model. The cover has the words "Patent Applied For" in raised letters. The float bowl drain screws into the carburetor body extension in the center of the bowl retaining nut. The carburetor gives the appearance of being a simplified 1912 model, however, if the part numbers are any indication, this is the earlier design.

The 1913 HOLLEY.

The 1914 Holley has everything that was ugly on any prior model and a horribly proportioned float bowl in addition. The mixing chamber cover is secured with three screws and the words "Patent Applied For" appear in raised letters on the cover. The idling screw stop is now integral with the body. The smooth air inlet horn provides the only feature of grace and beauty. The choke butterfly shaft has returned to the horizontal position as on the 1912 model. This is the first of the Holleys which we have been able to identify as the Model G from the literature. The earlier ones *may* have used this designation also. This

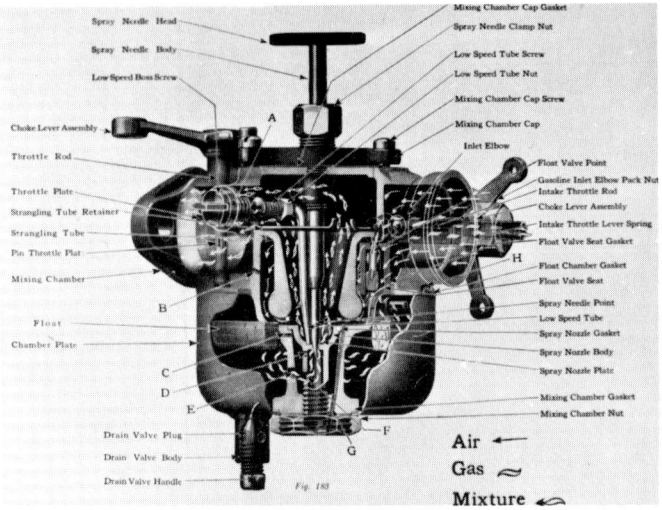

Typical of all of the Holleys from 1912 until the "NH", this phantom view shows the air and fuel flow patterns and and the general construction.

In the 1914 HOLLEY Model G, we return to the construction of the 1912 Holley. The same idling pickup tube, nestled along the side of the throat and secured by a small hex nut, is attached to a hollow screw which passes through the mixing chamber wall and directs fuel to the idling port near the throttle plate. A simplified wire retaining ring, introduced in 1913, secures the throat. The fuel jet is identical in appearance to the one used in the 1912 model. It no longer has the cylindrical extension around the mixture adjustment needle. The float bowl, still of brass, is larger than the previous models (3-7/16 inch diameter and 1-1/2 inch deep). The float is larger in diameter and of much smaller cross section than the 1913 model. A replaceable seat is installed in the carburetor body to accept the gasoline inlet needle. The bowl drain is mounted in the float bowl and uses a needle and seat. An extension of the drain needle serves to limit the downward travel of the float.

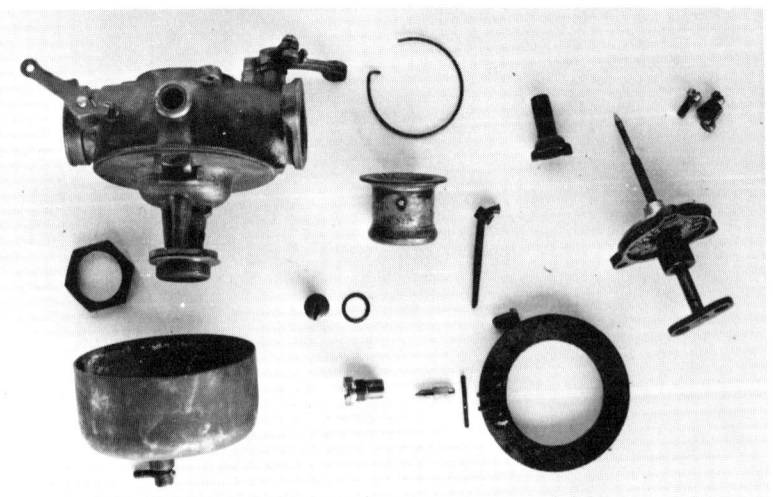

The 1914 HOLLEY.

model in identical configuration was used until January 1920. It is significant that in later years steel was substituted for brass. All parts are physically and functionally interchangeable from 1914 through 1919. All parts except the gasoline inlet needle, the cork float, the die cast throat, wire retaining ring and bowl retaining nut are of brass. This year model is the only one with the brass body and smooth air inlet. The later steel bodies, however, appear to have been cast from the same pattern.

The Holley Model G was continued for the 1915 model year with only minor changes in appearance. The brass mixing chamber cover for this and succeeding years now bears the words "Holley Detroit Patented Dec. 22, 1914". The float chamber bowl, identical in shape and size to the 1914 model, is now of steel. The air inlet horn has a stepped shape as may be seen in the illustration. Internally, this unit is identical to the 1914 model except that the jet has only drilled holes in the sides instead of the two keyhole slots that had been used.

The carburetor in this form was probably continued until about 1917. We are unable to find any clear indication of the dates when the various components were changed to steel, except that the choke levers of both the single lever and two lever variety have been found in steel. This tends to date the use of steel to the 1918 or earlier models.*

* Note: The two lever choke was introduced with the starter in 1919. The second lever was necessary so that the choke could be operated from the driver's seat. The steel single lever, therefore, would indicate that steel was used prior to the 1919 cars.

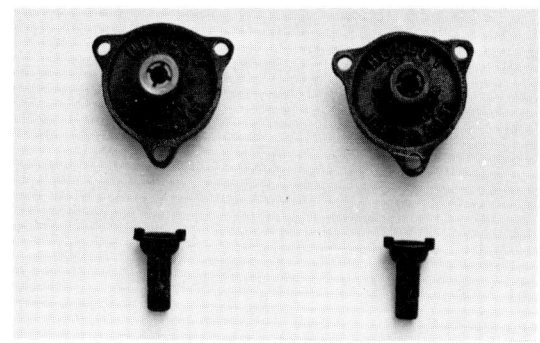

While interchangeable, the jets for the 1914 Holley have a slot cut into the side (left) while the 1915 version has only drilled holes (right).

The last of the Holley Model G were made almost entirely of steel. The use of brass was confined to the idling pickup tube and nut, the replaceable inlet fuel needle seat, and in the example we have found, the bowl retaining nut. The previous brass models used a steel bowl retaining nut. The steel body for this carburetor has a smooth inlet air horn, identical in appearance to the 1914 all-brass version. The throttle and choke levers are of cast steel, and in the case of the choke levers, both the single end and the double end types were furnished. This feature indicates that both the 1918 and 1919 model years used this unit, and in the absence of any information to the contrary, the years 1916 and 1917 could be included. The mixing chamber cover has only the words "Holley Patented Dec. 22, 1914" in raised letters.

The 1915 HOLLEY Model G. Similar to the 1914 style, the body and float bowl are now of iron and steel.

The 1918-19 HOLLEY Model G. Similar to the 1915 16 style, this carburetor is of all steel design and has a smooth air intake horn.

The 1915 Kingston is the Model L. The first of this model has a brass bowl, similar in appearance to the bowl used on the Model Y. On the Model L however, the gasoline inlet is in line with and centered directly under the air horn. A dashpot, or snubber, is screwed into the top of the air passage between the throttle lever and mixture adjusting screw. The petcock bowl drain similar to the previous models is retained. This petcock is open when the handle is horizontal; a feature which can be very frustrating if one tries to check the gasoline flow with the handle in the vertical position.

This unit, in keeping with the custom of the time, is nearly all brass. The air inlet horn has a slightly flared shape. A brass nameplate riveted to the engine side of the carburetor body has the words "Kingston L, Patent Applied For". The screw for retaining the flapper valve is on the right side of the air passage, just on top of the float chamber, and just forward of the mixture adjusting screw. On subsequent models with the gasoline inlet in the body, this screw is placed on the opposite side.

The picture shows the Model L disassembled. The mixture adjustment screw is removed by unscrewing the packing nut which surrounds it. The dashpot previously mentioned and shown in the picture, consists of a piston operating in an air chamber. It serves to cushion the air valve when it is raised on acceleration. The air valve is also shown, and is made of brass for this year.

The air valve is retained by a screw with an integral hinge pin. The float chamber is similar to that used in the Model Y of 1913 and 1914. The gasoline inlet needle and float pivot, along with the float, are installed as a subassembly with the float chamber.

We have found no reliable information to date the change from the first Model L to the second. The second version of the Model L places the gasoline inlet line in the carburetor body and uses a pressed steel bowl. Some of this style have a brass name plate riveted to the engine side of the body with the designation, "Kingston Patented May 3, 190- and March 6, 1916". Some have "Kingston Patent Applied For" and still others have no name plate, which leads to a possible 1916 usage date. All examples we have found have the cast brass, two lever choke arm. The throttle lever is still of cast brass. On this model the air valve, identical in shape to the previous model, is made of lead. The air valve retaining screw is now installed from the engine side. The air horn is smooth. In spite of the nameplate designation, this is probably the L-2 because it fits the description given in Dykes for the L-2. According to this source, the L-2 was used in 1917, 1918 and 1919. This carburetor uses the familiar short gasoline inlet elbow screwed into the carburetor body above the float bowl. The float is hinged to the body and a removeable inlet needle seat screws into the body. The screw-type drain valve is used in this model.

The 1915 KINGSTON Model L. This unit uses a brass "flapper" valve for low speed enrichment (or high speed leaning, depending on how you look at the subject). The carburetor body and bowl are also of brass.

The KINGSTON Model L-2 features a steel bowl; has the fuel inlet in the body, in line with the air horn; and all examples we have found have the two-arm choke lever.

The KINGSTON Model L-2, disassembled. Similar to the previous Model L, this one has a lead flapper valve. The Model L 2 was used in 1917, 1918 and 1919.

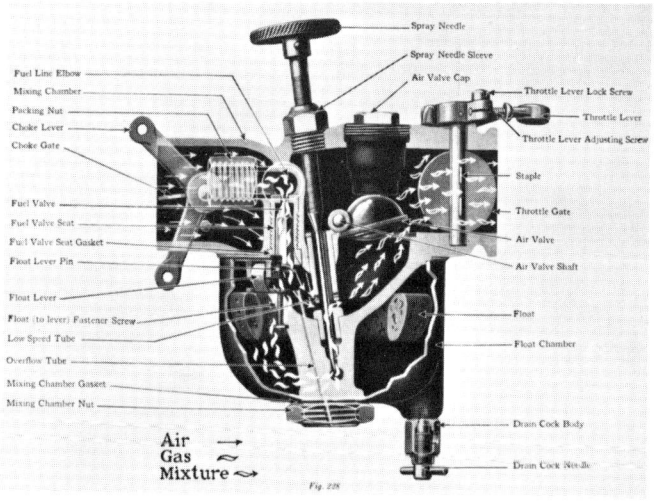

This phantom view of the L-2 shows the internal construction and air fuel flow patterns. This is typical of all the "L series" Kingstons.

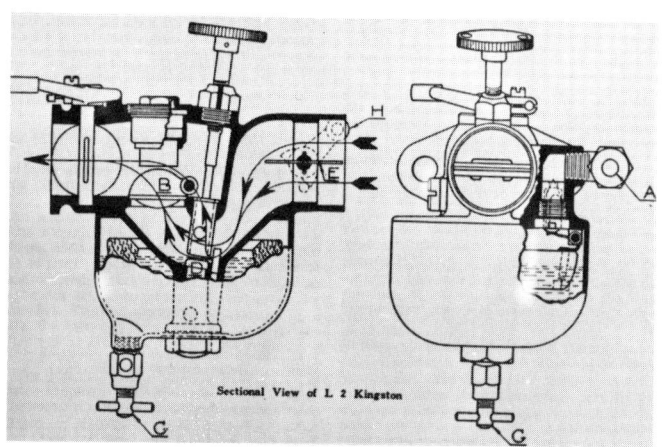

In January 1920, entirely new Holley and Kingston carburetors were supplied for Fords. Both had in common, hollow brass floats, which may be a clue as to why the older models were abandoned. The older cork floats would loose their coating and become gasoline soaked to render them ineffective. The lead air valve of the Kingston L-2 would wear and occasionally broke off. The Holley G was not up to the performance of the Kingston.

The new Kingston is the L-4. This carburetor is all steel except for the float, the gasoline inlet needle seat, the bowl retaining screw, the air valve and the mixture screw packing nut. This model is identified by a nearly straight-line design of the mixture outlet passage, and a small brass, slotted-head screw in the location of the dashpot of the previous models. A brass nameplate on the engine side of the body has the designation "Kingston Model L-4 Patented May 3, 190(?) and March 9, 1916 Made in USA." The air valve retaining screw is in line with and opposite the gasoline inlet fitting. The float bowl for the 1920 through 1923 models was essentially cylindrical in shape, with a nearly flat bottom, with the drain fitting in the bowl. The 1924 and later model has a hemispherical bowl bottom and the drain valve is integral with the bowl retaining screw.

The operating principle of this carburetor is identical to the previous Models L and L-2.

The picture of the disassembled L-4 shows the relatively few parts and a high degree of simplification. The dashpot consists of a cylindrical piece of cork approximately 1/4 inch in diameter. The throttle lever is pressed steel, and a locknut secures the idling adjustment screw. (Previous models used a separate clamping screw.) The air valve is all brass of a new design, shaped somewhat like a slab cut from the side of a cylinder. No example has been found of the 1924 and later model with the rounded bowl, for pictures.

The KINGSTON Model L-4, used from 1920 to 1923. The 1924 through 1926 models were similar but had a spherical float bowl, similar to that used on the Holley "NH" of the same era. The bowl drain was integral with the bowl retaining screw. The 1926 models had a new mixture adjustment fitting similar to the 1926 Holley. No examples of the later L-4's have been found for photos.

The Holley NH was introduced in 1920. This was an all new carburetor and at first glance appears almost identical to the Kingston L-4. The choke and throttle levers are of pressed steel and the idling adjustment is locked by spring action of a bent-over tab on the throttle lever. The only brass visible from the top is the mixture adjustment packing nut and the nameplate. This nameplate, which incidentally covers the idle vent plug, has the inscription "Holley Carburetor Co. Detroit, Michigan. Model NH, Patented (four patent dates) Other Patents Pending". The two and one-half inch diameter bowl is much smaller than the Model G and appears identical to the first Kingston L-4 bowl. It has the nearly flat bottom and the drain is in the bowl. This bowl was changed to the hemispherical lower end configuration at about 1923. This new bowl used a drain which was integral with the bowl retaining nut, similar to the late Kingston L-4's.

Internally, this carburetor is just as simple as the Kingston L-4. The only part which is readily removable from the top is the mixture adjusting screw and packing nut. Access to the jet is provided by removing the screw which secures the bowl. The bowl, bowl retaining screw and carburetor body may not be used interchangeably between the early and late versions of the Model NH.

The Holley NH is reputed to be one of the fastest of the conventional-equipment Model T carburetors. The Holley NH and the Kingston L-4 were both discontinued during 1926 production.

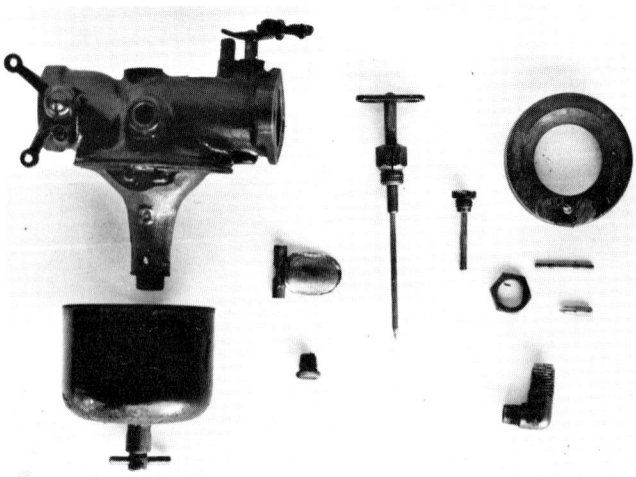

The L-4 disassembled shows fewer components; the dash pot of the earlier series had been discontinued.

Ford Model "NH" Carburetor

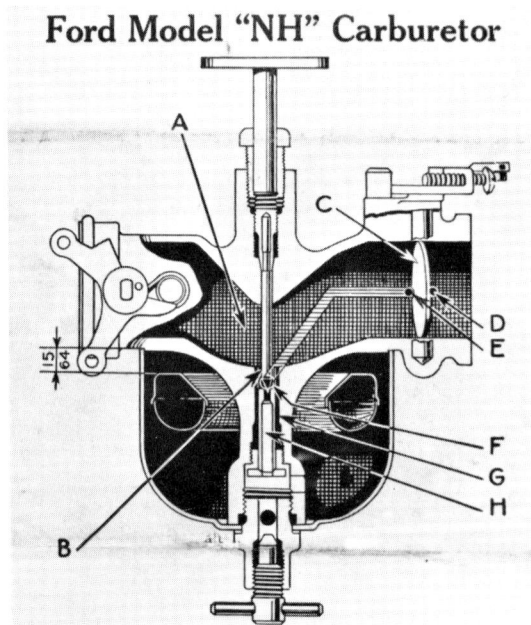

270

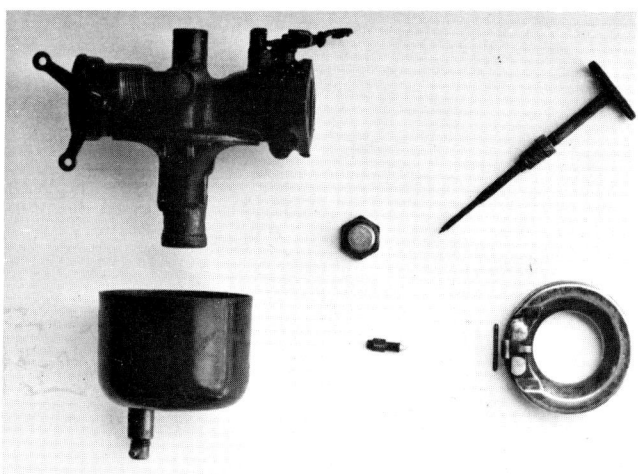

The HOLLEY "NH", used from 1920 to 1926 with only minor changes, was the simplest of any Ford carburetor. Not shown in the disassembled view are the main jet and the float valve seat, both removable. The idling tube was now integral with the body casting; is shown in the phantom view.

During 1923, the float bowl was changed to a spherical shape, and the drain made integral with the retaining screw. A new main jet adjuster was added in 1926.

In a last ditch effort to improve the sales appeal of the Model T, a new concept in carburetion was introduced in 1926. The new carburetor is the Holley Vaporizer, commonly known as the "Holley Hot Spot". The vaporizer is a complete system which integrated the carburetor, intake and exhaust manifolds into a unit. This assembly gives the appearance of a carburetor bowl in approximately the conventional location, suspended by a small pipe bolted to the exhaust manifold. In this unit, the exhaust manifold, contrary to prior Model T practice, is located below the intake manifold. At the upper end of the assembly is the air passage with the choke and throttle, attached directly to a simple parenthesis-shaped manifold. In this installation, the throttle lead rod passes over the engine instead of through the space between numbers two and three cylinders.

The disassembled vaporizer leaves the distinct impression that simplicity was no longer considered a virtue by Ford. The catalog lists

By far the most complex of all Model T carburetors, the Holley Hot Plate was also the most miserly in terms of fuel consumption. Of the air valve type, the first for Holley since the 1909 style, the unit heated the fuel as it was drawn past a heated plate on its way to the mixing chamber. During idle and low speed operation, air is drawn in through a hole near a heated plate on its way to the mixing chamber. When the choke is closed, air is drawn in through a hole near the choke valve and is drawn down to the main jet in the float bowl where it picks up a supply of fuel and raises to the mixing chamber. For idle and low speed operation, with the choke open, a similar process takes place, except that now the air valve acts as an automatic "choke" which opens as the engine speed increases.

Not a "new" idea at Ford — a similar device had been used on the Fordson tractor for years.

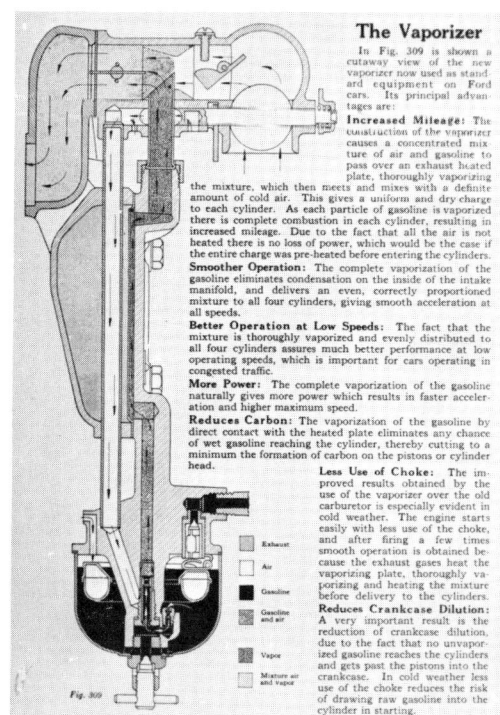

twice as many parts for this model as for the preceeding one. While this listing includes the intake and exhaust manifolds, listed separately for the prior carburetors, this unit is by far the most complex.

The interior of the float bowl and method of attachment are identical to the Holley NH. These parts as well as the float, gasoline inlet needle valve and removable seat all have the same part numbers.

Two vertical passages extend to the air inlet from the float bowl. One serves to carry the fuel vapor past a thin, heated plate and into the inlet throat. The other brings a small amount of heated air to the jet where the vaporizing process is initiated.

Among the unusual items found in this unit is the main jet discharge into the airstream. The jet is 7/16 inch diameter, and the venturi is only 9/16 inch diameter. Close examination of the unit reveals the fact that closing the choke butterfly also restricts airflow which brings preheated air to the jet in the carburetor bowl. This, no doubt to insure that the fuel will be lifted to the mixing section for cold starting. Contrary to prior Holley practice, this unit uses a weighted air valve, located between the choke butterfly and the venturi, to control the fuel-air mixture.

According to Ford advertisements, the vaporizer gives "over twenty-five miles per gallon under average conditions; official tests have shown thirty-five miles per gallon!" The surviving units still deliver twenty-five miles per gallon or more. This carburetor provided good, trouble free performance. Even so, there must have been some flaws in the system because Ford returned to a conventional carburetor with the introduction of the Model A in late 1927.

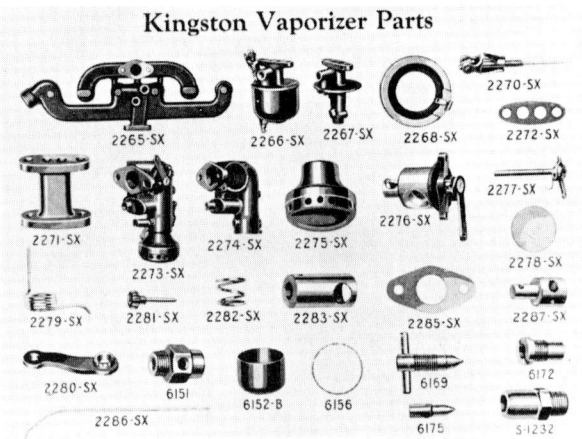

Kingston Vaporizer Parts

Information contained in this article has been supplied by many persons, over a period of several years. The author would like to thank, in particular, Glenn Rand, of Cuyahoga Falls, Ohio, and Warren LaBarre, of Portland, Oregon, for their help.

The Fords before the "T" —

— Models N, R and S

We have in the preceding chapters covered all the production models of the Model T Ford. Why not look at its immediate predecessors?

The Ford cars for 1906 were the Model F, a two-cylinder automobile; the Model K, a large six-cylinder one; and the Model N, a new four-cylinder design which was introduced in January of that year.

The Model F was similar in design to the earlier Models A and C. The engine was located under the seat in the fashion typical of the earlier automobiles. 1906 was to be the last year in which the Ford Motor Company was to supply a two-cylinder car.

The Model "K" was the deluxe automobile of the line. Large, powerful (for the time) and heavy, it was produced at a loss during its two to three year life span. It was built largely at the insistence of Alex Malcolmson, a major stockholder at the time. The majority of the automobile market at this period was in the higher-priced models; Malcolmson (and others) felt that this is where the profits were to be found. Sales were disappointing, overall profits declined; and in 1907 Ford's efforts were directed towards the newer, light and not-so-costly Model N.

The Model N was a success from the day of its introduction. While the Model K was to be

Two Model "N" cars. The upper picture from the 1906 catalog; the lower from the 1908. Changes were subtle. The headlamps on the 1908 car were optional equipment, as were the tops on both cars.

Engines stacked ready for installation. This photo was taken in 1906 at the Piquette Avenue plant. This, and the two other pictures of in-plant production, were used in the sales catalogs of 1906, 07 and 08, the captions changed to suit the date.

Model N chassis in the assembly area. This was long before the assembly line system was initiated.

continued into the 1908 model year, the N (and R,S) were to be the bread and butter models for the period. The N was advertised as being "Just automobile — all automobile." And that is just what it was. Fenders were simple wing-like attachments; there were no running boards. Items such as lights, top and windshield were optional extras.

In 1907, Ford offered the Model R, a deluxe version of the N. While the engine, chassis and running gear were identical, the R offered a slightly larger body, full fenders and running boards, in addition to larger wheels and tires (30 by 3 in place of the 28 by 2½). Approximately 2500 were built and the demand for the improved model exceeded the production. The Model N sold for $600; the R at $750.

Rather than re-tool for more of the Model R, Ford introduced the Model S. Still the same basic car, it was sort of a compromise between the N and R models. The Model S was to be *the* Ford car for the era. It sold for $700.

Later editions of the N and S were to see the introduction of Vanadium steel; these cars set the stage for the introduction of the Model T in October of 1908.

The N-R-S Fords were four-cylinder cars. The cylinders were cast in pairs and were bolted to an aluminum crankcase. The transmission was planetary, with the gears at the rear of the engine and enclosed only in a sheet metal shield. Lubrication was by external oilers. The car had a right-hand drive, typical for the time, and three foot pedals. The pedals were unique; two brakes and reverse! One of the brake pedals operated on the transmission brake, similar to the Model T; the other on the internal-expanding rear wheel brakes. The latter pedal could be held in the applied position by a latching device, to act as a parking brake. Low and high gears were controlled by a lever at the driver's right; pull back for low, center for neutral, forward for high.

Unique, in terms of modern practice, was the placement of the flywheel at the front of the engine. Fan blades were cast into the flywheel so that it doubled as the fan. One of the reasons for placing the flywheel at the front was to gain extra ground clearance to cope with the very poor roads of the day. Unfortunately, this location placed extra strain on the crankshaft due to the twisting action through the crankshaft as the flywheel would try to drive the engine (and car) under load changes.

Suspension was similar to the T in front, with the one transverse-mounted spring. The rear had a spring on each side, similar to present day practice except that they were full elliptic. Both front and rear axles featured radius rods, and except for the rear springs, the general design was carried over to the Model T.

Ignition was supplied by dry cell batteries; a magneto was not a part of the car's design.

But read on. The following is exactly what the Ford catalog of the day had to say.

A DAYS OUTPUT

SHIPPING ROOM

MODEL "R"

"Ever since the Ford Model "N" Runabout was first announced and more especially since the quality and powers of the car have become known to the world of motordom there has been a large and increasing demand for a car of similar construction, power and endurance, but more pretentious in outward appearance. A runabout more richly dressed and equipped with those frills and fussings that are dear to the hearts of more fastidious owners — persons who like something specially nice and to whom price, while a consideration, is a matter of secondary importance.

"Aware of this demand, solicitous competitor-friends have wondered and have asked repeatedly why the price of the Ford runabout was not set at a higher figure at first — say $800 or more, a figure which it was admitted we could sell all we could make in the next year or two at least. But Ford's plans are always known to his imitators — afterward.

"Anyone who has followed the development of the motor car in America has noticed that Ford has always been a year ahead. Each successive move he has made has suggested something to tardy imitators — an opportunity that had apparently escaped his keen eye. But while they are busy copying the latest Ford, behold! he brings forth another that leaves them hopelessly behind again. And this last is the product of the ripest experience — their's can at best be a poor copy and consequently an experiment so far as they are concerned. And thus the procession ever moves onward, Ford, the originator, the creator in the lead, imitators, copyists following his train, boastful but impotent.

"The Model "R" Ford Runabout is but the latest example of this habit Ford has of anticipating every move of those who would presume to compete with the Ford product.

"Waiting only until the motoring public had had time and opportunity to know the true value and the excellence of the Model "N" motor and chassis, he has proceeded to build a companion model to suit the more fastidious tastes and requirements of the class of buyers above indicated. Physicians, professional men in all branches, bankers and wealthy businessmen who already have one or more large touring cars but who feel a need for a light runabout that will emancipate them, on occasion, from the professional chauffeur — a car one can drive himself and derive keen pleasure from; one his wife or son or daughter can handle with equal ease and facility and which will negotiate congested city streets as well as country roads with greater safety and celerity than a more cumbersome runabout or touring car. Such a car is this latest Ford Model "R."

"In fact this latest model has been well described as "an edition deluxe of the Ford Model "N" Runabout."

"The Ford Model "N" motor and chassis has proven to have more strength and power than is necessary under any conditions for the size of the car. It was not necessary, therefore, to apply a larger motor or heavier axles, frame or transmission to produce the more pretentious appearing Model "R."

"The chief points of difference between the two models are as follows: 30 by 3" tires which enhance the speed qualities of the machine — forty-five miles an hour easily, down to four miles

on high gear by throttle control alone.

"Body is slightly larger, seats higher and more distance between seats and dash. Of the semi-individual type, seats are luxuriously upholstered in first grade M. B. leather and curled hair. Panels are more highly finished, tastefully striped and neatly ironed for top, the ironing following the contour of the seats.

"The beetle-back is rounded instead of pointed and is made larger to receive the larger extra tire.

"Large plow-share fenders at the front, the edges turned over in angle form to eliminate vibration and lend stiffness; rear fenders semi-enclosed and curved to follow the contour of the wheels, lend an imposing appearance to the machine. Fenders are connected by a wide rubber-covered running board with brass angle mouldings round the sides and ends.

"Ignition system is the best obtainable and the standard equipment includes a six-volt storage battery beside a set of six dry cell batteries.

"Add to the above a pair of handsome oil lamps, tail lamp and large French tube horn, brass operating lever, steering post and brass moulding around dash and you have one of the nattiest and tastiest cars ever turned out. And in performance — endurance, silence, ease of control, flexibility, speed and hill climbing ability, it has no rival, no equal at less than $1000 — and we know of none even at that figure. Price, $750, f.o.b., Detroit.

"A detailed description of the various features of design and construction follows. Additional information will be cheerfully furnished for the asking.

DETAILED DESCRIPTION

MOTOR

"Model "R" *(identical to Models N and S, Ed.)*— four-cylinder, vertical; located longitudinally under hood at the front. Cylinders cast in pairs. Bore, 3-3/4 inch; stroke 3-3/8 inch; rated in horse power at normal speed, 15. (Under series of tests connected with and driving dynamo develops 18.4 h.p.) Aluminum crank case. Crank shaft bearings, highest grade Babbitt metal; exceptionally long. Camshaft bearings, bronze.

"CRANK SHAFT — Drop-forged steel, specially heat-treated by our own process. All bearing surfaces ground to half-a-thousandth of an inch accuracy.

"CAM SHAFT — Drop-forged in one piece with all cams integral, from special high grade steel; cam surfaces case-hardened and all bearing surfaces ground.

"VALVES — Drop-forged, heads integral; seats and stems ground to micrometrical accuracy.

"CONNECTING RODS — Drop-forged from special steel *(Vanadium steel in 1908)* in "H" section. Lower bearing cap hinged. Provision for adjustment is made by the insertion of fibre*(!)* shims which can be removed and filed down for that purpose. Piston pin bearings, bronze; split bushing adjustable by tightening set screw. Large hand holes at the left side of motor, covered by removable plates, permit of easy inspection and adjustment of crank and piston pin bearings without otherwise disturbing the engine.

Fan fly wheel and Pistons

"PISTONS — Cast from fine grain grey iron, our own formula. First rough turned, then turned to within a few thousandths of size; are then annealed to relieve strains in the metal and effect such distortion as will result from heat. After cooling, are finished by grindings. Each piston provided with four rings of the eccentric type, split diagonally. Rings are ground on both sides and on the outer surface.

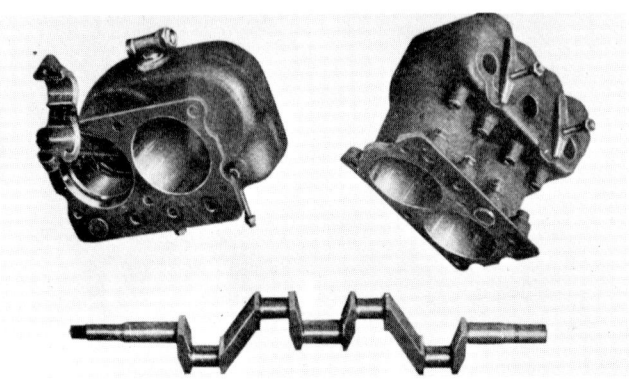

"CYLINDERS — Cast from the finest quality gray iron. After the first boring operation, cylinders are annealed to relieve strains and then rebored and finally reamed so as to secure an absolutely straight and round cylinder.

"PISTON PINS — Steel, hardened and ground.

LUBRICATION

"MECHANICAL OILER — A faultless lubrication system is afforded by a mechanical oiler with sight feeds for regulating the flow. One tube serves to maintain a uniform level in the engine base and the other leads to the ball-housing which encloses the universal joint in the cardon shaft. *(Cardon shaft is an obsolete term for the drive shaft. Cardon, or properly cardan, refers to the universal joint, named after its inventor, a man named Cardan.)* All engine parts — crank shaft and connecting rod bearings, piston pins, cylinders, cams and valve lifters, are lubricated by the "splash" system. Owing to the fact that the stroke of this engine is shorter than the bore and that the pistons project into the base at the end of each stroke, the splash system of lubrication leaves nothing to be desired. It is certain and simple. The oil begins to flow when the engine

starts and while it is running the supply is in direct proportion to the speed of the motor — in other words, to exactly meet its requirements. When the motor stops the oil ceases to run so that once the feed is regulated a constant level can be maintained in the engine base regardless of variation of speeds. A partition mid-way between front and rear of the engine base prevents the oil flooding the rear cylinders when climbing steep grades and keeps the two pairs equally lubricated. Oil cups are provided at every bearing point throughout the car — even at the spring connections. Provision is made both in the transmission gear and in the differential and bevel gear housing of the rear axle, to pack these parts with heavy grease, one supply of which will last for several weeks.

Ford Unit Power Plant—Motor and Transmission—Right Side

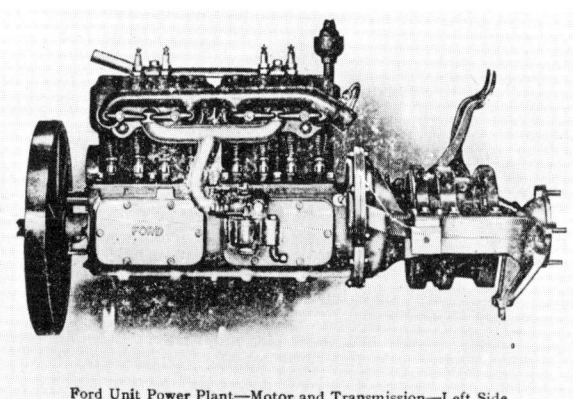
Ford Unit Power Plant—Motor and Transmission—Left Side

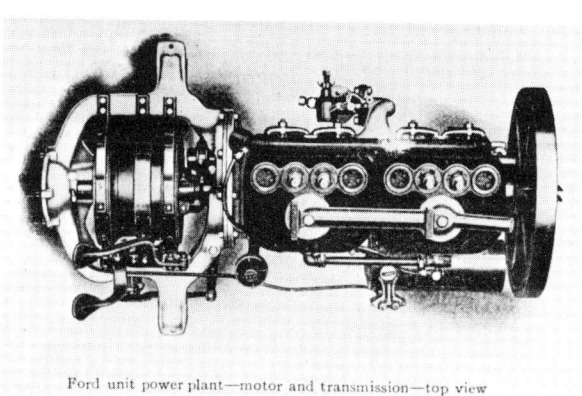
Ford unit power plant—motor and transmission—top view

"IGNITION — By jump spark; current supplied by batteries — standard equipment (Model "R") one set of six Columbia dry cells and one six-volt storage battery. *(Model "N" was furnished with two sets of the dry cells; no storage battery. The Model "S" was equipped like the "R".)*
Quadruple coil in handsome case located on the dash. Switch on front of case. Each coil unit is separate and complete in itself and any unit may be removed or replaced without disturbing the others. High tension wires well insulated and carried in fibre brackets so that disarrangement or short-circuiting is impossible.

"CARBURETOR — Float feed, automatic; specially designed for this car. Gasoline tank located under the seat with gravity feed to carburetor.

COOLING

"Perfect cooling under all conditions is afforded by a most efficient vertical tube radiator which forms the front of the hood and in which the centrifugal pump is incorporated. The circulation system has been carefully worked out so that the water is constantly in motion and it is impossible for the engine to overheat no matter how hot the weather or how long it may run idle or on the low gear.

TRANSMISSION

"The transmission is of the Ford spur-planetary type, nearly eight thousand of which are now in use and which have proven so wonderfully efficient and durable. Low speed and reverse clutches are of the fibre-lined, steel band type, which take hold smoothly and which spring away from the drums when disengaged so as to prevent "dragging" and the consequent waste of power. The high-

Ford spur-planetary transmission

speed clutch is of the multiple disc type with fibre discs interposed between smooth cast iron discs. A transmission gear is almost unnecessary on this Model "R" car as the excessive power of the engine enables the car to climb almost any hill or negotiate the muddiest or sandiest roads in high gear — and at a slow speed if the driver so desires. The low gear is seldom or never used except for the first twenty or thirty feet when starting from a stand-still. It will be seen, therefore, that this transmission should outwear almost any other part of the car.

"MOTOR SUSPENSION — The transmission gear is carried in a cast aluminum frame the front of which is bolted to the rear end of the motor, thereby forming the rear support of the latter. A bracket, cast integral with the front end of the engine base, rests on the front cross-member of the frame and this, with the two arms of the transmission frame which are bolted to the side frame members, gives an ideal three point suspension, and a rigid construction in engine and transmission. This construction is the reverse of most "three point suspension" systems, in all others of which two points of the triangle are at the front of the frame and the apex at the center. The Ford idea gives the maximum of flexibility while at the time relieving the transmission shaft of all twisting or distorting strains.

FINAL DRIVE

"The Ford triangular drive system is patented in every country in the world. It is the only system in which all driving shafts, universal joints, gears, and other moving parts are enclosed in a dust proof and oil tight housing from transmission gear to the hub caps of the wheels. The drive is direct to the center of the chassis regardless of whether the car is running straight or turning corners; and only one universal joint is necessary. A ball-and-socket connection between the tubular torsion member and the transmission frame allows the axle to oscillate in any direction and thereby relieves the passengers of all strains and shocks due to unevenness of the road. It also permits of the use of full elliptic springs, flexibly connected to the frame brackets instead of the rigid connection necessary when the driving strain must be transmitted through the medium of the springs. This system is broadly covered by letters patent in all countries and is used in all Ford models. The universal joint comprises four members — the two drop-forged steel sections and the halves of the split bronze retaining ring. It is, at the same time, the simplest, most efficient and most durable universal joint ever devised and it is automatically lubricated at all times, the owner "never knows it is in the car." The drive shaft bearings are of Babbitt, carefully reamed and fitted and the oil from the universal joint flows constantly down through these bearings and into the differential housing.

Universal Joint, Driving Gears and Differential

REAR AXLE

"The rear axle proper is the well known Ford design, the driving members being enclosed in a tubular steel housing, press-fitted and riveted to the cast steel sections of the differential case. Hyatt roller bearings of the indestructable type are fitted at both ends of the live members. The differential gear is of the three pinion, bevel type; all gears made from special high-grade, drop-forged, steel blanks. The driving pinion and main bevel gear are drop-forged from special chrome nickel steel *(Vanadium steel in 1908)*, teeth accurately planed and case hardened. The axle may be taken apart in a few minutes, differential gear and other parts removed and examined.

FRONT AXLE

"The front axle of the Model "R" is a marvel of the drop-forging art. The entire axle is drop-forged in one piece from special steel *(Vanadium steel in 1908)* and is specially treated after forging. It is in "I"-beam section — the form which gives the maximum of strength with the minimum of weight. The worst that can happen to this axle, even in a collision with a telegraph pole, is to bend it; and even if bent double, it can be heated in a blacksmith's forge and straightened without having suffered any actual injury. Steering knuckles and spindles, are drop-forged from special steel, in one piece. Front wheels are carried on large ball-bearings — balls being more suitable for supporting the end-thrusts occasioned by steering.

STEERING GEAR

"THE FORD REDUCTION-GEAR steering device is the only really new thing in this line that has been developed in several years. Like the rear axle, it is being patented in all countries, and we believe it is the most satisfactory solution of the steering problem that has yet appeared. It is just sufficiently irreversible to relieve the driver of all road worries and at the same time yields enough to irregularity of the ruts to save the car from the many shocks and twists from which it would otherwise suffer. The gears, instead of being located below the frame where they become clogged with mud and cut with grit and dust, are placed at the top of the post just within the hub of the steering wheel. Ball joints connect the steering arm with the transverse steering rod.

SPRINGS

"Full elliptic springs are the only satisfactory type for rough American roads and the imperfect block pavements of our cities — and Ford cars are built for hard service over such roads.

"The lightness of the Model "R" frame and

body and the disposition of the load — engine over front axle, passengers between front and rear — permits the use of very light, flexible rear springs — the result is the most perfect riding runabout ever built. Instead of the stiff side springs at the front, there is a single transverse spring shackled to forged integral bosses on the front axle. The front cross-frame member rests upon the center of this spring and there is, therefore, provided a three point suspension for the frame as well as for the motor and transmission gear. (For the enlightenment of those who would believe side springs would be superior to the single transverse spring, might we say we tried this out thoroughly before deciding to adopt the one we have. The difference in steering was not noticeable while the riding qualities of the transverse spring proved to be incomparably superior. In the thousands of cars now on the road, no weakness has ever developed in the spring construction so we can assert that for a light car, constructed as this one is, this spring suspension has no equal.)

CHASSIS MODEL N

FRAME

"The frame is of the approved pressed steel type, in channel section, and is made from the highest grade of special material. It is cold pressed and tapered toward the front and rear. The frame has a factor of safety many times the load which it will ever be called upon to sustain. This is also true of axles and every other part.

281

THREE POINT SUSPENSION

"While we are on the subject, it might be well to note that the "three point suspension" idea has been carried to what might be termed, its "logical conclusion" in this car. The driving forces are transmitted through tubular radius members from the outer ends of the rear axle, at a point just below the spring blocks, to a common center at the ball joint previously described; then, from a point almost directly below this ball joint is another from which diagonal tubular radius members convey the driving forces again to the ends of the front axle; the engine and transmission are supported at three points; and the frame also has a three point suspension on the two rear springs and the single transverse front spring previously outlined. The wonderment which everyone, after his first ride in a Ford runabout, expresses, is induced by the constructional factors above outlined.

BRAKES

"The Model "R" car is splendidly equipped with brakes. For service use, there is a contracting fibre-lined band brake operating on a special drum on the transmission shaft. For emergency use there are a pair of internal expanding, bronze rings contained within dust-proof, pressed steel drums attached to the rear hubs. Then the reverse clutch band, operated as it is by foot lever, may be used as a brake if desired. The service and emergency brakes, being also operated by foot levers, there are three foot levers, any one of which will slide the wheels on any kind of road surface.

TIRES

"The Model "R" is equipped with 30 by 3 inch clincher tires. *(1906-7 Model "N" cars were equipped with 28 by 2-1/2 clincher tires; later "N" and all Model "S" cars were supplied with 28 by 3 inch clincher tires.)* Owing to the fact that no one tire concern can supply us with our full requirements, it is impossible for us to give customers an option on make of tire — we must equip each day's output with whatever tires we have in stock. It is sufficient to say we buy the best there is and since the tire pool went to pieces, we have no difficulty in getting any brand we desire — in fact the scramble for the Ford tire business today is in sharp contrast to the attitude of some tire concerns a year ago when a concerted effort was made to prevent Ford carrying out his plans for a four-cylinder runabout at a reasonable price.

FENDERS

"The Model "R" car is equipped with fenders of ample proportions and front and rear fenders are connected by a broad running board. Brass angle mouldings all round running board and corrugated rubber mat gives a handsome appearance to this model. *(Model "N" cars had smaller, wing-like fenders; no running board. The later "S" was similar to the Model "R".)*

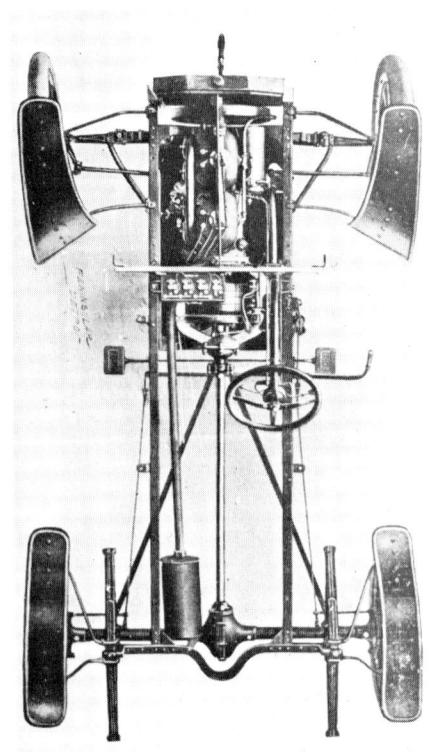

FUEL CAPACITY

"The gasoline tank is located under the seats and has a capacity of eight gallons. As this car averages about twenty-five miles per gallon of gasoline, this is sufficient for about two hundred miles of running over ordinary roads.

OPERATION AND CONTROL

"We believe we are justified in saying no other car in the world is as simple to master and easy to control as are the Ford Runabouts, Models "N" and "R." Hundreds of these cars are driven constantly by ladies and misses, not to mention the youths of fourteen to eighteen years of age who use them. So far as we know there has never been an accident which was in any way due to the inexperience of the driver or to any other cause, even remotely associated with the control of the machine. A single lever at the side operates the the low speed and the high, the movement being the simple backward and forward one with neutral position midway. The reverse is operated by a foot lever. Spark and throttle levers are located at the right and left side, respectively, of the steering post and just below the wheel, so that both can be operated by the index fingers without removing the hands from the steering wheel. Having excess of power to meet all conditions the car may be driven at any speed from four miles per hour to its maximum speed of about forty-five miles per hour by simple throttle and spark control alone. Even for driving in congested city streets it is seldom necessary to use the brake or to disengage the clutch. The motor is easy to start, so that a lady has no difficulty in this regard, whereas to start a single or even a two-cylinder motor of anything like the same horsepower would be an almost impossible task for a woman.

EQUIPMENT

"The Model "R" car is equipped with side oil lamps, tail lamp and French tubular horn and is ironed to receive a top. *(The "N" and "S" cars were not supplied "ironed" but the iron was available at five dollars extra. The 1908 catalog had this to say:*

"As 95 percent of all customers order tops fitted and as all owners want to attach them sooner or later; and as to iron finished body for top is expensive, we have adopted a plan of working all "N" seats for top, for which an extra charge of $5.00 is made. When top is ordered with car, cost of ironing is included in price of top."

BODY

"The Model "R" body is similar in general design to that of the Model "N", having a seating capacity of two. The seats are of a semi-individual type and are larger than formerly. Seats are also higher and there is more room between seats and dash, thus allowing for two very large persons. The "beetle back" is different in shape from the Model "N," being rounded at the rear and of larger proportions to permit of carrying the larger tires. This body is of very handsome appearance and there is ample body and leg room for two large persons. It is handsomely upholstered in first grade "M.B." leather, heavily tufted with curled hair.

MODEL "S"

"Mr. Ford's original aim in designing his now world-famous four-cylinder runabout was to build a stock model two passenger car that should combine the qualities of strength, lightness, power, speed and hill-climbing ability with those of endurance and economy of up-keep, and to clothe it in a body that should be "neat but not gaudy" and one which should meet as nearly as that is possible, the tastes of average buyers.

"In the matter of body design it might be said no two persons fully agree, so the designer must use his own judgment and compromise between what his broad experience teaches him the buyer should have, and those features which the buyer himself thinks he needs.

"The Model "N" was Mr. Ford's conception of a runabout that was "all automobile" — in other words, all efficiency with none of the frills or fussings so dear to the hearts of some motorists.

"The tremendous popularity of that model has proven Mr. Ford's judgment to have been correct, and to date he has found no reason to discontinue Model "N" — the $600 car.

"A demand soon manifested itself, however, for a car of more pretentious appearance, and the class of customers who wanted this were willing to pay the difference; so Model "R" with broad fenders, running board, larger wheels (30" by 3"), and somewhat larger body, was designed and the price fixed at $750 F.O.B. Detroit.

"It seemed as if 2500 of these would be ample for this season's needs, but we fell short of the mark. Every Model "R" now has left the factory and the only ones to be had are those which may be found here and there in the hands of agents and branches. It is too late to build more — we cannot make and finish bodies and wheels in time.

"What to do in this crisis was the problem, and as usual Mr. Ford solved it in a way that will be a delight to customers and enable us to take care of another demand which we have long felt but thought to ignore.

"The chassis of Models "N" and "R" are identical, as are engine and all other parts except

Body

Ford 4-cylinder—15-18 H. P. Runabout—Model "R"

Ford 4-Cylinder 15-18 H. P. Runabout—Model "S"

body, fenders and equipment. (N at $600 carries no equipment, it is "just automobile — all automobile.")

"So we now announce an intermediate model, a composite of the two former ones, at an intermediate price — $700 F.O.B. Detroit. This we call Model "S". Chassis standard 15 h.p. four-cylinder Ford runabout; wheels 28" shod with 3" clincher tires; broad steel fenders connected by running board, same as Model "R"; improved three feed mechanical oiler; lamps, horn and storage battery equipment same as Model "R."

"The body is a standard "N," but the seats have been raised, made larger and set further back from the dash than in the earlier ones. The pointed deck of the Model "N" has been much in favor among buyers and many liked it better than the round one which characterized the Model "R."

"So the "S" may be said to combine the choicest features of those two wonderfully popular models, at a cost of $50 less than Model "R."

"To distinguish them from the other two, Model "S" cars are painted Brewster Green as to body with cream running gear."

Colors are not definite. The only evidence we have is that the first Model "N" cars were finished in dark maroon, striped in black. There may have been other colors added during the production run of three years.

We are all indebted to Warren LaBarre for his assistance in preparing this article. He has supplied the pictures taken during the restoration process, as well as his own commentary which is included below.

STURDY, DEPENDABLE, INEXPENSIVE

Henry Ford's Model T was a car that most American families could afford to own. Yet, just before the Model T was put into production, the Ford Motor Company manufactured an attractive two-seater with a "mother in law" seat. This fancy little car was completely opposite the Model T in all mechanical parts. It had a right hand drive and a lever on the right which "shifted the gears." Pedals were on the floor but the left pedal was reverse; the middle pedal for the transmission brake, and the right hand pedal actuated the rear brakes.

The flywheel was located in the front of the engine instead of at the rear as in the "T". The timer was attached to the rear of the engine between the block and the transmission — which meant the differential and transmission had to be disengaged in order to remove the timer.

The connecting rods could be adjusted through two removable plates on the left side of the engine. The crankcase held only one quart of oil. An oiler with three pumps oiled the front and rear main bearings and also pumped oil into the engine. The connecting rod bearing caps were secured by a bolt on one side with a hinge on the other side, instead of having bolts on both sides. This made it easy to adjust bearings. Another unique feature was the wrist pin bushings, which were split for easy adjustment.

Instead of having a tapered axle with nuts, this model came with a straight axle. The hubs were secured with 3/8-inch round pins which in turn were kept in place by the hub caps. *(The early Model T's used the same arrangement. Ed.)* If a cap happened to come off while the car was being driven, the pin might fall out, thus permitting the wheel to come off.

Just below the hand crank, the water pump was visible as it was part of the radiator and was geared with a fibre gear to a bronze gear on the crankshaft.

The spark lever was on the right hand and the throttle on the left side of the steering column.

The Model S did not come with headlamps or top. However, they could be purchased as accessories. Under the rear bucket seat were two tool compartments. The rear seat hinged toward the front for the top compartment with a long pin locking device. The lower compartment was opened by leaving the top compartment locked and by disengaging a lower pin locking device.

It was my good fortune to obtain a Model S which had been stored indoors for years by a gentleman in Portland, Oregon. It was his fond wish to restore this and other antique cars which he had obtained through the years. However, it became necessary for him to sell some of these and only keep a few. I was lucky enough to have been first to ask to buy the Model S. Before I had gotten home with it on the trailer, the phone was ringing at my shop with offers to buy the car from me. I felt the "S" and I were meant for each other, though.

The restoration was very interesting and took about two and a half years. This was a complete original car, both metal and wood. Each piece was removed and carefully inspected. When it was all disassembled, every part was thoroughly cleaned and the engine was completely rebuilt. While disassembling the body I removed the serial number plate (which was number 3361) from the kick board of the front seat. The original body paint was under this plate so that I could duplicate the original color.

The leather upholstering was dried and shrunk and had to be replaced. The top, which in 1908 had to be purchased as an accessory, was not with the car. It took months to find top bows and hinges in order to complete the top.

The headlights, sidelights and taillight were on the car but in very bad condition. There was no windshield as this particular model came without one.

An interesting accessory on the car was a sprag. This attachment is fastened to the frame with a hinge that is operated by the driver so that it may be lowered as a safety device should the engine fail. The sprag will hold the car from backing down hill.

When compared with the early Model T, it is not difficult to trace the ancestry. The manifolds and carburetor (a five-ball Kingston) are almost exactly alike, but just reversed.

The box at the side of the engine is the oil pump. Driven by a small belt from the crankshaft, it supplies oil to the main bearings and crankcase.

The wheels were similar, too, to the early Ts. This was before the usual Ford script appeared; hubcaps carried the name in the block letters which were also used in the early Ts.

The coil box and coils are Heinze. The high tension leads come out the bottom of the box rather that through the rear. This same assembly appeared on the first 1909 Model Ts.

At a glance, the differential appears similar to the 1915 and later Fords. It seems strange that Ford discarded this design with the introduction of the T. The truss rod was standard equipment.

Front axle was similar to, but not the same as, the Model T. One-piece spindles were featured.

The rear axles were not tapered; had a key and a pin to prevent the wheel from coming off. The pin was held in place by the hub cap. This system was not very practical; the keyway and key wore making a loose fit after a time. Ford went over to a tapered axle during the 1911 model year.

Serial Numbers

The accepted method of dating a Model T Ford is to check the serial (engine) number against one of the published lists which indicated the date on which a given number was produced. We have compiled this list after considerable research, and believe it to be as accurate as is possible at this late date. Actually, we have two lists.

You will notice that there are differences between the two lists. A few of the reasons for the differences are explained later. We should add, however, that in fact neither of these lists are absolutely correct, and that both should be used only as a guide. Why? Well it just seems incredible that Ford could have ended each month with an even number. It was a well known fact that Henry Ford had little use for statistics. No doubt that feeling was reflected in what appears to be a "close enough" list of numbers published during the days of the Model T Ford.

If you have studied the lists of Model T serial numbers that have appeared in different publications you may have noticed that they don't all agree. Even the Ford Motor Company isn't consistent in the lists they published during the days of the Model T.

We have compiled a list which we feel is as close as possible, with the information that we have been able to gather. You will note that there are some differences from the lists appearing elsewhere. Our list was compiled from a combination of the Ford Service Bulletins, the 1926 Ford Sales Data Book and a number of other similar sources.

One source of errors is in the interpretation of the original information. For instance, the 1926 Sales Data Book says that in September, 1910, Ford built serial numbers 31000 to 31900. In October it says 31900 to 32500. Some writers took this to mean: September, 31000 to 31899; October, 31900 to 32499. Others said; September, 30999 to 31900; October, 31901 to 32500. Who knows what the actual numbers were? The point is, all three are close and unless you happen to have a car with one of those numbers, what difference does it really make? No doubt all three are wrong anyway!

The *Ford Service Bulletins* show, from October 1, 1912 to September 30, 1913, *Two* sets of serial numbers. One set runs from 169,452 to 370,147; the other set runs from B1 to B12247. The last number produced in September of 1912 was 157,205. There is, therefore, a gap of 12247 motors in the serial number sequence — exactly the number of "B" numbered cars built. Just why there were these "B" numbered cars is an unanswered question. All we know for sure is that they were built in Detroit (rather than Highland Park). They may have been for export. We have included these numbers, and the "gap" in our list. Strangely, the 1926 Sales Data Book shows no gap in the numbers but does mention the "B" numbered engines.

The first Model T's had both a motor number and a body number. Ford placed no significance on the body number and discontinued it in April of 1915. We have included these numbers. Note that they do not necessarily agree with the motor numbers. We have no evidence that they *ever* agreed after September of 1911.

Perhaps the most interesting facet of the list is the lack of cars produced in January of 1921. December of 1920 ended with number 4,698,415; February of 1921 picked up from there. What happened?

During 1919, when Henry Ford bought out the last of the original stockholders, he had to borrow the money. At that time he felt that business would be so good that he could pay off the notes with ease from the profits of the Company. But, there was a recession shortly thereafter and things looked pretty bad when the notes were due to be paid. What to do?

During the last months of 1920, Ford bought all the material he could (on credit) and built all the cars he could build. When the parts supply was exhausted he closed the plant (January of 1921) and shipped the cars out to his dealers. These cars had not been ordered by the dealers, and were shipped COD, freight collect (as was the custom then). Any dealer who objected could refuse shipment, of course, but when reminded that there were other people in his town who would be pleased to have the Ford dealership, most of them took the cars. Many had to borrow the money to pay for the shipment. Henry Ford ended up with more than enough cash to pay his creditors. Today, this sort of a deal would probably be illegal, but in 1921, it was Ford's way.

It would be interesting to tie down more facts relating to the serial numbers — such as, when were the open-valve blocks discontinued — or at what number did the starter engines begin.

Early in the Model T era, Ford's fiscal year was from October 1st through September 30th. Later, through a number of shifts, it became August 1st through July 31st. Did the Model Year coincide with the Fiscal Year? There is some evidence that it did; the 1926 "New Ford" was introduced in July of 1925, for example.

There must be a world of information among you readers — let's hear from you. . . .

We have provided two lists. One consists of the numbers produced during Ford's fiscal years (except for a brief transitional period during 1915), and the other lists the monthly production. We have not listed the monthly numbers prior to August of 1915 because none of our sources agree with the yearly lists published by Ford in 1919, and since these other sources are later, we feel the 1919 is more likely to be the most accurate.

OCTOBER 1, 1908 TO SEPTEMBER 30, 1909
Car and Motor No.   1 to 11,100

OCTOBER 1, 1909 TO SEPTEMBER 30, 1910
Car and Motor No.   11,101 to 31,900

OCTOBER 1, 1910 TO SEPTEMBER 30, 1911
Car and Motor No.   31,901 to 69,876

OCTOBER 1, 1911 TO SEPTEMBER 30, 1912
Motor No.   69,877 to 157,205
Car No.   80,000 to 150,000

OCTOBER 1, 1912 TO SEPTEMBER 30, 1913
Motor No.   B1 to B12,247
Motor No.   169,452 to 370,147
Car No.   150,001 to 332,500

OCTOBER 1, 1913 TO JULY 31, 1914
Motor No.   370,148 to 570,790
Car No.   332,501 to 539,000

AUGUST 1, 1914 TO APRIL 30, 1915
Motor No.   570,791 to 773,487
Car No.   539,001 to 742,313

MAY 1, 1915 TO JULY 31, 1915
Motor No.   773,488 to 855,500

AUGUST 1, 1915 TO JULY 31, 1916
Motor No.   855,501 to 1,362,200

AUGUST 1, 1916 TO JULY 31, 1917
Motor No.   1,362,201 to 2,113,500

AUGUST 1, 1917 TO JULY 31, 1918
Motor No.   2,113,501 to 2,756,251

AUGUST 1, 1918 TO JULY 31, 1919
Motor No.   2,756,252 to 3,277,851

AUGUST 1, 1919 TO JULY 31, 1920
Motor No.   3,277,852 to 4,233,350

AUGUST 1, 1920 TO JULY 31, 1921
Motor No.   4,233,351 to 5,223,135

AUGUST 1, 1921 TO JULY 31, 1922
Motor No.   5,223,136 to 6,334,196

AUGUST 1, 1922 TO JULY 31, 1923
Motor No.   6,334,197 to 8,122,674

AUGUST 1, 1923 TO JULY 31, 1924
Motor No.   8,122,675 to 10,266,471

AUGUST 1, 1924 TO JULY 31, 1925
Motor No.   10,266,472 to 12,222,528

AUGUST 1, 1925 TO JULY 31, 1926
Motor No.   12,222,529 to 14,049,029

AUGUST 1, 1926 TO MAY 31, 1927
Motor No.   14,049,030 to 15,007,033

1915
AUGUST	855,501 to 881,000
SEPTEMBER	881,001 to 913,000
OCTOBER	913,001 to 949,000
NOVEMBER	949,001 to 985,400
DECEMBER	985,401 to 1,029,200

1916
JANUARY	1,029,201 to 1,071,800
FEBRUARY	1,071,801 to 1,119,000
MARCH	1,119,001 to 1,167,900
APRIL	1,167,901 to 1,219,400
MAY	1,219,401 to 1,272,000
JUNE	1,272,001 to 1,326,900
JULY	1,326,901 to 1,362,213
AUGUST	1,362,214 to 1,400,900
SEPTEMBER	1,400,901 to 1,452,200
OCTOBER	1,452,201 to 1,510,500
NOVEMBER	1,510,501 to 1,570,700
DECEMBER	1,570,701 to 1,614,600

1917
JANUARY	1,614,601 to 1,680,000
FEBRUARY	1,680,001 to 1,739,900
MARCH	1,739,901 to 1,812,000
APRIL	1,812,001 to 1,888,000
MAY	1,888,001 to 1,968,629
JUNE	1,968,630 to 2,044,100
JULY	2,044,101 to 2,113,500
AUGUST	2,113,501 to 2,162,800
SEPTEMBER	2,162,801 to 2,231,000
OCTOBER	2,231,001 to 2,310,400
NOVEMBER	2,310,401 to 2,383,900
DECEMBER	2,383,901 to 2,449,100

1918
JANUARY	2,449,101 to 2,503,200
FEBRUARY	2,503,201 to 2,558,200
MARCH	2,558,201 to 2,611,400
APRIL	2,611,401 to 2,657,500
MAY	2,657,501 to 2,700,800
JUNE	2,700,801 to 2,735,700
JULY	2,735,701 to 2,756,250
AUGUST	2,756,251 to 2,774,600
SEPTEMBER	2,774,601 to 2,787,800
OCTOBER	2,787,801 to 2,792,300
NOVEMBER	2,792,301 to 2,805,100
DECEMBER	2,805,101 to 2,831,400

1919
JANUARY	2,831,401 to 2,880,170
FEBRUARY	2,880,171 to 2,933,000
MARCH	2,933,001 to 2,997,100
APRIL	2,997,101 to 3,067,700
MAY	3,067,701 to 3,140,000
JUNE	3,140,001 to 3,210,800
JULY	3,210,801 to 3,277,850
AUGUST	3,277,851 to 3,346,900
SEPTEMBER	3,346,901 to 3,429,400
OCTOBER	3,429,401 to 3,515,431
NOVEMBER	3,515,432 to 3,588,000
DECEMBER	3,588,001 to 3,659,970

1920
JANUARY	3,659,971 to 3,743,075
FEBRUARY	3,743,076 to 3,817,430
MARCH	3,817,431 to 3,910,000
APRIL	3,910,001 to 3,969,150
MAY	3,969,151 to 4,055,280
JUNE	4,055,281 to 4,141,450
JULY	4,141,451 to 4,233,350
AUGUST	4,233,351 to 4,329,900
SEPTEMBER	4,329,901 to 4,426,385
OCTOBER	4,426,386 to 4,526,540
NOVEMBER	4,526,541 to 4,617,925
DECEMBER	4,617,926 to 4,698,415

1921
JANUARY	None built
FEBRUARY	4,698,416 to 4,736,430
MARCH	4,736,431 to 4,810,010
APRIL	4,810,011 to 4,907,500
MAY	4,907,501 to 5,008,000
JUNE	5,008,001 to 5,114,530
JULY	5,114,531 to 5,223,135
AUGUST	5,223,136 to 5,337,545
SEPTEMBER	5,337,546 to 5,447,816
OCTOBER	5,447,817 to 5,529,519
NOVEMBER	5,529,520 to 5,602,301
DECEMBER	5,602,302 to 5,638,071

1922
JANUARY	5,638,072 to 5,683,808
FEBRUARY	5,683,809 to 5,736,278
MARCH	5,736,279 to 5,812,608
APRIL	5,812,609 to 5,922,968
MAY	5,922,969 to 6,058,671
JUNE	6,058,672 to 6,199,796
JULY	6,199,797 to 6,334,196
AUGUST	6,334,197 to 6,473,195
SEPTEMBER	6,473,196 to 6,582,724
OCTOBER	6,582,725 to 6,713,881
NOVEMBER	6,713,882 to 6,844,681
DECEMBER	6,844,682 to 6,953,071

1923
JANUARY	6,953,072 to 7,084,225
FEBRUARY	7,084,226 to 7,217,971
MARCH	7,217,972 to 7,386,111
APRIL	7,386,112 to 7,564,111
MAY	7,564,112 to 7,738,372
JUNE	7,738,373 to 7,927,374
JULY	7,927,375 to 8,122,674
AUGUST	8,122,675 to 8,311,581
SEPTEMBER	8,311,582 to 8,477,681
OCTOBER	8,477,682 to 8,664,281
NOVEMBER	8,664,282 to 8,843,065
DECEMBER	8,843,066 to 9,008,381

1924
JANUARY	9,008,382 to 9,232,671
FEBRUARY	9,232,672 to 9,427,721
MARCH	9,427,722 to 9,622,521
APRIL	9,622,522 to 9,814,521
MAY	9,814,522 to 9,984,771
JUNE	9,984,772 to 10,126,671
JULY	10,126,672 to 10,266,471
AUGUST	10,266,472 to 10,404,822
SEPTEMBER	10,404,823 to 10,560,821
OCTOBER	10,560,822 to 10,734,504
NOVEMBER	10,734,505 to 10,886,259
DECEMBER	10,886,260 to 10,999,900

1925
JANUARY	10,999,901 to 11,135,308
FEBRUARY	11,135,309 to 11,302,019
MARCH	11,302,020 to 11,477,655
APRIL	11,477,656 to 11,688,647
MAY	11,688,648 to 11,869,207
JUNE	11,869,208 to 12,062,486
JULY	12,062,487 to 12,222,528
AUGUST	12,222,529 to 12,290,760
SEPTEMBER	12,290,761 to 12,399,496
OCTOBER	12,399,497 to 12,621,501
NOVEMBER	12,621,502 to 12,823,126
DECEMBER	12,823,127 to 12,990,055

1926
JANUARY	12,990,056 to 13,138,675
FEBRUARY	13,138,676 to 13,286,289
MARCH	13,286,290 to 13,454,890
APRIL	13,454,891 to 13,619,705
MAY	13,619,706 to 13,769,814
JUNE	13,769,815 to 13,912,754
JULY	13,912,755 to 14,049,029
AUGUST	14,049,030 to 14,194,489
SEPTEMBER	14,194,490 to 14,331,152
OCTOBER	14,331,153 to 14,472,253
NOVEMBER	14,472,254 to 14,577,135
DECEMBER	14,577,136 to 14,619,254

1927
JANUARY	14,619,255 to 14,623,502
FEBRUARY	14,623,503 to 14,762,945
MARCH	14,762,946 to 14,851,445
APRIL	14,851,446 to 14,927,495
MAY	14,927,496 to 15,007,033

The Defeat of Obscurity.....

It might seem strange that of the over fifteen million Model T Fords produced, we ordinarily see so few. On reflection though, this is the truly normal result of the technological process to which we have been conditioned. For our lives have become attuned to the newest, the fastest and the more "modern", and the advertising agencies of Madison Avenue successfully produce an annual dissatisfaction with our current automobile.

It was always thus, but in the Model T's time, there was another, perhaps more potent force adding to the owner's desire to replace his car. During its lifetime, the yearly improvements and changes were hardly sufficient to justify a change in ownership, but during this lifespan, Model T witnessed the development of automotive *transportation* as an important and significant part of our way of life. As cars were improved, so were the roads, gasolines, service stations, accommodations and, in other cars, physical comfort.

So, when Henry Ford was forced, in 1927, to concede the need for a newer and more nearly current car, the changes that he incorporated into his new Model A were so drastic, so differing, so great, from his Model T that this car became immediately obsolete. Even the diehard multitude of loyalists were forced to concede their positions. As a result, later, when Model T did "wear out," it was rarely, if ever, replaced with another Model T. The scrapyards and wrecking yards began, in 1928, to see the start of an influx of tired Model T Fords.

By 1939, ten years later, we found ourselves "up to here" with scrapped cars, many of them the elderly Model T Fords. Due to the limited markets, during the Thirties, for automobiles, we were happy to send these tired old bones abroad to be used later in foreign production of steel. Those few which escaped that fate were shortly to be threatened by the domestic need for scrap metal during the years of World War II. Few escaped this end.

As they wore out, especially in rural areas where space was less confining, Model T Fords were often left abandoned in back lots, barns, indoors and outdoors — wherever they were when they "gave up the ghost." In contemporary times, since they were available, even in running condition, for only a few dollars, it hardly seemed worth the while to take them to wrecking yards to try to salvage more than just a few loose parts. Cars were far too plentiful for that. Added to this was a host of loyal owner-drivers whose confidence in the Model T had raised the car to the status of a full family member. These people, in many cases, simply could not bear to part with their favorites.

There have always been those few among us whose interest prompted the restoration of the many excellent, complete cars available. As the supply of these cars diminished, prices of antique automobiles — including the Model T Ford — rose steadily. As newly interested hobbiests entered the field, the market for available cars grew to levels beyond the means of many people. Thus the increasing interest in the Model T Ford, whose parts are so readily interchangeable and whose supply has remained comparatively so common, and whose bones still littered the countryside.

In the late 1950's, the increasing number of enthusiasts were swelled by a multitude of people whose affluence afforded them the opportunity to acquire a "toy" which would lend pleasure in the achievements of Restoration and the perils of Driving. The passing of time heightened the effect of the sight of an occasional Model T Ford on its way home from errands, etc., and fed the spiraling interest in the cars. Clubs were formed to encourage and preserve the Model T; Clubs that were not, as is generally the case, all-inclusive, but which were limited to Membership interested in the Model T Ford.

In addition to the multitude of regional, local, or unaffiliated groups, there now are two powerful National clubs; *The Model T Ford Club of America*, (Tarzana, Calif.), and *The Model T Ford Club International*, (Chicago, Ill.), which together are comprised of over 6000 owners and enthusiasts. As a matter of interest, qualified sources have estimated the number of Model T Fords still on the road at over 50,000, and every year, due to the constructive efforts of devoted part-time mechanics, more, not fewer, cars join the tally. Many of these cars are assembled, generally authentically, out of parts that are accumulated from many sources. When complete, though, their beauty and authenticity can hardly be challenged.

It is the dream of most interested people to find a whole, unrestored, original, complete Model T "in a barn somewhere." Well, such is still a very real possibility for there remain tucked away in barns, sheds, back lots, garages and carriage houses many such examples. A year does not pass that authenticated reports of such events are not still reported.

So it goes. The cycle is complete. The Model T was designed, built, mass-produced, run reliably and long, scrapped, forgotten, and now it is being resurrected. Truly a *Defeat of Obscurity*.